Communications
in Computer and Information Science 470

Frances Cleary · Massimo Felici (Eds.)

Cyber Security and Privacy

Third Cyber Security and Privacy EU Forum,
CSP Forum 2014
Athens, Greece, May 21–22, 2014
Revised Selected Papers

 Springer

Editors
Frances Cleary
Waterford Institute of Technology
Waterford
Ireland

Massimo Felici
Hewlett-Packard Laboratories
Bristol
UK

ISSN 1865-0929   ISSN 1865-0937 (electronic)
Communications in Computer and Information Science
ISBN 978-3-319-12573-2   ISBN 978-3-319-12574-9 (eBook)
DOI 10.1007/978-3-319-12574-9

Library of Congress Control Number: 2014954582

Springer Cham Heidelberg New York Dordrecht London
© Springer International Publishing Switzerland 2014

Printed on acid-free paper

Springer International Publishing AG Switzerland is part of Springer Science+Business Media
(www.springer.com)

Foreword By Seccord

The CSP Forum initiative[1] (funded by the EU FP7 SecCord[2] CSA project) has a core objective of enabling enhanced collaboration through effective clustering of EU funded trust and security research projects. Funded research projects contribute to the larger work program of the commission. The CSP forum through its promotion of collaboration, encourages trust and security focused projects to work to create syner-gies, coming together as a community for greater impact.

Projects need to prove collectively that as a program they have delivered good results with a high impact potential. This in turn clearly conveys to the decision/policy makers the need for such research and provides evidence of the potential and real impact of such funded research activities. Highlighting such a need for future investment in this research domain area demonstrates the continued need to have trust and security embedded in future EU work programs.

With ICT technologies advancing at a rapid pace globally, this has a knock-on effect regarding policy and regulation. It is imperative that the ICT trust and security community demonstrate how they are contributing to this ever-changing and technically challenging world. The CSP forum continues in its analysis and clustering activities to pro-vide the bigger picture of what we are doing collectively, through the ongoing partici-pation and contributions from individual projects carrying out the research work.

Horizon 2020 (H2020)[3] EU flagship initiative, aimed at securing Europe's global competitiveness, actively works to couple research and innovation with a core goal to ensure that Europe produces world-class science, and removes existing barriers to innova-tion, providing an environment for both private and public sectors to come together for greater impact. The CSP forum through its ongoing activities aligns its activities with the H2020 objective and innovation/impact focus by

- Providing an overview of the EU trust and security research portfolio (focusing on outputs/success stories with real marketable impact/potential)
- Addressing Policy in the Making – Assessing funded projects activities and their relation to the Cybersecurity Strategy – "Impact on Europe," EU data pro-tection reform – "protecting your personal data/privacy"
- Assessing economic barriers of trust and security technology uptake – "How to access the market more effectively," Research to Industry impact – "How to improve, implement, and succeed"
- Aligning trust and security EU initiatives with focused Member state initiatives – "Investigating How to work together better."

---

[1] https://www.cspforum.eu/

[2] http://www.seccord.eu/

[3] http://ec.europa.eu/programmes/horizon2020/

Proceedings from the Annual Cyber Security and Privacy (CSP) Forum Conference 2014[4] are included in this volume. The CSP Forum conference 2014 in partnership with Pripare[5] colocated with "The Annual Privacy Forum conference 2014"[6] in Athens, Greece during May 21–22, 2014. The CSP forum conference provided an opportunity for projects to come together to disseminate to the wider community their research out-puts, highlighting the potential innovative market opportunities and impact of EC funded Cyber Security and Privacy research activities.

August 2014   Frances Cleary

---

[4] https://www.cspforum.eu/2014
[5] http://pripareproject.eu/
[6] http://privacyforum.eu/

Preface

This volume consists of the selected revised papers based on the presentations at the Cyber Security and Privacy (CSP) Forum 2014, collocated with The Annual Privacy Forum conference, held in Athens, Greece, during May 21–22, 2014. This volume builds on the experience of the volume of the CSP FORUM 2013 (published by Springer, CCIS 182). It is edited with the intention and ambition to develop a "portfolio" of European research. It aims to disseminate research outcomes beyond research communities by proving a single access point for different stakeholders.

This volume captures ongoing research activities and results carried out within European projects mostly funded within the EU's framework research programs. The conference program consisted of 15 different tracks involving a variety of presentations and panel discussions covering the key challenges and strategies available to effectively manage employee, citizen, and corporate trust. The conference provided an opportunity for those in business, public sector, research, and government who are involved in the policy, security, systems, and processes surrounding security and pri-vacy technologies. The papers collected in this volume highlight research conducted by the following EU projects (in alphabetical order):

- A4Cloud
  Accountability for Cloud and other Future Internet Services
  FP7-317550
- ABC4Trust
  Attribute-based Credentials for Trust
  FP7-257782
- Aniketos
  Project Full Title: Secure and Trustworthy Composite Services
  FP7-257930
- FINESCE
  Future Internet Smart Utility Services
  FP7-604677
- FI-WARE
  Future Internet Core Platform
  FP7-285248
- IPACSO
  Innovation Framework for Privacy and Cyber Security Market Opportunities
  FP7-609892
- PRIPARE
  PReparing Industry to Privacy-by-design by supporting its Application in Research
  FP7-610613
- SecCord
  SECurity and trust COoRDination and enhanced collaboration
  FP7-316622

- SECONOMICS
  Socio-Economics meets Security
  FP7-285223
- SECURED
  SECURity at the network EDge
  FP7-611458
- TRESCCA
  TRustworthy Embedded systems for Secure Cloud Computing Applications
  FP7-318036

This two-day conference organized by the SecCord project invited presenters, panellists, and exhibitors to contribute to this collection of selected papers. Two types of papers were solicited to be published in the post-proceedings of the conference:

- Practical Experience Reports and Tools presenting in-depth description of practitioner experiences, case studies, and tools
- Research Papers presenting recent original research results providing new insights into the community.

Papers submitted were peer-reviewed by (at least two to three) Program Committee members and experts. The peer-review process provided authors with valuable feedback in order to improve their papers. The selected papers grouped into thematic parts of these proceedings capture just a snapshot of the two-day conference, which provided an opportunity to present and debate ongoing cyber security and privacy re-search and development in Europe. These proceedings intend to inform researchers, practitioners, and policy-makers about research developments and technological oppor-tunities for innovation in cyber security and privacy.

We would like to thank all the people who made the publication of these proceedings possible, in particular the authors, the Program Committee members and reviewers, the conference organizers, and the supporting organizations.

August 2014   Frances Cleary
                                                                   Massimo Felici

Organisation

Organising Committee

Frances Cleary	Waterford Institute of Technology, Ireland
Michele Bezzi	SAP, France
Massimo Felici	HP Labs, UK
Olga Gadyatskaya	University of Trento, Italy
Fabio Massacci	University of Trento, Italy
Aljosa Pasic	ATOS, Spain
Alan Ryan	Waterford Institute of Technology, Ireland
Nick Wainwright	HP Labs, UK

Program Committee Members and Reviewers

Claudio Agostino Ardagna	Università degli Studi di Milano - Italy
Ermanno Battista	University of Naples Federico II, Italy
Karin Bernsmed	SINTEF ICT, Norway
Michele Bezzi	SAP Research Sophia-Antipolis, France
Claudio Caimi	HP, Italy
Valentina Casola	University of Naples "Federico II", Italy
Frances Cleary	Waterford Institute of Technology, Ireland
Jorge Cuellar	Siemens, (AG, Germany)
Ernesto Damiani	University of Milan, Italy
Alessandra De Benedictis	University of Naples Federico II, Italy
Francesco Di Cerbo	SAP Research Sophia-Antipolis, France
Zeta Dooly	Waterford Institute of Technology, Ireland
Hisain Elshaafi	Waterford Institute of Technology, Ireland
Massimo Felici	HP Labs, UK
Olga Gadyatskaya	University Trento, Italy
Antonio Gómez Skarmeta	Universidad de Murcia, Spain
Jose Luis Hernández	University of Murcia, Spain
Mario Hoffmann	Fraunhofer AISEC, Germany
Kazim Hussain	ATOS, Spain
Dharm Kapletia	HP Labs, UK
Jim Longstaff	Teesside University, UK
Emil Lupu	Imperial College, UK
Evangelos Markatos	ICS/FORTH, Greece
Fabio Martinelli	IIT-CNR, Italy
Maria Victoria Moreno	University of Murcia, Spain
Stefano Paraboschi	Universita di Bergamo, Italy

Aneel Rahim   Waterford Institute of Technology, Ireland
Alan Ryan   Waterford Institute of Technology, Ireland
Yannis Stamatiou   RACTI, Greece
Vasilis Tountopoulos   ATC Innovation Lab, Greece
Mauro Turtur   University of Sannio, Italy

Contents

Research and Innovation

Security

Ensuring Trustworthiness and Security in Service Compositions

Vasilios Tountopoulos[1(✉)], Ira Giannakoudaki[2],
Konstantinos Giannakakis[1], Lefteris Korres[2],
and Leonidas Kallipolitis[1]

[1] Athens Technology Center S.A, Halandri, Athens, Greece
{v.tountopoulos,k.giannakakis,l.kallipolitis}@atc.gr
[2] DAEM, Athens, Greece
{i.giannakoudaki,l.korres}@daem.gr

Abstract. Future Internet applications can be dynamically composed of atomic services, which exhibit different trustworthiness and security requirements, when being integrated into complex service chains. In that respect, research in the security field works around solutions that can ensure that security characteristics are well addressed in modern, Web-based, ICT environments, aiming to establish a level of trust and confidence on the service consumers. Towards this direction, this paper showcases the results of the EU-funded FP7 Aniketos project, in order to support the secure development life cycle of Web-based service compositions. It elaborates on the design time and runtime capabilities of the Aniketos platform to support security and trust in the specification of composite service processes, by offering service developers the ability to efficiently express their security requirements and service providers the capability to track security breaches and threats and support decisions on the appropriate mitigation actions.

Keywords: Secure service development · Composition of public services · Trust property

1 Introduction

Secure service composition plays a key role in Future Internet Applications, since the value of the service delivery process increases with the importance of the involved data and their security requirements. Different types of multi-source information are integrated into distributed ICT platforms and services to facilitate the needs of multiple cross discipline business domains, which require the composition of public and private service processes. However, the integration of any type of data in complex service provisioning paradigms raises valid concerns on the security and privacy vulnerabilities of data systems to maintain the value of the offered information content [1].

As a consequence, end users appear to be reluctant in using such ICT systems and they expect to increase their perceived confidence by setting specific trust and security requirements that should be met. In this context, this paper approaches the problem of security by design to support the development and execution of data driven composite

© Springer International Publishing Switzerland 2014
F. Cleary and M. Felici (Eds.): CSP Forum 2014, CCIS 470, pp. 3–15, 2014.
DOI: 10.1007/978-3-319-12574-9_1

services, which are consumed in critical business domains to build secure Web-based applications.

The paper presents the results of the FP7 Aniketos project [2] to address the problem of the design time support of security properties in the provision of sensitive data in composite service processes, with application to a variety of business sectors. More specifically, it demonstrates how specific end user security and trust requirements are evolving to system level security mechanisms to deliver complex interactive Web service-based applications that require the integration of critical information, which is subject to various security classifications.

In a nutshell, the scope of the paper is to present the applicability of the research work conducted in the context of the Aniketos project on domain specific application scenarios, which raise certain security concerns that have to be effectively addressed in the design, development, deployment and execution of secure composite services. In that respect, the paper is structured as follows: Sect. 2 gives an overview of the technical aspects of the Aniketos project and, presents the Aniketos methodology for developing secure composite service specifications and integrating them in operational and highly business-oriented Web applications. Then, Sect. 3 introduces the software packages comprising the Aniketos platform, which is the main outcome of the Aniketos project by providing software level implementation details. Then, Sect. 4 elaborates on how the platform has been used to develop secure composite services in the context of an e-Government application, which exhibits certain security and trust requirements. This section, also, introduces the main results collected as feedback from the evaluation of the Aniketos design time and runtime capabilities. Finally, Sect. 5 concludes this paper.

2 Overview of the Aniketos Project

This section makes an introduction to the objectives of the Aniketos platform and introduces the technical directions, towards which the Aniketos work delivers significant results to advance the current state-of-the-art in the area of secure service engineering. This section, also, presents the methodology that is adopted to realise the Aniketos research in real application scenarios.

2.1 Introduction to the Project Objectives

The main objective of the Aniketos Project is to establish and maintain security and trustworthiness in composite services. The project delivers a platform that builds upon existing environment solutions, such as service composition, service runtime execution and service storage, and extends them to offer the security and trust dimension when designing, implementing, deploying and running composite services.

In more details, the Aniketos platform aims to advance the state-of-the-art in the area of service composition by creating and maintaining secure and trusted composite services. Through the appropriate specification of methods and development of tools and services, the Aniketos platform supports the whole service life cycle in service engineering, ranging from service implementation, discovery and composition to service management, adaptation and reconfiguration.

As Future Internet services can be dynamically composed or evolved, the Aniketos platform defines trust models and security policies, through which the interested stakeholders can define, validate and monitor trustworthiness and security properties. These properties can be used as the building blocks for developing the security descriptors for the composed services and contract related artefacts, as well as be exploited to identify and overcome the shortcomings in service engineering when dealing with security violation issues.

Security violations can occur when systems and services are vulnerable to intruders, which may affect the set security standards and the quality of experience received by the users. Towards this direction, the Aniketos platform tries to address potential loss on service availability and end user trust by efficiently analysing, solving and sharing information on how new threats and vulnerabilities can affect service compositions and can be mitigated [3], so that the composed services can be (semi-) automatically adapted to the new runtime conditions.

On top of that, the Aniketos platform adds a socio-technical perspective to the way that security and trustworthiness requirements are addressed in service engineering. Since service and service-based systems target highly business-oriented environments, the respective business processes, which are being supported through the deployment of the appropriate composite services, are governed from both technical and social aspects. Such aspects should be tackled together once security and trust are considered.

2.2 The Aniketos Methodology

The adoption of the Aniketos concepts is based on existing secure software development methodologies. Our approach extends them to provide the roadmap on how the innovative technologies of the Aniketos platform can be integrated in order to advance compositions of data critical services to be more secure, reliable and trusted.

As data driven future Internet services can be dynamically composed or evolved, the Aniketos platform gives emphasis on the definition of both human readable and machine readable security policies, through which the involved stakeholders in a service chain can validate the offered security properties and monitor the trustworthiness of the associated providers. These properties affect the availability of sensitive data and can be used for the implementation of the security descriptors of the composed services and contract related artefacts, as well as be exploited to identify and overcome the shortcomings in service engineering when dealing with security violation issues at runtime.

More specifically, the Aniketos platform capabilities are realized through three distinct phases, as depicted in Fig. 1. As a first step, we show how the Aniketos platform relates to the secure service development of data driven composite services and applications by enabling domain security experts and service designers and developers in the design-time service process specifications taking into account security and trust requirements [4, 5]. The requirements are expressed in the form of security consumer policies with respect to how data is provided and shared among participating data holders and consumers.

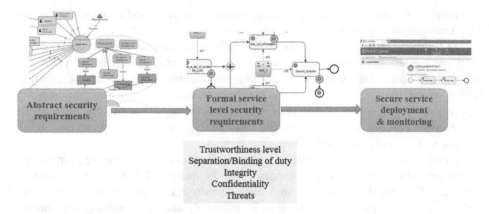

Fig. 1. The methodology for the use of the Aniketos platform

The requirements can be described in a high level XML like specification language, which can, then, be mapped to a formal service specification language, like Business Process Modelling and Notation (BPMN) [6]. Based on the defined security policies, the Aniketos design time methodology prompts service developers in linking service processes with actual atomic services, which satisfy these policies. Thus, the composition of the service process chain is verified on the security assertions that the target service consumers have declared as requirements [7]. The development of the secure service compositions is based on the Activiti Modeler[1].

At runtime, the designed specification of the secure service composition is deployed, so that it can be exploited in domain specific application development. During the announcement phase, the service developer can define a set of rules to accompany the service contract and which can potential drive the runtime behaviour of the service execution, in order to handle security violations and threat exposures. The deployment and execution of the composite service specifications is performed through the Activiti Engine (see Footnote 1). As a last step of our approach, the Aniketos platform enables monitoring of the runtime execution for the relevant composite services to ensure that the provisions of the security contract are respected and that the potential exposure of threats is well addressed [8]. In case of violations, the platform enacts automatic service adaptation mechanisms, through re-composition or re-configuration.

3   The Offerings of the Aniketos Platform

The Aniketos platform has followed a modular approach for the architectural design, which enables the platform to be installed either as a platform as a whole or as separate components. This gives the target users the advantage to choose the functionalities that they want to install.

---

[1] http://www.activiti.org

The Aniketos Platform and Environment components have been grouped to software packages, which better facilitate the delivery of the Aniketos platform functionalities to the target user groups. The platform architecture has been based on the OSGi framework[2], which is a standardised technology, fully documented, that defines a dynamic modular system for Java applications [9, 10].

Thus, here we introduce the potentials for grouping the Aniketos provisions into software packages, which can be commercialised directly to the target markets and facilitate real life needs for supporting security and trustworthiness in a variety of (cross-discipline) application domains. The packaging takes into account the details of the components, their licensing scheme and their position in the Aniketos methodology presented above, including the security service development lifecycle.

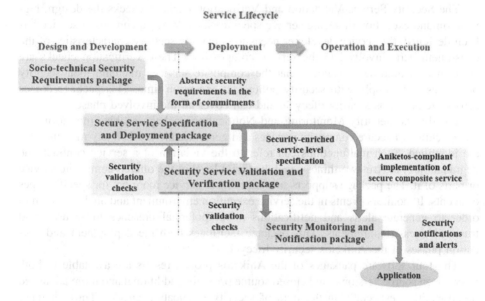

Fig. 2. The software packages of the Aniketos platform

As shown in Fig. 2, the Aniketos platform is provided as four distinct software packages, which are summarised in the following lines.

The Socio-technical Security (STS) Requirements package offers the ability to model the security requirements in complex services [11]. The language and tools allow us to represent the agents and the roles involved in the service execution, the goals they should achieve, the trust and security relationships among them, and the documents specifying the achievement of these goals. This package generates security requirements for services, whether they are developed from scratch or already exist and need to conform to certain security rules and organisational policies. By using this package, we can involve different stakeholders and specify our security requirements

---

[2] OSGi Alliance Specifications - http://www.osgi.org/Specifications/HomePage.

by exploiting close to real world modelling practices. This package facilitates the design phase of the Aniketos security lifecycle.

The Secure Service Specification and Deployment package enables business process modelling of composite services and configuration of the security requirements, which can be retrieved from the previous package or defined from scratch. The package allows easy deployment of the composite services in a runtime environment. For each service part, the functional specification is enriched with security characteristics, detailing the level of security that should be supported [12]. The package offers the possibility to publish services to a service registry and supports searching in this registry to discover the most appropriate atomic services to be associated with the composite service. This package facilitates both the development and deployment phases of the Aniketos security lifecycle.

The Security Service Validation and Verification package checks the design, registration and execution of secure service specifications. When a composite service has been designed, the service developer needs to check the security characteristics of the constituent parts involved in the service composition. These verification checks are performed at runtime to validate that the composite services maintain their security properties and comply with security policies at execution time. This package comes across the Aniketos security lifecycle and can cover all the involved phases.

Finally, the Security Monitoring and Notification package enables monitoring of the execution of secure composite services and generates alerts when any malfunctions are identified. Such malfunctions can refer to the violation of a service contract, the degradation in the trustworthiness, and the threat level of the offered composite service or parts of it. The package supports subscriptions to service monitors for specific types of events. It monitors events in the service execution environment and analyses them in order to generate alerts and notifications about potential breaches to security and trustworthiness requirements. This package facilitates both the deployment and execution phases of the Aniketos security lifecycle.

The four software packages of the Aniketos project results are available in both basic, open source versions[3] and closed source providing additional and more advanced functionalities, especially in the field of security verification checks. Through these packages, the Aniketos platform offers design time and runtime support of security and trustworthiness properties in the provision of composite services. More details about the Aniketos software packages can be found in [2].

The platform capabilities address the needs of different stakeholders, including service and application developers and service providers. The service developers can exploit the Aniketos platform at design time to define trustworthiness and risk-based security properties over and between external service components. By adopting the Aniketos design time methodologies and tools, as presented above, they are able to create composite secure service specifications, discover and select the most appropriate secure service components and evaluate the compliance of service compositions with respect to set security user requirements and service properties.

---

[3] Available at github.com/AniketosEU.

At runtime, the Aniketos platform offers software packages, which enable the service providers to publish their composite service specifications and operate their secure and trusted services, and application developers to monitor the operational behaviour of composite service executions and efficiently react in cases of contextual environmental changes and security violations. Thus, when changes occur that have an impact in the proper and secure service execution, the Aniketos packaged platform is notified to take the appropriate actions and potentially proceed with service recomposition and reconfiguration, according to the best service adaptation potential.

4 Building Secure Service-Based Applications

This section describes the way that the Aniketos platform is used to develop secure composite services that can be consumed in business-oriented applications. The section introduces the steps that should be adopted by the involved service designers, developers and providers during the whole service lifecycle. This section is concluded with some initial remarks arising from the evaluation of the Aniketos platform through the realisation of a use case facilitating the needs of an e-Government scenario.

4.1 Development of a Use Case Application

In the scope of this paper, we exploit the capabilities of the Aniketos platform to showcase their applicability in real life examples and evaluate the practicality of the platform functionalities in commercially critical environments. For our case, we select an example from the e-Government regime, which constitutes a demanding case of public and confidential information being integrated into a secure service based application. This example aims to address the citizens' security concerns when participating in e-Government online public services following a security-by-design implementation approach.

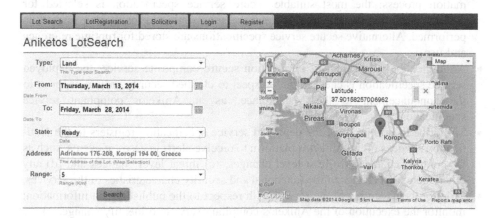

Fig. 3. A screenshot of the Web application for the e-Government domain

More specifically, in order to evaluate the Aniketos methodology towards supporting the design time specification of secure service compositions and the deployment of Aniketos compliant composite services, we have used the Aniketos platform to develop a set of composite services that have been consumed in this e-Government Web application, facilitating the task for publishing the lot information residing in a given area (see Fig. 3 for the end user view of this application). The development process has been made aiming to evaluate the capability of the platform to provide the necessary level of abstraction and enable (not necessarily security skilled) service designers and developers define their security and trustworthiness requirements in the specification of complex public services.

The functionalities that have been exposed by the platform and have been used to develop this e-Government application are analysed in the following steps, which implement the Aniketos approach to build secure service-based business applications:

- Build security requirements-based service specification for publishing lot information scenario: an initial structure of the Aniketos compliant specification is built, based on abstract security requirements (see Fig. 4), being defined through the STS package, and after their transformation to concrete service specification resources.
- Define security policies for the publishing lot information service tasks: the Aniketos compliant specification is enriched with more security requirements at the level of the formal service specification.
- Create candidate compositions by discovering existing services to facilitate the publishing lot information process: the tasks associated to a composite service specification are linked to actual service components, which are discovered from the Marketplace, based on functional and security characteristics.
- Analyse service properties: the Marketplace requests for the validation of the security properties of a service with certain functional characteristics.
- Perform design time service verification: the list of candidate service specifications are verified to ensure compliance of service security properties with defined consumer policies.
- Deploy the Aniketos compliant service specification for the publishing lot information process: the most suitable secure service specification is selected for deployment to the runtime platform and the subscription to monitoring services is performed. Alternative secure service specifications are stored for runtime reference and use.
- Announce the publishing lot information secure composite service: the deployed service specification is checked with respect to claimed security properties, prior to the announcement to the Marketplace, as an Aniketos compliant service specification.
- Subscribe to notifications: the deployed service specification registers to the Notification services of the Aniketos platform to receive alerts in cases of events, such as (a) contract changes, (b) trust level changes, (c) threat level changes and (d) any other contextual change of the functional and security characteristics of the services.
- Monitor the execution of the service with respect to the publishing lot information: monitor the execution of the Aniketos compliant service to identify changes in the proper runtime behaviour, based on the Agreement Template.

- Perform runtime service verification: in case of any violations, the properties of the composite service are verified at runtime to identify the type of violation and provide reasoning over the appropriate actions to be followed.
- Invoke service re-composition to maintain the security and trust policies for the publishing lot information process: the necessary actions towards re-composition of the runtime behaviour of the service are performed. The execution of the service is not interrupted.
- In case that re-composition fails, invoke service re-configuration: the necessary actions towards re-configuration of the composite service specification for the publishing lot information process are performed. The execution of the service may be interrupted.

Based on these steps, we have managed to develop a composite service specification, as shown in Fig. 5, which facilitates the publishing lot information scenario,

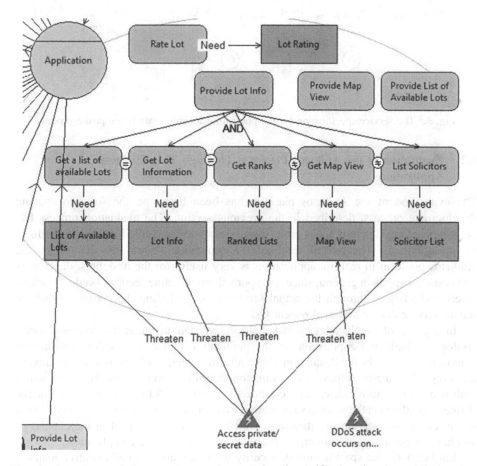

Fig. 4. An extract of the security requirements-based specification for the publishing lot information composite process

with a set of given security and trust properties applied to it. This composite service process has been consumed in a Web-based application, to offer the runtime realisation of the execution level capabilities of the Aniketos platform.

In order to facilitate the proper operation of the Web application through the Aniketos platform, we have performed different test scenarios at runtime, which include the conduction of various trigger events to form and emulate a violation of the specified security agreement. Thus, the application is tested to observe the runtime behavior for different configurations of the service execution, aiming to showcase how and when service re-composition and reconfiguration occurs, in accordance to the specific runtime rules.

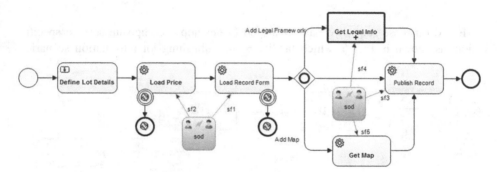

Fig. 5. The service specification for the publishing lot information composite process

4.2   Evaluation of the Aniketos Platform Through This Business Application

The evaluation of the Aniketos platform has been based on the scenario specific development process, described in the previous section. The evaluation process has been evolved through both focus group discussions and structured feedback in the form of questionnaires. The overall result of the evaluation shows that the use of the Aniketos platform in real life applications is very useful for the designers, developers and domain experts in general, since it supports them to define security needs at various levels and navigate through the actual service process, hiding the complexity of the secure service design and deployment tasks.

In a group of highly relevant stakeholders, we demonstrated the Aniketos methodology to build the application for the publication of lot information. During the demonstration and in the discussion phase after it, specific advantages and disadvantages regarding the usefulness of the Aniketos capabilities were discussed, while issues with respect to future extensions were raised. A very useful overall outcome for the Aniketos platform is the seamless integration from the design time to the deployment of secure composite service specifications, which can, then, be reused in the context of another composition and, subsequently, be consumed in another application.

Furthermore, the specification of security requirements in a collaborative manner, in which you have different stakeholders sitting together in order to define the complex process is another asset for the Aniketos platform and the level of expertise from the these stakeholders that needs to be captured in the platform. This, also, drives how security is applied as part of the high level concept of the application, which is, then, mapped to specific service processes with certain security restrictions.

Despite the positive points raised in the evaluation feedback, some missing aspects have been spotted down as well. Of particular interest for future work is the fact that the evaluators would like to see the whole set of security properties that you define at the design phase to be populated after the deployment phase as well. Emphasizing on the security properties lifecycle, it would be of great importance for the service providers to be able to visually track the evolution of the security property values at runtime. For example, if you specify a trustworthiness level during the development of a service composition to be greater than 0.5, you should be able to monitor whether the provided services offer a trustworthiness level greater than 0.7 or not.

Another important feature that has been suggested during the evaluation refers to the ranking of the available candidate compositions at the development phase. One should be able to balance the algorithm of the ranking, by giving specific weights over, for example, the trustworthiness and the credibility criteria, resulting to a hybrid ranking experience. This might be useful when you have different security requirements along your process and the service designer should be able to define the balance on the ranking across these security requirements.

As an overall evaluation statement, using the Aniketos platform, it turns that service composition can be enhanced, enabling the involved stakeholders establishing a sense of trust when using the respective software packages. In the e-Government domain, service composition is subject to security restrictions and concerns, which are potentially driven by legal limitations. Thus, in this specific domain, in which citizens and enterprises' trust on ICT systems owned by the local authorities lowers with the credibility of the public bodies, the need for a third party "certification" of best practice development is necessary. The same is applicable to an extended list of paradigms in various business sectors, in which the exploitation of the Aniketos platform provisions can eventually minimize the final costs for developing future Internet applications, paying specific attention to security concerns existing in them.

5 Conclusions

Today's ICT systems are evolved within a service-based space, in which data plays a key role as a valuable asset of the service engineering process. Web content is continuously made available and is being provided through Web services, which are autonomously or synergistically operate to feed the business execution of any kind of organisation, including commercial branches, industries, and governments. As the value the involved data streams increases, the need for protecting the composition of the service delivery processes is increased as well, aiming to offer innovative services for the consumers of Future Internet applications and systems.

In this paper, we presented the security by design concepts built in the Aniketos project, when developing composite services, focusing on an example from the public service delivery domain. We elaborated on the Aniketos methodology to deliver security solutions that are bound to the actual needs of the service development life-cycle, in which service developers can express specific high level security requirements and translate them to service process level requirements, which are associated with the secure service specifications being constructed in a formal language (namely secure BPMN).

By defining own security policies, service developers can investigate on the appropriate combination of atomic services in a composite service process chain and enact the execution of the composite service process to monitor that at runtime the specified security attributes are compliant to the expressed security policies. In that respect, the paper offered realisation on how the development and deployment of Aniketos compliant composite services in the context of business level applications, and in our case for the e-Government domain, can be affected by the security provisions of individual service components.

At this point, we would like to mention that this work is partially funded by the European Commission under the FP7 Framework Programme and Grant Agreement 257930 Aniketos project [2]. We would like to thank all Aniketos partners in contributing to the design, specification, development and evaluation of the Aniketos capabilities and the delivery of the Aniketos platform, which was the basis for the work in this paper.

References

1. Meland, P.H., Guerenabarrena, J.B., Llewellyn-Jones, D.: The challenges of secure and trustworthy service composition in the Future Internet. In: 2011 6th International Conference on Proceeding of System of Systems Engineering (SoSE). IEEE Computer Society (2011)
2. FP7-257930 Aniketos project. www.aniketos.eu
3. Georgia Institute of Technology, "Emerging Cyber Threats Report 2014". Georgia Tech Cyber Security Summit 2013
4. Pajaa, E., Choprab, A.K., Giorgini, P.: Trust-based specification of sociotechnical systems. Data Knowl. Eng. **87**, 339–353 (2013). doi:10.1016/j.datak.2012.12.005. Elsevier
5. Paja, E., Dalpiaz, F., Giorgini, P.: Managing security requirements conflicts in socio-technical systems. In: Ng, W., Storey, V.C., Trujillo, J.C. (eds.) ER 2013. LNCS, vol. 8217, pp. 270–283. Springer, Heidelberg (2013)
6. Object Management Group(OMG), Business Process Modelling and Notation (BPMN) specification v2.0, January 2011. www.bpmn.org
7. Brucker, A.D., Malmignati, F., Merabti, M., Qi, S., Bo, Z.: A Framework for Secure Service Composition. In: Proceedings of the International Conference on Social Computing 2013 (SocialCom), IEEE, pp. 647–652, doi:10.1109/SocialCom.2013.97
8. Ayed, D., Asim, M., Llewellyn-Jones, D.: An event processing approach for threats monitoring of service compositions. In: Proceedings of the 2013 International Conference on Risks and Security of Internet and Systems (CRiSIS), IEEE, pp. 1–10, doi:10.1109/CRiSIS. 2013.6766363
9. Hall, R.S., Pauls, K., McCulloch, S., Savage, D.: OSGi in Action. Manning Publications Co., Greenwich (2011)
10. Cummins, H., Ward, T.: Enterprise OSGi in Action. Manning Publications Co., Birmingham (2013)

11. Dalpiaz, F., Paja, E., Giorgini, P.: Security requirements engineering via commitments. In: Proceedings of STAST'11, pp. 1–8 (2011)
12. Brucker, A.D.: Integrating security aspects into business process models. IT Inf. Technol. **55** (6), 239–246 (2013). ISSN: 2196-7032. doi:10.1524/itit.2013.2004. http://www.brucker.ch/bibliography/abstract/brucker-securebpmn-2013. Special Issue on Security in Business Processes

Exploiting the Network
for Securing Personal Devices

Chris Dalton[1], Antonio Lioy[2](✉),
Diego Lopez[3], Fulvio Risso[2], and Roberto Sassu[2]

[1] HP Laboratories, Bristol, UK
[2] Dipartimento di Automatica e Informatica, Politecnico di Torino, Torino, Italy
lioy@polito.it
[3] Teléfonica I+D, Madrid, Spain

Abstract. Personal devices (such as smartphones and laptops) often experience incoherent levels of security due to the different protection applications available on the various devices. This paper presents a novel approach that consists in offloading security applications from personal devices and relocating them inside the network; this will be achieved by enriching network devices with the appropriate computational capabilities to execute generic security applications. This approach is fostered by the SECURED project, which will define the architecture, data and protocols needed to turn this vision into reality.

Keywords: Network-based personal security · Personal security protection · Remote attestation · Network functions virtualization

1 Introduction

The recent years have witnessed an increasing number of user terminals (such as laptops and smartphones) being connected to the Internet and we foresee an even more exciting growth in the coming years, due to new functions such as car infotainment systems, smart Internet-of-Things (IoT) devices, and more. This scenario encompasses a high number of devices with very different capabilities and hence poses significant challenges in terms of security, particularly with respect to protection from external threats.

First, many devices have limited resources, particularly embedded and mobile devices, and are often further constrained by severe limitations in terms of power consumption. As a consequence, complex protection applications (like anti-virus or VPN client with strong encryption) may not be executed on all devices.

Second, users can access the network from anywhere, hence they experience different levels of protection depending on the network they are connected to. For example, a user is typically exposed to more threats when connecting from a public hotspot than when connecting from the corporate network (as it usually includes a sophisticated border firewall).

© Springer International Publishing Switzerland 2014
F. Cleary and M. Felici (Eds.): CSP Forum 2014, CCIS 470, pp. 16–27, 2014.
DOI: 10.1007/978-3-319-12574-9_2

Last but not least, the level of protection depends upon the security applications available for a specific terminal. For example, a laptop can be equipped with a powerful parental control, while the same software may not be available when browsing the Internet from a smart TV, hence leaving kids unprotected.

This paper proposes a possible solution to the above problems, based on a *network application offloading* approach [7]. In a nutshell, we move protection from the user terminal to the (closest) network edge device (NED), which can be represented by an access point, switch or router, augmented with the computing capabilities required to run the offloaded security applications. According to this approach, users will configure the desired security countermeasures (applications and policies) only once, then they will be applied automatically by all NEDs regardless of the user terminal and network connection.

The main advantage of this approach consists in transforming protection from device- or network-based into a new user-centric paradigm, hence delivering personalized protection independent from the user's device and location. In addition, this would no longer require to install specific software on each terminal, which simplifies management and reduces power consumption, hence offering to devices with limited capabilities the same level of protection of more complex platforms. This approach is fostered by the project SECURED[1], which is currently designing the technical framework to turn this vision into reality.

2 Requirements

Running personal security applications into the network is a sensitive action and several requirements must be met by an architecture aiming to reach this target.

2.1 Security Requirements

Trust. Since applications would be executed at a node not under the control of the end user, a verification mechanism is needed to provide evidence that the NED can be trusted to run the applications. In particular, a NED should provide the following guarantees.

First, it must prove to be an original device and not one simulating the SECURED behaviour (for example by reproducing the same output upon a request); the consequence of trusting a fake device could be that its owner could manipulate the traffic of the victim at his will.

Second, a NED must prove that the traffic of a given user is processed by the applications he requested and not by some malicious software (that could, for example, forward all user's traffic to an attacker's favourite location).

Note that trust should come from the evaluation of these guarantees, but we do not exclude the possibility to accept other sources of trust. For instance, the user might be satisfied with trust originating from non-technical considerations, such as having the physical control of his home gateway or a contractual agreement (and corresponding liability) with his ISP.

---

[1] http://www.secured-fp7.eu/

Channel protection. If the user trusts a NED, he must also create a protected channel with it, so that attackers cannot manipulate the traffic. In addition, he must ensure that the other channel endpoint is the same entity that presented the trust proofs, otherwise an attacker could perform a man-in-the-middle attack by relaying the proofs requests and replies to a trusted device.

Isolation. As a NED could be multi-tenant (e.g. many users connected at the same time to a public WiFi access point), it must ensure the proper separation of traffic of the different users and must bind each flow only to the applications selected by that user. Since applications could misbehave (e.g. due to a bug or a vulnerability exploited through a malformed packet), a NED must properly confine each application so that a misbehaving one does not affect the others.

2.2 Technical Requirements

User authentication. To deliver protection to the right user, a NED must have the capability to recognize who is currently connecting to it with a standard authentication procedure (e.g. a username/password pair). It is worth noting that this is not a mechanism for network access control, although the NED could use information exchanged during that phase. Rather, authentication is needed to retrieve the user's profile (applications and policies) so that a NED knows how the traffic of this user must be processed.

Standardized platform. Since a security application could run on an arbitrary NED (e.g. home gateway or corporate switch, depending on the location a user connect from), it must be designed to support different environments. This requirement could be met by designing applications in a platform-independent way (e.g. as Java byte-code) or ensuring that a NED could run the environment required by an application (e.g. through virtualization).

Standardized policies. Typically applications that accomplish similar tasks for different platforms offer different configuration options, thus increasing complexity for a user to obtain the same behaviour. To overcome this problem, a user should have the possibility to express how his traffic must be processed with an application-independent policy language.

Scalability. Since the NED is primarily a networking device (although augmented with computational capabilities) supporting a massive number of concurrent tenants connected to it, all the NED components executing user applications should be as lightweight as possible, with fast primitive operations oriented to network processing, such as packet filtering and segment/payload reassembling.

3   The SECURED Infrastructure

3.1   NED Deployment Scenarios

Figure 1 presents the possible implementation options of the NED according to three orthogonal dimensions, namely the hardware architecture, the type of deployment, and how the user traffic is delivered to the NED.

The first dimension considers two possible hardware options: components engineered for data plane processing (e.g. network processors, hierarchical memory architectures, hardware accelerators) versus standard components (e.g. general purpose processors, mainstream memories). The former is more appropriate for high speed processing, while the latter offers a better price/performance ratio and looks more appropriate to integrate the NED in a cloud-like infrastructure.

Concerning the second dimension, we distinguish the NED as a monolithic component that implements all the core functions from the case in which the NED functions are distributed across multiple elements. For example, a traditional router without advanced computing capabilities might redirect the user traffic (e.g. through OpenFlow [5]) to a server that takes care of the required processing. The monolithic flavour looks simpler to deploy and manage (e.g. the procedure to verify the hardware/software integrity has to handle a single box), while the distributed model can guarantee better scalability and is more oriented to cloud-like environments.

The third dimension refers to the way the user traffic is redirected to the NED. While the preferred incarnation of this project assumes that the network is SECURED-aware and hence the traffic is automatically handled by the (first) network device encountered ("transparent" traffic steering), we foresee also the case of a user connecting to an untrusted or legacy network. In this case we provide a small agent operating on the user device to establish a secure tunnel to a remote NED and delivers all the user traffic to it ("explicit" traffic steering).

The Cartesian product of these three dimensions (with two options each) generates the eight points in Fig. 1, corresponding to possible deployment scenarios. Among the different possibilities, labelled (A) – (H) in the figure, we discuss now those that we consider most promising (Fig. 2).

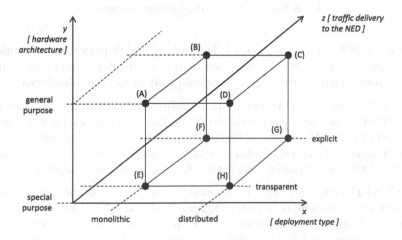

Fig. 1. Dimensions for the possible NED deployment scenarios.

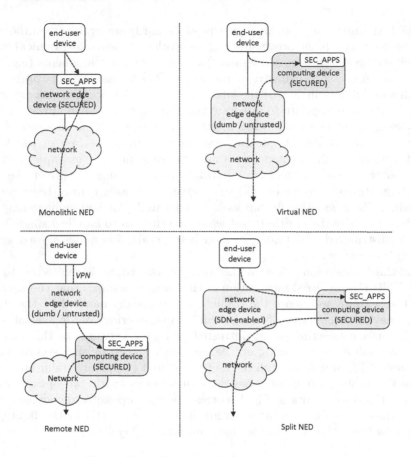

Fig. 2. Some SECURED deployment scenarios.

Monolithic NED (case E). This is the case of a high performance appliance (e.g. HP 3800 series) directly connected with the user device and containing a network router with a custom computational unit in the same hardware box.

Split NED (case D). This represents a traditional access router directly connected with the user device and redirecting the traffic to a general purpose server (e.g. via SDN technologies such as OpenFlow), which executes the security applications. This model could work also on legacy networks, when traditional routers are coupled with a companion server that takes care of the processing.

Virtual NED (case C). This is the case where a local compute node, under user control (e.g. a home desktop), is equipped with the NED software and acts as a communication gateway for all user's devices. User terminals have to connect directly to the virtual NED (via the local network, if trusted by the user, or by means of a secure channel) by explicitly redirecting their traffic to this box.

Remote NED (case B). This point represents the case in which the user terminal explicitly connects to a remote NED through a secure channel (e.g. a traditional virtual private network): in this case we would depart from our philosophy of not requiring any modification to the client as we need to install a custom application at the user terminal. This approach would incur penalties both in management (necessity of a VPN client) and performance (additional computations performed at the terminal and non optimized routing through the remote NED). However we consider this case as a form of "last resort" option if the user connects to a legacy network without SECURED capabilities: this case should be rare as many modern routers already support some protocols that enable the implementation at least of the split NED option.

3.2   Providing Trust

Regardless of how the infrastructure is implemented, the most important aspect from the user's perspective is that the NED must be able to process the traffic as expected and must prove this to the user. The problem is how to guarantee to a user that, when he connects to a network, the traffic will be processed by a SECURED device. Indeed, a user may connect to a legacy network (without NEDs) or to a NED that has been previously compromised: in these cases users are exposed to possible threats. To avoid this situation, SECURED exploits the Trusted Computing technology, in particular the *remote attestation* procedure.

The Trusted Computing Group (TCG) defined the specifications of a cryptographic chip, the Trusted Platform Module (TPM) [4], which uniquely identifies a Trusted Platform (TP). The TPM contains the necessary primitives to record measurements (i.e. fingerprints) of hardware and software components, to protect measurements integrity while they are stored at the TP, and to securely transmit them to a verifier. The latter can evaluate, from received data, if the TP will perform the requested tasks as expected: this procedure is known as remote attestation.

If the user remotely attests a NED before sending network traffic to it, this prevents the threats described above:

- in case of a legacy network, a device cannot prove to the user that it belongs to a SECURED infrastructure since this proof requires the use of an asymmetric key (Attestation Identity Key), which belongs to a unique TPM and whose private part is never exposed outside this chip;
- in case of a compromised NED, the TCG methodology ensures that the user can reliably detect if the accessed device will not properly process his traffic.

However, the sole attestation of the NED is not enough to protect users against attacks from other users connected to the same network. Indeed, attackers may try to intercept or modify the communication between the user and the attested NED. Although a secure channel is appropriate to overcome this problem, this does not ensure that the endpoint contacted by the user is the attested NED: as pointed out in [2], the endpoint may be a device controlled by an attacker relying the attestation to a NED. To fight this threat, SECURED employs a trusted channel between the user terminal and the NED and investigates which solution is the best fit for this goal (e.g. [1] or [8]).

3.3   Security Policies

SECURED allows to describe user security requirements via a High-level Security Policy Language (HSPL). HSPL is a user-oriented language suitable for expressing concepts related to end-point protection, which represents a departure from current languages that are either related to network filters (for border firewalls) or to access control (for database and applications). This language is appropriate for capturing the user requirements but cannot be directly implemented by security controls. As a consequence, we translate HSPL into a medium-level security policy language (MSPL) which conveys the same information in an application-independent format suitable for configuring security controls, typically an ordered sequence of permit and deny actions related to matching packets or payloads. A final translation step is needed from the MSPL to the application-dependent languages that are needed to configure the actual security controls (e.g. the Linux iptables firewall or the Snort intrusion detection system).

The Security Policy Management service (SPM) allows users to create, delete, edit, view, store and save their security policies. Each user may have more than one set of policies (associated to different personae) to differentiate the level of protection according to the security level required for a certain type of work. The SPM is also the main user interface to select security applications (or Personal Security Applications, PSA in short), either directly (in case of an expert user that prefers an application-driven security configuration) or indirectly (in case of a user preferring a policy-driven security configuration and thus selecting applications among those that offer the capabilities needed by his policy).

Once the policy has been specified with MSPL statements and PSAs with the required capabilities have been selected, we still need to create the configuration files for the PSAs. This is done by invoking the Medium-to-Low level (M2L) translation service associated to each PSA: it transforms a policy expressed in MSPL in the configuration format required by the specific application.

4   The SECURED Architecture

Figure 3 displays the SECURED architecture. We now proceed to explain how the application offloading can be realized, examining first modifications at the user terminals (to recognize if it is attached to a SECURED network) and then introducing the main components inside the NED. Finally, we describe at high level the steps required for a user to setup a network connection with SECURED.

4.1   User Terminal

If the user may access either a SECURED infrastructure or a legacy network, he must install on his devices a small monitoring application, the SECURED app. This application is activated each time the device attaches to a new network to check that the connection is to a trusted and secure NED. In case this condition is not verified, the SECURED app establishes a remote connection (e.g. VPN) to

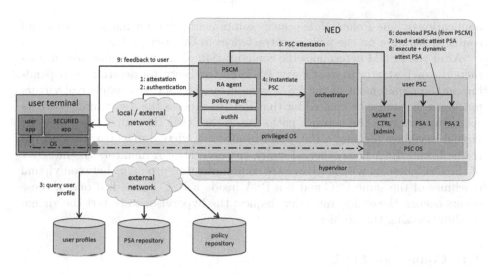

Fig. 3. Overview of the SECURED architecture.

a trusted NED and redirects all the traffic of the user terminal to the remote network node, hence guaranteeing the expected level of protection although with a higher latency.

It is worth nothing that the above application is not mandatory. For instance, we foresee the case of devices which cannot install this application. These devices are still compatible with the SECURED model, although they may not have access to additional features such as the possibility to trust the NED or to automatically connect to a remote NED in case of a legacy network.

4.2   The NED

Within the NED, each user is provided with a Personal Security Controller (PSC), a logical container of execution environments (e.g. virtual machines) that will coordinate the execution of his security applications into the network.

The PSC can run either directly on the network device (monolithic NED) or on a separate computational unit (split NED) When a user connects to the network, the NED will create a new PSC and download on the created container the security applications (PSAs). When ready, the new PSC will operate on the sole traffic of the user.

Two main NED components are involved in configuring the PSC: the Personal Security Controller Management service (PSCM) and an orchestrator.

The PSCM is the component contacted by users to setup a connection with SECURED and contains three main modules. A *Remote Attestation Agent* is in charge of executing the remote attestation protocol with the user and reporting the integrity status of a NED. An *Authentication Module* requests to a connecting user a proof of his identity to retrieve the user profile (policies and applications). The *Policy Management* component performs harmonization and conflict resolution on the policies extracted from the user profile.

After the PSCM determines the configuration of the user connection, it contacts the orchestrator to start a new PSC. The orchestrator determines, depending on the requirement of the PSAs chosen by the user, the number of virtual machines that must be created for that PSC to process the user traffic. Also, its role is to configure the network paths inside the NED (to connect together the virtual machines forming a PSC) and inside each virtual machine (to send the traffic from a PSA to another). Finally, the orchestrator monitors the integrity of the PSC, detects whether there are communication problems between virtual machines of the same PSC and if a PSA inside a PSC crashed; if one of these events occurs, the orchestrator may request the hypervisor to restart the virtual machine causing the problem.

4.3   Connection Set-Up

When a device connects to a NED the following steps are performed to create a protected network connection.

1. Front-end attestation. The user terminal has to perform a remote attestation pass toward the NED to verify that is connected to a trusted device running the expected software.

2. User authentication. This step aims at discovering the identity of the user connecting to the network, which is needed to retrieve his personal security profile. This could be integrated with existing authentication mechanisms that are already active for network access, such as the 802.1x protocol[2] or SIM-based authentication in mobile networks. This way the user would perform a single authentication, both for network access (not requested by SECURED) and to retrieve the user profile.

3. Retrieval of the user profile. Upon successful identification of the user, the PSCM fetches from a server the user security profile, which contains the list of PSAs to be executed and their calling order. Then the PSCM contacts the PSA repository to retrieve the application characteristics, such as their execution model (e.g. full fledged virtual machine, Java virtual machine, Linux container) and hardware requirements (e.g. CPU and memory). This information is needed to create a precise view of the computing/networking primitives to be set up, which includes the execution environment themselves, the PSAs, and the network connections between the previous components to satisfy the desired service order.

4. Setup of the user PSC. Giving the execution graph created in the previous step, the orchestrator issues the proper commands to create the required computing resources and properly connect them. These resources are grouped

---

[2] While the 802.1x protocol was originally intended to perform device authentication (e.g. based on the MAC address of the user terminal), recent extensions allow to perform this step based on user-defined credentials, such as username and password.

under the term Personal Security Controller (PSC), which may include different execution environments based on the requirements of the PSAs. In this step no PSAs are installed, as the user has to perform an additional verification step to make sure that his PSC has been set up properly.

5. Attestation of the PSC. The user completes a remote attestation phase to verify the correctness of the PSC (albeit limited to computing and networking resources), making sure that the execution environments are trusted and that traffic will traverse those components in the expected order.

6. Download and install applications and policies. PSAs are downloaded from the repository and installed in the execution environment. Furthermore, policies are retrieved from the user profile and applied to the applications.

7. Loading and attestation of the PSAs. PSAs are loaded in memory and are statically attested to verify the correctness of the applications themselves.

8. PSA execution. PSAs are launched and operate on the user traffic. Possibly, a dynamic attestation step can be carried out on the whole PSC (execution environments, network connections, PSAs) to detect run-time attacks.

9. Feedback to the user. Finally, the user is notified that all steps have been successfully completed and the user PSAs are operating properly. A dynamic feedback is optional but strongly desirable to notify users about possible changes (e.g. when moving from a network to another, hence the PSC moves to a different NED, or in case of any problem such as a crashed PSA or network issues).

Note that the user is required to complete the setup of his profile before being able to connect to a NED. This requires the user registration in the profile server with a valid account, selection of the proper PSAs and definition of the desired policies (following either the policy-driven or application-driven approach).

5 Evaluation and Conclusions

As evident from the discussion above, the execution model chosen for our network application offloading schema is compatible with the service model proposed in ETSI by the Network Functions Virtualization (NFV) group. This is a recent framework for the provision of network services by virtualization techniques [6] and many operators are looking at it with increasing interest. As such, it is of high interest also to SECURED as a target environment for its implementation. NFV is based on the availability of a homogeneous infrastructure, supporting the deployment, replication and mobility of software-based implementations of the different network functions, named VNF (Virtual Network Function). Network services are built by composing VNFs and deployed by the NFV Orchestrator upon the virtualized infrastructure.

NFV can support an additional SECURED model, the **Distributed NED**, which can be seen as the generalization of the Split one. In this case the NED is composed by several distinct processing components deployed in different locations, such as a dedicated server in the enterprise domain, the edge point-of-presence of the network operator, and/or a centralized datacenter. Each critical component (PSC, PSCM) is mapped to a separate VNF, while PSAs are mapped onto VNF elements, the so-called VNFCs (VNF components).

There are mutual benefits in a relationship between SECURED and NFV. First, the NED faces a scalability problem as it may have to cope with hundreds of simultaneous users, but this is not an issue for NFV as new VNF can easily be deployed as needed. Second, since VNF is a technology being currently adopted by telecom and network providers, its mapping with SECURED implies an easy implementation path for those parties wishing to offer SECURED services. Last but not least, as SECURED pays special attention to the trust and security aspects of the NED, there are several techniques (such as remote attestation for distributed systems) that could be adopted to improve the NFV framework.

In addition to NFV, the adoption of "industry standard" components, such as OpenFlow (for networking) and KVM/OpenStack (for the computation part), enables our solution to be integrated in cloud-oriented platforms, hence guaranteeing synergies between different services of a network operator. Moreover, this allows a NED to offload part of its workload to other machines, such as servers operating in a datacenter, which can guarantee almost unlimited computational power in addition to cost savings (even when the NFV approach is not taken). Our architecture does not mandate the use of a single option, but leaves freedom to choose the most appropriate technology depending on the deployment scenario: a single NED may be appropriate for a home network or a small company infrastructure, while a cloud/NFV architecture may be used by a mobile operator to handle the network traffic of its customers.

Offloading applications to the network gives important advantages. In many cases, our approach ensures better performance in terms of responsiveness and throughput because of the limited resources available at the user terminal. Second, it saves resources at the user terminal, that may be dedicated to other purposes (entertainment, work) or to save power. Third, it provides *personal* security protection, independent from the physical terminal in use. Finally, our approach breaks the paradigm that the highest security standards are available only on high-end platforms: a user could have many and heavy applications operating on his traffic even if his terminal does not satisfy the technical requirements (e.g. CPU frequency, amount of memory) for those applications.

Among the costs that need to be paid for our solution, we mention the increased amount of time needed for connecting (securely) to the network, in addition to the overhead generated by exchanging additional data between the user terminal and the NED. For instance, the trusted channel between the user terminal and the NED, one of the key elements described in Sect. 4, requires either performing encryption/decryption of network packets at each channel side[3] and repeatedly fetching and evaluating the integrity measurements performed by the NED. It is worth noting that the above overhead does not apply in all scenarios; for example, the trusted channel can be avoided if the user trusts the network he is connected to (i.e. other entities are not considered as

---

[3] This step could be avoided in case the access network already uses encryption, such as a WPA-protected WiFi hotspot.

adversaries or the user is directly connected to the NED with a cable). In this case, the network performance would be the same as if applications are run at the user's terminal. Another possible drawback of our solution is the difficulty, for PSAs running in the NED, to access the information available inside the user terminal, such as the application that generated a given packet, in order to implement per-application security policies. While currently we are not addressing this issue, we are confident that a solution can be envisioned based on [3], which requires an additional software in the user terminal that monitors the traffic and transfers the *<network session ID - process ID>* pairs to a PSA running in the NED.

We think that the results of this preliminary evaluation are promising. The proposed architecture opens an interesting opportunity to offer user-centric protection (as opposed to the current device- and network-centric approaches) and enables also new business models, such as a marketplace for security applications (PSAs) and ISP contracts including PSA execution.

Acknowledgement. The research described in this paper is part of the SECURED project, co-funded by the European Commission (FP7 grant agreement no. 611458).

References

1. Armknecht, F., Gasmi, Y., Sadeghi, A.R., Stewin, P., Unger, M., Ramunno, G., Vernizzi, D.: An efficient implementation of trusted channels based on OpenSSL. In: ACM Workshop on Scalable Trusted Computing, pp. 41–50 (2008)
2. Goldman, K., Perez, R., Sailer, R.: Linking remote attestation to secure tunnel endpoints. In: ACM Workshop on Scalable Trusted Computing, pp. 21–24 (2006)
3. Gringoli, F., Salgarelli, L., Dusi, M., Cascarano, N., Risso, F., Claffy, K.: GT: picking up the truth from the ground for Internet traffic. ACM SIGCOMM Comput. Commun. Rev. **39**(5), 12–18 (2009)
4. Trusted Computing Group: TPM Main Specification, Version 1.2, Revision 103 (2007). https://www.trustedcomputinggroup.org
5. McKeown, N., Anderson, T., Balakrishnan, H., Parulkar, G., Peterson, L., Rexford, J., Shenker, S., Turner, J.: Openflow: enabling innovation in campus networks. SIG-COMM Comput. Commun. Rev. **38**(2), 69–74 (2008)
6. Network Functions Virtualisation Industry Specification Group (NFV ISG): Network Functions Virtualisation - update white paper, October 2013. http://portal.etsi.org/NFV/NFV_White_Paper2.pdf
7. Risso, F., Cerrato, I.: Customizing data-plane processing in edge routers. In: European Workshop on Software Defined Networks, pp. 114–120 (2012)
8. Sadeghi, A.-R., Schulz, S.: Extending IPsec for efficient remote attestation. In: Sion, R., Curtmola, R., Dietrich, S., Kiayias, A., Miret, J.M., Sako, K., Sebé, F. (eds.) FC 2010 Workshops. LNCS, vol. 6054, pp. 150–165. Springer, Heidelberg (2010)

A Performance Analysis of ARM Virtual Machines Secured Using SELinux

Michele Paolino$^{(\boxtimes)}$, Mian M. Hamayun, and Daniel Raho

Virtual Open Systems, Grenoble, France
{m.paolino,m.hamayun,s.raho}@virtualopensystems.com
http://www.virtualopensystems.com

Abstract. Virtualization of the ARM architecture is becoming increasingly popular in several domains. Thus security is one of the main concerns in modern virtualized embedded platforms. An effective way to enhance the security of these platforms is through a combination of virtualization and Mandatory Access Control (MAC) security policies. The aim of this paper is to discuss the performance overhead of MAC-secured virtual machines. We compare the I/O performance of a KVM/ARM guest running on a SELinux host with the one of a non-secured VM. The result of the comparison is unexpected, since the performance of the SELinux based VM is better than the non-secured VM. We present a detailed analysis based on a modified version of SELinux running on an ARM core, and highlight the main causes of the observed performance improvement.

Keywords: ARM virtualization · SELinux · KVM ARM · VM security · MAC virtual machines · Mandatory access control (MAC)

1 Introduction

The ARM architecture is expanding from embedded systems to server, automotive and High Performance Computing (HPC) platforms. The use of virtualization is rapidly increasing in these platforms to save power through consolidation, to isolate applications and to deploy multiple operating system instances on shared hardware resources. As the use of virtualization technology becomes common place in enterprise and end-user markets *e.g.* Data Centers, NFV (Network Functions Virtualization) systems, Android devices, CPS (Cyber Physical Systems) *etc.*, new security aspects have emerged, such as protecting virtual machines from potential host based attacks.

A hypervisor or Virtual Machine Monitor (VMM) creates virtual instances of the CPUs, memory and interrupts to provide an illusion of a real machine in software. When the VMM implements full virtualization, it provides hardware isolation for these resources exploiting hardware features *e.g.* Virtualization Extensions, IOMMU and GIC in ARM platforms. Other resources such as

© Springer International Publishing Switzerland 2014
F. Cleary and M. Felici (Eds.): CSP Forum 2014, CCIS 470, pp. 28–36, 2014.
DOI: 10.1007/978-3-319-12574-9_3

device peripherals (network, disks *etc.*) or shared memory are isolated in software by the hypervisor and virtualized through emulation or para-virtualization. This constitutes the concept of isolation using virtualization, which is valid from the guest point of view but not from the host perspective. Especially for a privileged user in a standard Discretionary Access Control (DAC) environment, VM's resources are accessible without any restrictions. This means that a cloud administrator may read the disk data and sniff network traffic of its customers' virtual machines. Moreover, an attacker can compromise the host system (even from a virtual environment) and perform un-authorized operations over the resources that belong to the VMs.

Security issues that specifically affect virtual environments have been classified as: communication between VMs or between VMs and host, VM escape, VM monitoring from the host, VM monitoring from another VM, denial of service, guest-to-guest attacks, external modification of a VM and external modification of the hypervisor [14]. Most of these security threats, aim to compromise isolation between guests or between guest and host *e.g.* using the CPU cache [23] or directly assigned devices [13] to gain privileges or access un-authorized data. To mitigate these threats, hypervisors are provided with strong access control mechanisms [22] like the Mandatory Access Control (MAC) and Role Based Access Control (RBAC) [12]. In fact, in every virtualized system such as a cloud, the primary challenges for data security are the separation of sensitive data and access control mechanisms [20].

This paper presents a performance overview of the KVM/ARM VMs that leverage MAC policies to secure virtual resources. The Linux kernel provides different alternative implementations of MAC security policy such as SELinux, TOMOYO, AppArmor and SMACK. None of these is clearly better than the others but SELinux is considered the most mature and widely deployed amongst Linux enhanced security mechanisms [17]. The KVM hypervisor has been selected for this evaluation as it exploits the standard SELinux implementation. In fact, the most important alternative VMM for ARM *i.e.* XEN, has its own MAC implementation wrapped in Xen Security Modules (XSM) [2].

We compare the performance of two VMs: one running on a host using the DAC security policy and the other executed in SELinux environment. This comparison shows unexpected results, as the performance of SELinux based VM is better than the non-secure VM. We isolate and discuss the key factors behind this behavior using a modified version of SELinux. To the best of our knowledge, this is the first SELinux based performance analysis for KVM/ARM virtual machines.

This paper is organized as follows: Sect. 2 describes SELinux and the Linux Security Modules (LSM). Section 3 gives details on the hardware and software platform used to gather test results that are presented in Sect. 4. Related work is described in Sect. 5 and potential future directions are given in Sect. 6.

2   Security in the Linux Kernel

By default the Linux kernel uses DAC security policy, which is based on users and groups. This policy is easy to use but has significant drawbacks. In fact,

DAC allows the owner of a resource to freely delegate rights over it. Moreover, only two types of roles are supported: super user and normal users. The former (also known as root), may be a security threat as it has complete control of the system. This is particularly undesirable in multi-user, multi-tenancy systems such as cloud, server, NFV and CPS environments.

To overcome the security issues of DAC, Linux combines it with the MAC security policy, where a system-wide mechanism controls access to objects *e.g.* a socket, a disk file *etc.*, and an individual subject *e.g.* a process, a VM *etc.*, cannot alter it [6].

2.1 Linux Security Modules and SELinux

To avoid the proliferation of security solutions that perform invasive modifications to the Linux kernel, support for security solutions has been provided through an abstraction layer known as the Linux Security Modules (LSM). It enables the implementation of MAC policies as loadable kernel modules avoiding the necessity to deal with long and difficult to maintain patches. LSM allows modules to mediate access to kernel objects by placing hooks in the kernel code just ahead of access to them [25]. These hooks are scattered through-out the kernel and have been classified as task, program loading, file-system, IPC, module and network hooks [24]. A security module implements some or all of these hooks.

In 2001 SELinux was initially presented to the open source community as a kernel patch by the National Security Agency(NSA), and was later re-implemented as LSM module [19]. It is an implementation of the Flask OS security architecture [5] and its MAC policy is based on Type Enforcement (TE) that can also provide Role Based Access Control (RBAC). The Flask OS's main capability is to separate security access control decisions from their enforcement [1]. This feature has been inherited in SELinux, where the Security Server takes the security access control decisions and the LSM hooks enforce them [7]. Furthermore, SELinux has

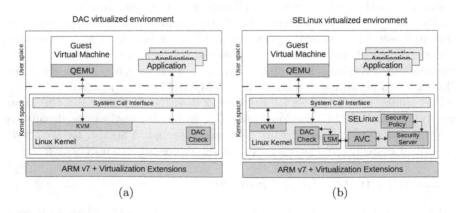

Fig. 1. DAC and SELinux based virtualization environments

a third component known as Access Vector Cache (AVC), which is designed to speed-up the access validation decisions. The AVC maintains a cache of decisions made by the Security Server for subsequent accesses [7]. Figure 1 shows the DAC and SELinux based virtualization environments.

2.2   Disabling the SELinux AVC

When comparing a guest in a DAC virtualization environment (Fig. 1a) with a VM in a SELinux host (Fig. 1b), the later shows better I/O performance. This result is unexpected given that SELinux introduces at-least two different sources of overhead: the first one comes from the LSM layer and the second is due to the access control decision making infrastructure *i.e.* SELinux performs a security check every time a subject wants to execute an operation on an object. So this additional cost *should* lower the performance of SELinux host VMs. In order to explain these results and evaluate its performance impact on the overall security system, we *disable* the main component designed to improve the SELinux performance *i.e.* the AVC.

We modify the avc_has_perm_noaudit() function, which performs permissions checks in every access. The permission check is firstly delegated to the AVC cache and if the result is not found (an AVC miss), the request is forwarded to the Security Server. In order to oblige the Linux kernel to always go through the Security Server, we force a cache miss for each request. To include the lookup time in our measurements, we force the cache miss *after* the AVC lookup function. This modification aims to keep the SELinux source code changes as simple as possible. In fact, a complete removal of the AVC would result in important modifications to the existing code as it has been included in SELinux from very early stages, and it is fully integrated into it. In addition, this enables us to measure the AVC cache miss influence on an implementation that is very similar to the mainline SELinux.

3   Hardware/Software Platform and Benchmarks

The Texas Instruments OMAP5-uEVM board has been used to perform these tests. It is equipped with two ARM Cortex-A15 MPCore (1.5 GHz), 2 GB of DDR3L RAM and a 16 GB MicroSD card (Class 6). Although Ubuntu 12.04 is the most widely used distribution on ARM, it does not officially support SELinux so we installed Fedora 20 as a host on the OMAP platform. To create and manage virtual machines we used QEMU 1.7.91 and libvirt 1.2.2 [10]. The mainline kernel v3.14.0 is used for the host; for the DAC virtualization environment (Fig. 1a) it is compiled without any security support (*i.e.* no LSM) and for the MAC secured virtualization environment (Fig. 1b), it is compiled with SELinux support and booted in targeted enforcing mode.

The VM runs Ubuntu 12.04 (kernel v3.12.0-rc7) with 256 MB of RAM and is pinned to a physical processor. The virtio para-virtual drivers have been used for both network and disks. The VM's disk image is stored on the host local storage. The *noop* I/O scheduler and EXT4 file-system have been used in both guest and host systems.

The *iozone* and *netperf* software benchmarks are used for the guest file-system and network tests, respectively. In fact, I/O is the most important reason for interactions between the guest and host systems. The disk tests have been performed with different file sizes *i.e.* 4 KB, 100 KB, 1 MB, 2 MB and 10 MB. The smallest file size is equal to the block size of EXT4 file-system, while the higher values are small-to-medium sizes that are commonly found in different use-cases. To prevent any caching mechanism between the VM and host, we disable caches in the *virtio* and *iozone* configurations. The performance evaluation of SELinux within the virtual machines is out-of-scope of this paper.

4   Performance Evaluation and Results

In this section we present some experimental results on I/O performance of the ARM virtual machines. All of the disk performance figures show the average results of 13 file-system operations for 5 different file sizes (65 in total), and each test has been repeated 30 times. In Figs. 2 and 3, a negative result means that the VM on SELinux host is faster as compared to the DAC host VM. Figure 2 presents a comparison between two guests: the first running in a DAC environment and the second on a SELinux host. In this case, the SELinux host based VM is faster in 38 out of 65 tests (58 % negative results).

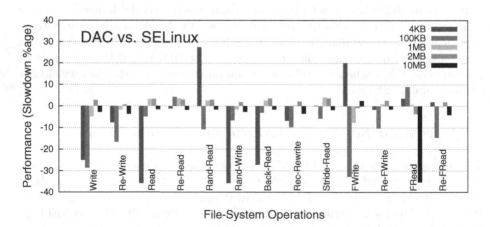

Fig. 2. VM disk performance with a standard SELinux host (with AVC)

These results are unexpected for the reasons discussed in Sect. 2.2. So we neutralize the SELinux AVC cache and obtain the results shown in Fig. 3. These results highlight the overall impact of AVC cache on the disk performance. It is interesting to see that 8 out of 65 results are still negative (12 %), where 7 results are greater than −8 % of slowdown percentage and the most negative one

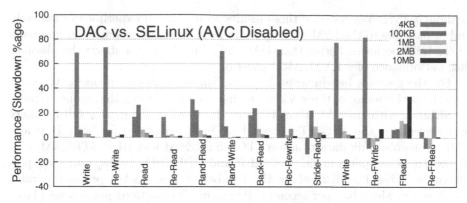

Fig. 3. VM disk performance with a SELinux host (AVC disabled)

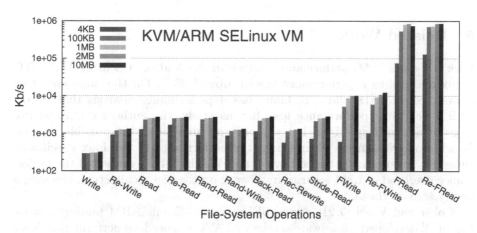

Fig. 4. VM absolute disk performance on SELinux host (with AVC)

Table 1. VM streaming I/O performance results (*netperf*)

	SELinux (with AVC)	SELinux (AVC disabled)	DAC host
TCP_STREAM	45.96 Mbps	14.23 Mbps	41.79 Mbps
UDP_STREAM	114.57 Mbps	23.99 Mbps	81.75 Mbps

Table 2. VM request/response I/O performance results (*netperf*)

	SELinux (with AVC)	SELinux (AVC disabled)	DAC host
TCP_RR	630.37 Tps	362.50 Tps	615.07 Tps
UDP_RR	653.93 Tps	377.01 Tps	641.18 Tps

is about −13 %. We consider these results as mostly an experimental anomaly and in part due to the LSM framework. In fact, there are examples in literature where LSM performs better than DAC [25]. Finally, Fig. 4 shows the absolute disk performance of a KVM/ARM guest on a SELinux host.

For the network benchmarks, a similar approach has been taken. We compare the performance of three VMs: the first on a DAC host, the second running on SELinux with the AVC disabled, and the third running on a full SELinux host (leveraging the AVC). Two tests have been performed for both TCP and UDP protocols: bulk data transfers (TCP_STREAM and UDP_STREAM) and request/response performance (TCP_RR and UDP_RR). These results are presented in Tables 1 and 2, where the bandwidth and packet processing rates are shown in Mega-bits per second (Mbps) and Transactions per second (Tps), respectively. In both cases, similar to the disk benchmark results, we can claim that SELinux VM is faster than the DAC guest. These results also show that AVC has a significant impact over the network performance of the guest VMs.

5   Related Work

Park [11] did a MAC performance analysis of the Android OS using TOMOYO Linux and claims a performance loss of around 25 %. On the same operating system, Shabtai [18] did a SELinux based performance analysis that results with a negligible performance loss. In this study, the authors confirmed two cases of SELinux speed-up, but without any analysis of the possible reasons. In addition, Nakamura [9] measured the performance of SELinux specifically tuned for resource-constrained devices and Wright [24,25] measured the performance overhead of LSM security framework on the x86 architecture, claiming a nearly zero overhead.

Coker and Vogel [3,21] ported SELinux to different ARM platforms while Fiorin [4] developed a hardware accelerated AVC to speed-up performance. None of these works take into account virtualized environments.

Other studies include the Mandatory Access Control implementation directly in the hypervisor (vHype and XEN, Sailer [15,16]) to improve the management and run-time security of the system. Lastly, Nahari [8] proposed a secure embedded Linux architecture by means of virtualization, SELinux and ARM TrustZone.

6   Conclusions and Future Work

We provided a detailed I/O performance analysis of a KVM/ARM guest running on a SELinux host. We compared these results with a guest running without any security enhancements *i.e.* on a DAC host. Our test results show that virtual machines running in a DAC environment are slower than virtual machines running on a SELinux host. We discussed the main causes of this performance improvement, and finally we strongly recommend the use of SELinux in any virtualized environment *e.g.* Data Centers, NFV systems, Android devices, CPS *etc.*, for both security and performance enhancement.

Future work will include an analysis of the LSM framework impact on the guests performance in systems enhanced with MAC security policies. In addition, it will be interesting to study the scalability of KVM/ARM VMs on SELinux hosts, analyzing the performance while increasing number of guests in the system. Finally we will investigate acceleration methods for those systems which cannot exploit MAC security.

Acknowledgment. This research work has been supported by the FP7 TRESCCA project under the grant number 318036.

References

1. Barr, J.: The Flask Security Architecture. Comput. Sci. **574**, 6 (2002)
2. Coker, G.: Xen security modules (XSM). Xen Summit, pp. 1–33 (2006)
3. Coker, R.: Porting NSA security enhanced linux to hand-held devices. In: Proceedings of the Linux Symposium, Ottawa Linux Symposium (2003)
4. Fiorin, L., Ferrante, A., Padarnitsas, K., Regazzoni, F.: Security enhanced linux on embedded systems: a hardware-accelerated implementation. In: 17th Asia and South Pacific Design Automation Conference (ASP-DAC), pp. 29–34. IEEE (2012)
5. Lepreau, J., Spencer, R., Smalley, S., Loscocco, P., Hibler, M., Andersen, D.: The flask security architecture: system support for diverse security policies. In: SSYM'99 Proceedings of the 8th conference on USENIX Security Symposium (2006)
6. Lindqvist, H.: Mandatory access control. Master's Thesis in Computing Science, Umea University, Department of Computing Science, SE-901 87 (2006)
7. Mayer, F., Caplan, D., MacMillan, K.: SELinux by Example: Using Security Enhanced Linux. Pearson Education, Prentice Hall (2006)
8. Nahari, H.: Trusted secure embedded linux. In: Proceedings of 2007 Linux Symposium, pp. 79–85. Citeseer, Ottawa Ontario, Canada:[sn] (2007)
9. Nakamura, Y., Sameshima, Y.: SELinux for consumer electronics devices. In: Proceedings of Linux Symposium, pp. 125–133 (2008)
10. Paolino, M.: sVirt Security for KVM Virtualization on OMAP5 uEVM. http://www.virtualopensystems.com/en/solutions/guides/kvm-svirt-omap5/
11. Park, J., Kim, B., Kim, S.R., Yoon, J.H., Cho, Y.: Performance analysis of security enforcement on android operating system. In: Proceedings of the 2011 ACM Symposium on Research in Applied Computation, pp. 282–286. ACM (2011)
12. Pék, G., Bencsáth, B., et al.: A survey of security issues in hardware virtualization. ACM Comput. Surv. (CSUR) **45**(3), 40 (2013)
13. Pék, G., Lanzi, A., Srivastava, A., Balzarotti, D., Francillon, A., Neumann, C.: On the feasibility of software attacks on commodity virtual machine monitors via direct device assignment. In: ACM Symposium on Information, Computer and Communications Security (ASIACCS) (2014)
14. Reuben, J.S.: A survey on virtual machine security. Helsinki University of Technology (2007)

15. Sailer, R., Jaeger, T., Valdez, E., Caceres, R., Perez, R., Berger, S., Griffin, J.L., van Doorn, L.: Building a MAC-based security architecture for the xen open-source hypervisor. In: 21st Annual Computer Security Applications Conference, 10 pp. IEEE (2005)
16. Sailer, R., Valdez, E., Jaeger, T., Perez, R., Van Doorn, L., Griffin, J.L., Berger, S., Sailer, R., Valdez, E., Jaeger, T., et al.: sHype: secure hypervisor approach to trusted virtualized systems. Technical report, RC23511 (2005)
17. Schreuders, Z.C., McGill, T., Payne, C.: Empowering end users to confine their own applications: the results of a usability study comparing SELinux, AppArmor, and FBAC-LSM. ACM Trans. Inf. Syst. Secur. (TISSEC) **14**(2), 19 (2011)
18. Shabtai, A., Fledel, Y., Elovici, Y.: Securing android-powered mobile devices using SELinux. IEEE Secur. Priv. **8**(3), 36–44 (2010)
19. Smalley, S., Vance, C., Salamon, W.: Implementing SELinux as a linux security module. NAI Labs Rep. **1**, 43 (2001)
20. Thapliyal, M., Mandoria, H.L., Garg, N.: Data security analysis in cloud environment: a review. Int. J. Innovations Adv. Comput. Sci. **2**(1), 14–19 (2014)
21. Vogel, B., Steinke, B.: Using SELinux security enforcement in linux-based embedded devices. In: Proceedings of the 1st international Conference on MOBILe Wireless MiddleWARE, Operating Systems, and Applications, ICST (Institute for Computer Sciences, Social-Informatics and Telecommunications Engineering), p. 15 (2008)
22. Vollmar, W., Harris, T., Long Jr., L., Green, R.: Hypervisor security in cloud computing systems. ACM Comput. Surv., 1–22 (2014)
23. Weiß, M., Heinz, B., Stumpf, F.: A cache timing attack on AES in virtualization environments. In: Keromytis, A.D. (ed.) FC 2012. LNCS, vol. 7397, pp. 314–328. Springer, Heidelberg (2012)
24. Wright, C., Cowan, C., Morris, J., Smalley, S., Kroah-Hartman, G.: Linux security module framework. In: Ottawa Linux Symposium. vol. 8032 (2002)
25. Wright, C., Morris, J., Kroah-Hartman, G., Cowan, C., Smalley, S.: Linux security modules: general security support for the linux kernel. In: Foundations of Intrusion Tolerant Systems (OASIS'03), p. 213. IEEE Computer Society (2003)

Airports as Critical Transportation Infrastructures Increasingly Impacted by Cyberattacks: A Case Study

Alessandro Pollini[1(✉)], Alessandra Tedeschi[1], and Lorenzo Falciani[2]

[1] Deep Blue, Piazza Buenos Aires 20, 00198 Rome, Italy
{alessandro.pollini,alessandra.tedeschi}@dblue.it
[2] George Washington University, 2121 St NW, Washington, DC, USA
Lorenzo@alumni.gwu.edu

Abstract. The current state of cyber security in today's critical infrastructures reveals that there have been a limited but growing number of incidents in which the defences of safety-critical applications have been penetrated. In this work we concentrate on airports' infrastructures and investigate how airport authorities are concerned with emerging terrorist threats, such as cyber threats, against airport installations and systems, and security gain and risk perception of passengers. A review of actual attacks and real issues in the airport infrastructures allowed us to build projections or potential future scenarios. In the context of the present research, we analyzed in a deeper detail these factors, developed an emerging threat scenario, and calibrated a prediction model on our findings.

Keywords: Airport · Security · Cyberthreat · Transport · Infrastructure

1 Introduction[1]

The current state of cyber security in today's critical infrastructures reveals that there have been a limited but growing number of incidents in which the defences of safety-critical applications have been penetrated, including Air Traffic Management infrastructures, Airport infrastructures, Fire and Rescue dispatch systems and Maritime monitoring applications. The first step is to identify what the new and emerging threats are. Despite the reluctance of private and public companies to report cyber attacks, especially those that have been successful, a number of precedents can be found in both old and recent media reports. Old reports show that the cyber security problem is not a novelty and can be rooted back to the very introduction of analogue remote access methods. New media reports help characterize the current state of cyber security identifying existing threats and attack vectors. In this work we concentrate on airports' infrastructures and investigate how the airport authorities are concerned with emerging terrorist threats, such as cyber threats, against airport installations and systems, and security gain and risk perception of passengers. As a way to mitigate the impact of such new menace, some technical, procedural and organizational countermeasures are being

---

[1] The views expressed in this article are those of the authors and do not necessarily represent the views of, and should not be attributed to, their respective companies and organizations.

© Springer International Publishing Switzerland 2014
F. Cleary and M. Felici (Eds.): CSP Forum 2014, CCIS 470, pp. 37–48, 2014.
DOI: 10.1007/978-3-319-12574-9_4

implemented. Even though it is hard to assess the risks posed by cyberattacks, the impact of the attacks is also captured in this study, both in terms of the probability of an attack and the consequences for safety and security [1]. The review of actual attacks and real issues in the airport infrastructures allowed us to build projections or potential future scenarios. The identified scenario is representative of the airport environment, and the risks are representative of emerging threats.

Cyber security emerging threats for airports are those threats that have already been identified, at least in one instance, as feasible on information systems, and are poised to become more impactful, or more widespread, or to migrate in the airport infrastructure, contributing to the overall risk of the airport's assets, operations or users. The threat and the threat agents vectors included in the selected scenario are identified as part of the list of 10 emerging threats for Critical Infrastructure [2], including the airport environment (i.e. includes aircraft, air traffic control systems, commercial and military airports, heliports, and landing strips) as officially appointed in the U.S. National Infrastructure Protection Plan (NIPP) [6]. While risks and impacts of a cyber attack are most intimately connected with the target environment, resources, and function; the motives, threat agents, and threats can be drawn back to reasonably small and consistent sets that span unaltered across sectors (public and private), industries (financial, manufacturing, transportation, etc.), and level of informatization of targets (low technology and low maturity to highly coupled technological infrastructures).

The socio-economic models are built on the basis of the developed scenarios. The intention of these models is not to accurately predict future modes of attack. In contrast, the aim is to advise airport security decision makers by providing them with an optimal portfolio of security investments. The Adversarial Risk Analysis (ARA) modeling approach [3] has been used to build the Cyberthreat model. According to the ARA approach, two intelligent adversaries' (the Defender and the Attacker) decisions and actions are modeled. The utility functions, aggregating all relevant information about costs, revenues, payoffs, etc., are used with the goal of modeling each adversary's preferences and utilities. Utility functions are built from the costs and revenues relevant for each actor. Non-monetary rewards can be included in the revenue function as well (e.g., the revenues in terms of fame, recognition among peers, etc. might be considered). Both adversaries are expected to be utility maximizers, i.e. they both will try to obtain the maximum profit from their actions, making the corresponding decisions. The final output of the model will be to give advice to airport authorities for devising a security plan, i.e. providing them with an optimal portfolio of defensive measures.

The research questions guiding the investigation of the airport security scenarios are:

- Do the current security regulations adequately and appropriately ensure that airports mitigate the risks and optimize resource allocation?
- Different sized airports: what is the difference from security cost and decision perspective?
- What is the impact related to the risk perception of passengers, of airport operators, or the social acceptance of security measures; and how can it be modeled?
- What is the balance between new security measures and emerging threats, in terms of cost and technology, security gain and risk perception of passengers?

These questions form the key requirements of this work. By utilizing the threats and the scenarios identified in the present report we aim to answer the questions presented above and build socio-economic models based upon those answers.

This paper presents a literature of recent cyber disruptions of critical infrastructures (Sect. 1) and airports' attacks (Sect. 2). Cyberthreat scenarios are then described in detail (Sect. 3) and the selection and validation processes that they underwent is addressed (Sect. 4). As concluding section, the modeling approach and the future steps are also presented (Sect. 5).

2   Recent Cyber Disruptions of Critical Infrastructures

The first step in the identification of the relevant scenarios has been to identify what is the current state of cyber security in today's airports' infrastructures, and to identify emerging threats. Despite the reluctance of private and public companies to report cyber attacks, especially those that have been successful, a number of precedents can be found in both old and recent media reports. Old reports show that the cyber security problem is not a novelty and can be rooted back to the very introduction of analog remote access methods. New media reports help characterizing the current state of cyber security identifying current threats and attack vectors.

Rationale for selecting the following references is:

(1) The problem that they present is not new, it is connected to the very presence of the IT infrastructure,
(2) Successful attacks inflicted large consequences even in a less interconnected (and slower) world.

Table 1. Cyberattack

Year	Description	Reference
1982	Devastating Explosion in Siberian Gas Pipeline Caused by Logic Bomb – The result was *the most monumental non-nuclear explosion and fire ever seen from space* (Thomas Reed, Former AF Secretary)	http://en.wikipedia.org/wiki/ Siberian_pipeline_sabotage
1997	Hacker launched a cyber attack that resulted in the disruption of all local police and fire 911 services as well as the ability of incoming aircraft to activate the runway lights at the Worcester, MA airport. The telephone service was out at the airport tower for six hours	http://www.gpo.gov/fdsys/pkg/ CHRG-106shrg68563/html/ CHRG-106shrg68563.htm

(Continued)

Table 1. (*Continued*)

Year	Description	Reference
2000	264,000 gallons of sewage intentionally released by the "insider" Vitek Boden who gained access into the controls of the sewer system of Australia's Maroochy Shire Council	http://www.aci-na.org/sites/default/files/larry_jaffe.pdf
2003	Slammer worm intrusion into Davis-Besse Ohio Nuclear Plant network. It rendered the network useless	http://www.aci-na.org/sites/default/files/larry_jaffe.pdf
2003	Worm infects CSX telecommunications network that supported both their signal system and dispatch system. Passenger and freight train traffic halted in 23 US states	http://www.aci-na.org/sites/default/files/larry_jaffe.pdf
2009–2010	StuxNet Worm Attack Targets Iranian Nuclear Program. Also, Infects India and Pakistan affecting SCADA targeting capability. Stuxnet uses two compromised security certificates (stolen from firms in Taiwan) and a previously unknown security hole in Windows to launch itself automatically from a memory stick. Targets particular Siemens controllers and a specific configuration of devices	http://www.theguardian.com/world/2012/jun/01/obama-sped-up-cyberattack-iran
2012	An unidentified group of hackers targeted various natural gas pipeline companies gained access to and exfiltrated data on how their control systems work	http://money.cnn.com/2013/01/09/technology/security/infrastructure-cyberattacks/

From the analysis of the cases reported in Table 1 it is possible to conclude that:

(1) Critical infrastructures can be and are attacked with success,
(2) Threat agents are various and diverse,
(3) Resources needed to successfully attack the CIs can be significant, but not always.

2.1 Airports Have Suffered Too

Selected incident reports of cyberattacks targeting Airports are:

2012	The National Technical Research Organisation (NTRO) officials alerted the Airports Authority of India (AAI) to serious vulnerabilities in its cargo management system at Chennai, Coimbatore, Kolkata, Amritsar, Lucknow and Guwahati airports. Weak passwords and outdated operating systems were the main problems. These six airports handled 311,000 metric tonne of international cargo in 2010/11. A single day's disruption would have sent 853 tonnes of cargo to the wrong destinations. "The economic impact would have been immense had the systems been penetrated by unscrupulous elements," says P.K. Kapoor, Executive Director (Information Technology), AAI.
2013	CBI believes a cyberattack led to IGI airport's technical problems, provoking the failure of the passenger processing system and impacting 50 flights delayed and their passengers had to be manually checked in.
2013	Boston digital security firm Trusteer says it uncovered malware hidden in the private network of a major non-U.S. international airport. The company says "the threat could have compromised everything from employees' personal information to the safety of passengers. [...] The attack used Citadel Trojan malware—which computer users can unknowingly install simply by clicking on a Web link—to read the screens of employees who logged in remotely to the airport's virtual private network (VPN). It also allowed the cybercriminals to capture the username, password, and one-time passcode of the victims with a form-grabbing technology".

The following conclusions may be drawn:

- Despite the secrecy around security breaches and especially on their impacts, we know that airports have been breached,
- Again, as for the Critical Infrastructures (CIs), resources needed to accomplish the breaches vary greatly, as well as the skill level of the attackers, The news contains often only partial impact assessments.

2.2 Cutting Edge Cyber Security

A search on academic resources and research products related to the field of airports' cyber security did not return many results. Much research and literature has been produced on airport security as a whole socio-technical system, considering cyber security as a single high level item, but without ascertaining in depth its contribution as a single point of failure for the airport infrastructure, neither in terms of direct impact nor economic risk, for both the operator and the users [4].

However, this should not be seen as a lack of research or attention to the problem. Information security includes the major families: people, processes and technology. In the context of airports, the people and processes will vary because of the specific context; however the technological family will mirror other industries, and is consistent with general IT security research, as IT systems and concepts are transversal. It is this connection that allows us to understand the IT security problem in airport, and allows us to use general IT references and studies.

3 Airport Security Cyberattack Scenarios

The information presented above identifies a number of current cyber security threats already 'in the wild', and then a subset of those attacks that previously hit airport infrastructures. The reported events are all actual attacks and real issues, not projections or potential scenarios. Considering that the trend of cyber threats, with respect to their targets and their frequency, has been found to be consistent across many sectors, on the basis of past events it's possible to argue that such attacks will increase and target also airports.

In the context of the SECONOMICS research project [5], it is inevitable to analyze in a deeper detail exactly these factors. For this purpose, three scenarios will be identified, and a prediction model will be developed, calibrated, and run on them.

The identified scenarios aim to be representative of the airport environment, and the risks should be representative of emerging threats. The present paper doesn't attempt to identify new and innovative way to perpetrate cyber attacks. While such an exercise may have a great value in developing a long term strategic view, such an approach lacks the evidence and hard reference data needed to plan actual defence and security measures. Cyber security emerging threats for airports are those threats that have already been identified, at least in one instance, as feasible on information systems, and are poised to have a significant impact, to become more widespread, or to migrate in the airport infrastructure, contributing to the overall risk of the airport's assets, operations or users.

The following scenarios fit the requirements set forth above and relate to the airport context. Within the context of the present research the following three scenarios will be deepened into details, validated through the involvement of the stakeholders and used to leverage the socioeconomic models building.

3.1 Scenario 1: Targeted Cyber Attack

This first scenario is an example of how technology can be used to create damage even where it is minimally used and by an attacker with a limited IT and/or security knowledge.

Scenario: An example in today's Europe would be a hacktivist group wishing to stop pollution by airplanes in a particular zone. It may be also a foreign state or terrorist group trying to disrupt commercial flight operations. The important thing to consider is that the technological knowledge required to successfully perpetrate a targeted cyber attack is limited and, if successful the attack can have the most extensive impact on the IT infrastructure. An iteration of this scenario can see a green hacktivist group gathering intelligence on two sets of airport employees, managing directors and IT system administrators. When enough intelligence has been gathered, they proceed to forge ad hoc emails to those people. The probability that those emails containing links or documents are opened by the receivers is relatively high. The infected attached documents or links then give a backdoor in the systems to the attacker, possibly with the target access privileges. The attacker then gains a foothold in the system with limited chances to be discovered by eventual Intrusion Detection Systems (IDS)/Intrusion Protection Systems IPSs placed in the network.

Threat agent: Since the complexity of the attack is terms of IT knowledge is limited, virtually any group with sufficient motive can enact it. Intelligence gathering can take some time, which is why this attack is usually perpetrated by groups that can count on more elements to collect data effectively in s short amount of time.

Threat: The name for this type of threat has already been coded with "spear phishing attack". It is a targeted attack to a specific person. It usually involves a phone call to a subordinate or an email sent from a person in the circle of trust of the receiver. Intelligence gathered in advance serves the purpose of avoiding rendering the email suspicious to the eyes of the receiver.

Threat vector: The threat vector is usually a specifically crafted email. It may contain malware, a link to an infected site, or an infected documented. If the target doesn't recognize the attack in time, the system and/or the network used to open the email are at risk. If the target is a system administrator or a manager with extensive access capabilities, the attacker may not even need to escalate privileges or to attack other systems in the network. However, if technical knowledge is available to the group, and the target is not just data, but airport sensitive systems, the intrusion can be used as starting point to launch internal attacks and reach other parts of the network. Even if disconnected from internet access, segregated network segments can be reached.

Vulnerability: The major vulnerabilities for this type of attack are lack of awareness and lack of training for the subject being targeted. However, a well forged email is almost undistinguishable from a legitimate one, and other measures need to be in place to keep this risk at bay. Networks should implement the principle of defence in depth to limit the damage a targeted attack can do to the infrastructure.

Impact: Switch back to manual procedures, loss of control or reliability of information systems.

3.2   Scenario 2: Operation Payback

Disgruntled employees are harmful to any organization and they do exist is a quote from a recent article in Forbes magazine (7/23/2012, The Power Of The Disgruntled Employee). There are many security controls that deal directly with this problem, starting from preventive controls like background checks, to monitoring and deterring controls like auditing and fully integrated Identity Management (IdM) solutions, to emergency and physical controls like fast user de-provisioning and escorting out of the premises in case of termination. This scenario is based on events that happen daily at any type of business and across all industries.

Scenario: The airport is in the need to scale down personnel and terminates a number of employees. One of these employees decides to make its former employer to pay for this decision and s/he is also knowledgeable about IT. S/he knows decides that stealing personal data would be the perfect punishment for the former employer, as that would result in a big lawsuit, damaging the airport reputation, and it will be expensive to settle against the strict European rules regarding the protection of personal data. The disgruntled employee doesn't even need physical access to the premise, because the airport implements remote access capabilities. The day after the termination s/he unlawfully connects to the airport systems from a coffee shop, finds out that the account is still active, authenticates to the system, escalates the user privileges, and exfiltrates the personal data of all the airport personnel.

Threat agent: A disgruntled employee. The scenario described above assumes the termination, but it is worth noting that many occurrences of disgruntled employees still employed with the target firm have been recorded, and with much more serious impacts.

Threat: unauthorized access to systems and data or illicit use of company property. A disgruntled employee can act on a multitude of assets: recently an Italian disgruntled employee destroyed the complete Brunello wine production of his employer of the last 4 years for a total damage worth millions of Euros, another one, in Poland, continuously damaged computers and servers for 3 years with chemical cleaning products, until he was caught by surveillance cameras. In this scenario we focus on those that directly exploit the IT systems of the airport. It is important to note that the scenario can be construed with a threat that can be either internal, if still employed, or external, if already terminated.

Threat vector: Internet facing systems and especially remote access systems in case of the external threat, otherwise any type of IT internal system, since the threat vector is actually authorized to access those systems. Where the actor doesn't have all the necessary privileges to access its target, but enough to log into a system, the required privileges can easily be escalated if a thorough, efficient, and consistent patch management and change management program are not in place.

Vulnerability: In the case of the internal threat, any vulnerability in any system can be exploited to the advantage of the attacker. If a monitoring and auditing system is not in place, it may be impossible to identify and track down the perpetrator of an internal attack. In the case of an external threat, i.e. a former employee, there range of system that can be used is more limited but not necessarily better protected. For example, a slow user de-provisioning system can allow the terminated employee to access company resources after termination. The same can happen if group accounts are in place.

Impact: Loss of personal data, identity theft, legal risks.

3.3   Scenario 3: Dark Night

Attacks to SCADA networks and engineering systems are occurring in all major critical infrastructures. There is consensus that soon they will multiply also at airports, and small to medium airports should be on the watch. This scenario ultimately means that automated SCADA exploits are more common, available to a broader public, and can be weaponized more easily. This scenario is based on events that already took place in a different industry, and that can be transposed in an airport context due to the identified cyber trends and evolution.

Scenario: The attacker crafts a piece of malware that is then used to infiltrate the internal IT system of the airport without affecting its operations or tripping monitoring devices. This is considered feasible for various classes of attackers. The malware is delivered and is not discovered by the security staff as it doesn't affect the internal network or its systems. The malware payload contains one or more specific exploits for the airport ground support lights system, which is necessary for safely landing airplanes and is connected with the internal network. It may use an Out of Band (OOB) channel or a maintenance monitoring port. From this moment on, an undetected unauthorized external entity has the capability to command those lights.

Threat agent: A possible attacker is an adversary nation state trying to deny airspace access to commercial flights, to inflict harm to the target country commercial interests, or a terrorist group trying to crash planes or disrupt airport operations to gain media attention.

Threat: The scenario can be set on by various cyber attack threats. A specifically crafted malware would be the threat of choice by the identified threat agent. The sophistication required for this type of threat is quite high, and the resources needed to implement it are medium, making it an affordable attack also for groups, should not be considered a prerogative of nation states.

Threat vector: The attack works on two different steps, infection of the internal network and infection of the SCADA/engineering system. The vector for the first step is any external connection to the internal network, whereas the vector for the second step is the connection between the two systems. The network and SCADA malware can be built upon a number of different issues and can target other systems as well.

Vulnerability: To be successful this attack will need to exploit multiple vulnerabilities, however these are not necessarily high risk vulnerabilities per se, and can be often found in most networks. Furthermore, different attack vectors can be used depending on which vulnerability can actually be identified in the target airport. Vulnerabilities allowing the first step of the attack could be an un-patched endpoint, the lack of defence in depth measures, untrained staff, improperly configured IDSs, etc. While vulnerabilities allowing the second step may include a poor network design, lack of structured processes for maintenance, etc. Vulnerabilities in engineering systems and SCADA are not uncommon.

Impact: Diversion of flights, critical services outage, physical damage/incident.

4   Selection and Validation Process

Section 4 describes the process of selection that the scenarios underwent and the validation according to stakeholders' judgement and contribution. One scenario has been selected to ground the development of socioeconomic models to support decision-making in airport security.

4.1 Scenario Selection

Airport security stakeholders initially reviewed and evaluated the early formulation of scenarios, and later validated and selected the revised version of the scenarios. Figure 1 summarizes the two phases.

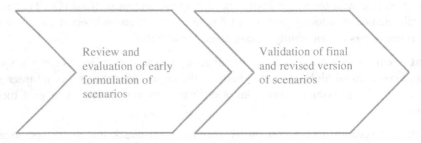

Fig. 1. Scenario selection process

In order to select proper scenarios to steer the modelling and development of a socio-economics security framework and tools, this study focuses on low level Airport Security scenarios that describe how local decisions are affected by the implementation of single security measures by decision makers at the airport. The picture below shows the scenarios' development and selection process (Fig. 2).

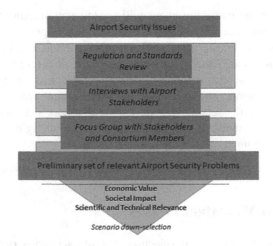

Fig. 2. Process of scenarios development and selection

The Scenario 1: Targeted cyber attack was selected among the three scenarios since it was evaluated to have the greatest impact in the Airport Security domain since it envisions an information security attack that is widespread in many critical infrastructures and that could easily affect airport security in the near future.

4.2 Scenarios Validation

Scenario 1, as well as other Airport Security scenarios (i.e. development of security regulation and physical attack to the control tower) has been presented and discussed with relevant stakeholders in the Airport Security domain, then refined iteratively by consortium partners.

Iterative meetings with two Security Instructors certified by the International Air Transport Association (IATA) have been organized to collect information to feed preliminary models versions, to steer and review the intermediate models, and to evaluate final versions of the models and discuss the results provided. A number of conference calls and phone interviews have been carried out with Operational and Security experts from Esjberg (DK), Brno (CZ) and Pescara (IT) Airports. Policy makers and decision makers at national (i.e. Ente Nazionale per l'Aviazione Civile – ENAC, the Italian CAA) and international levels (i.e. Eurocontrol and the Airport Council International - ACI Europe) have been involved as well.

A cyber-security expert has been involved in the refinement and assessment of Scenario 1.

The following activities have been carried out in order to evaluate and evolve the whole set of operational Airport Security scenarios developed:

- Interview with one Civil Aviation Authority Security Instructors,
- Informal contact with ICT Airport Security Solution Industry,
- Questionnaires for Airport Security Managers (total of 22 Questionnaires sent, 10 Questionnaires back),
- Skype Interviews with Airport Security Managers (3 Interviews done).

Different techniques, like informal contacts, structured and focused interviews as well as multiple choice questionnaires are some of the techniques used to support the stakeholders' engagement in the validation process. The results of these activities have been analyzed and elaborated as input into the socio-economics models.

In particular, Scenario 1 has been evaluated towards the actual collaborative decision making in airport security. 76 % respondents of the Questionnaire thought that the scenario is well structured with respect to both content and completeness of information. In particular, the scenario, originated as an United States specific case, is currently applicable and valuable in Europe as well, since the member states still lack ad hoc regulations on cybersecurity.

Scenario 1 is very innovative and interesting for the involved Policy Makers. ACI Europe is carrying out an in-depth research about cyber-security in Airport and comparing IT security level of different airports (linked to their size and to the national regulations on the topic) and they are studying the European Cyber-Security Strategy to understand how to apply it to the Airport domain to further inform relevant Policy

Makers in the Aviation domain for future Regulations on the topic (currently almost uncovered).

The impact of this scenario needs to be better specified since it could be even worse than the ones currently foreseen. According to the expert judges, the impact of an IT attack needs to put safety and security into relation.

A prologue describing the overall context of emerging threats could be useful. The major need is to prevent the eventual impact of a future threat (like biothreats and powder and chemical substances attacks). In order to reach this aim, the definition of the security scenario may need to be specified through a live example taking into account new security measures and future emerging threats.

5 Conclusions

In this report, the operational airport security cyberattack scenarios developed in this research are described. Through the participatory approach adopted, Airport security stakeholders have been involved in presentation, discussion and iterative refinement of working and final versions of the models and the scenarios.

Possible risks and limitations of the study have been highlighted, and the most appreciated and valuable results of the project are described. The complexity and the innovation of the proposed scenarios make the process of validating them a challenging task. The security, social and economic issues addressed by this project are heterogeneous, and the results of the research will be likewise heterogeneous, ranging from theoretical models to policy guidelines and software toolkit for decision support. The full coverage of security, social and economic issues will be assured by the data collection phase that will inform the development of model. In particular costs related to social issues (e.g. image cost, acceptance of security measures, etc.) will be included in the model aiming at explicitly integrating social and economic issues and developing a socio-economical understanding of the airport security.

References

1. Johnson, C.W.: Preparing for cyber-attacks on air traffic management infrastructures: Cyber-safety scenario generation. In: Proceedings of the 7th IET Conference on Systems Safety and Cyber-Security, Edinburgh, Scotland, 15–18 October 2012. IET, Savoy Place (2012)
2. ENISA Threat Landscape - Responding to the Evolving Threat Environment (2013). http://www.enisa.europa.eu/activities/risk-management/evolving-threat-environment/enisa-threat-landscape-2013-overview-of-current-and-emerging-cyber-threats
3. Rios Insua, D., Rios, J., Banks, D.: Adversarial risk analysis. J. Am. Stat. Assoc. **104**(486), 841–854 (2009)
4. Foster, C.E., Hoey, J.: Airport security complexity: Problems with the information security components. In: Van de Walle, B., Carle, B. (eds.) 2nd International ISCRAM Conference, pp. 61–66. LeMoyne College Business Department, Brussels (2005). ISBN: 9076971099
5. SECONOMICS website. http://www.seconomicsproject.eu
6. United States National Infrastructure Protection Plan (NIPP). http://www.dhs.gov/transportation-systems-sector

Preserving Compliance with Security Requirements in Socio-Technical Systems

Mattia Salnitri$^{(\boxtimes)}$, Elda Paja, and Paolo Giorgini

University of Trento, Trento, Italy
{mattia.salnitri,elda.paja,paolo.giorgini}@unitn.it

Abstract. Socio-technical systems are an interplay of social (humans and organizations) and technical components interacting with one another to achieve their objectives. Security is a central issue in such complex systems, and it cannot be tackled only through technical mechanisms: the encryption of sensitive data while being transmitted, does not assure that the receiver will not disclose them to unauthorized parties. Therefore, dealing with security in socio-technical systems requires an analysis: (i) from a social and organizational perspective, to elicit the objectives and security requirements of each component; (ii) from a procedural perspective, to define how the actors behave and interact with each other. But, socio-technical systems need to adapt to changes of the external environment, making the need to deal with security a problem that has to be faced during all the systems' life-cycle. We propose an iterative and incremental process to elicit security requirements and verify the socio-technical system's compliance with such requirements throughout the systems' life cycle.

Keywords: Socio-technical systems · Security requirements · Security policies · Compliance · Business processes

1 Introduction

Socio-technical systems are complex systems where social (human and organizational) and technical components interact with each other to achieve common objectives. Examples of socio-technical systems are healthcare systems, smart cities, air traffic management, etc. In a smart city citizens constantly exchange information with e-governmental systems such as tax-payment. The amount of information exchanged in such systems is considerable, and quite often part of such information is sensitive, i.e., should be protected. Apart from information, other types of assets are relevant when dealing with socio-technical systems. In a smart city, examples of other assets are the services being offered, such as the tax verification and monitoring service.

An analysis of security aspects is crucial to avoid severe consequences [3,7,13] such as loss of privacy and law infringement. Security is typically dealt with technical security mechanisms. For instance, encryption mechanisms are

© Springer International Publishing Switzerland 2014
F. Cleary and M. Felici (Eds.): CSP Forum 2014, CCIS 470, pp. 49–61, 2014.
DOI: 10.1007/978-3-319-12574-9_5

used to protect data confidentiality. However, such mechanisms cannot protect information from misuse by authorized users. As a result, security analysis in socio-technical systems calls for an analysis of social and organizational aspects along technical ones.

An analysis of social and organizational aspects allows to capture the objectives of each stakeholder and their business policies, how stakeholders pursue their objectives, to then check if some of these business policies might threaten stakeholders' assets (or those of their interacting parties) with respect to security. For example, citizens might want the non-disclosure of their social security number, but the employees of the tax-payment system may need to use this information for statistical purposes. In this case, there is a conflict between stakeholders' need, which can be detected only through an analysis of social and organizational aspects. Starting from stakeholders' needs, and after dealing with possible conflicts one can obtain a consistent security requirements specification.

But an analysis of social and organizational aspects to security requirements engineering is not enough, verifying whether the socio-technical system is compliant with such requirements is crucial too. To perform such verification, we need to analyse the overall socio-technical system, the involved stakeholders, their behavior and interactions with others to check whether the procedures and activities underlying the system comply with the specified security requirements. Indeed, the analysis of procedural aspects allows to verify if the security requirements are satisfied by the socio-technical system. For instance, in a smart city, citizens require the non-disclosure of their social security numbers. An analysis of the flow of activities and the information flow, via business processes [12], allows verifying whether there is a flow of information containing the social security number, which does not start from the citizen, capturing in this way a breach with respect to non-disclosure of such information.

The need socio-technical systems have to adapt, has a high impact over their capability to remain compliant with security requirements. For example, the business process executed to coordinate the tax-payment system with the provision of the smart city services, is drastically changed because new technologies are employed to minimize the effort of the smart city employees. Before the deployment of the adapted business process, all security policies shall be verified, to avoid security breaches.

In this paper, we propose a process to guide security designers in capturing security requirements in socio-technical systems and preserving compliance with them. As far as our knowledge goes, no similar processes have been proposed in the literature to guide security designers in maintaining business processes running in a socio-technical system compliant with social and organizational security requirements. Specifically, we rely on the STS-ml [8,18] (Socio-Technical Security modeling language), an actor and goal-oriented modeling language, for the modeling of social and organizational aspects of socio-technical systems, and SecBPMN [25] (Secure BPMN), an extension of Business Process Modeling and Notation (BPMN) for modeling procedural aspects of socio-technical systems. The process proposed in this paper guides security designers in the specification of SecBPMN security policies from STS-ml security requirements, and in maintaining compliance with security policies, while preserving in this way compliance with security requirements.

The paper is structured as follows. Section 2 gives an overview of the proposed process, while Sect. 3 provides a detailed description of the steps of the process, with references to the chosen languages. Section 4 discusses related work, and Sect. 5 summarizes the paper and concludes.

2 Incremental Design Process for Socio-Technical Systems

We propose an iterative and incremental process to verify the continuous compliance of evolving and adaptable socio-technical systems with security requirements for the said system. The process is iterative, because it cycles various times, and incremental, because it allows security requirement engineers to refine and extend the model during its iterations. It receives in input the security specification of a socio-technical system and, during its iterations, it ensures compliance with security requirements.

The process, illustrated in Fig. 1, is divided in two phases, the first phase is executed by security requirement engineers and it regards the elicitation of security requirements considering social and organizational aspects, while the second phase is executed by security designers and it regards verifying compliance via procedural aspects of socio-technical systems. The process can be used: (i) before deployment, to guide the definition of the business processes (procedural) executed by the socio-technical system; (ii) after the deployment, to help preserving compliance of the socio-technical system during its life-cycle.

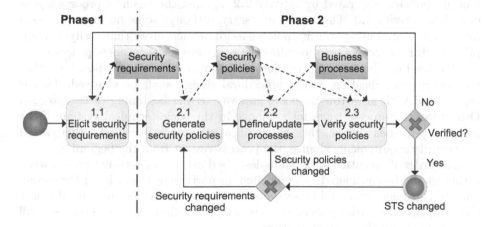

Fig. 1. Incremental design process

2.1   Phase 1

The first phase consists of only one activity, namely **1.1 Elicit security requirements**, and it is concerned with the extraction of security requirements for the considered socio-technical system. The set of security requirements is represented with the data object "Security requirements"; the dashed arrow from the activity to the data object means the activity creates or modifies this data object. Section 3.1 describes the elicitation activity in more detail.

2.2   Phase 2

The activities in the second phase are executed to verify if security requirements captured through Phase 1 are satisfied by the business processes of the socio-technical system. For this, security requirements are transformed in security policies, i.e., security constraints in terms of business process concepts.

The activity **2.1. Generate security policies** consists in generating security policies from security requirements. In this step, a set of transformation rules, presented in [27], is used to transform security requirements in security policies in a semi-automated fashion. This activity receives in input (see the incoming dashed arrow, Fig. 1) a set of security requirements and it results in a set of security policies (data object "Security policies") in output.

The activity **2.2. Define/update processes** consists in the definition of new business processes, or the modification of existing ones. This activity receives in input the security policies generated by the previous activity: the definition or modification of processes will be guided by the security policies they should comply with. The activity produces a set of business processes, represented with the data object "Business processes".

The activity **2.3. Verify security policies** consists in the verification of the security policies, generated by activity **2.2**, against the business processes generated by activity **2.3**. This step is necessary, although some business processes have been created using security policies as guidelines, given that verifying compliance with security policies requires the complete set of business processes.

If at least one business process does not comply with security policies, either the security specification or the procedural design shall be changed. This is represented with an arrow from the gateway to the beginning of the process. Otherwise, the process waits for a change in the socio-technical system: if the business processes change, then the verification step is executed, otherwise, if the security requirements change, the process restart from the beginning.

The order of execution of the steps described in the process is not prescriptive, rather should be considered as a guideline. In particular, the order of the second and the third activity could be swapped: frequently processes are defined before the definition of security policies. In this case, the definition of the processes will not be guided by the security policies.

3   The Process in Action

We describe how the process is executed with the help of a motivating example. We use the SWIM[1] Air Traffic Management (ATM) socio-technical system[2] as a motivating example for our process. It consists of a large number of autonomous and heterogeneous components (stakeholders), such as pilots, airports personnel, national airspace managers, meteo services, radars, etc., which interact with each other to enable air traffic management operations. In such a complex system, ensuring security is critical, for security leaks may result in severe consequences on, for example, safety. For instance, a successful attack to the control tower, the core component of every airport, can paralyse an airport for hours or days, with severe consequences on managing flights and consequently on passengers.

3.1   Phase One: Eliciting Security Requirements

The elicitation of security requirements is concerned with the analysis of social and organizational aspects in the said socio-technical system to derive a consistent security requirements specification. To execute this activity we have adopted STS-ml [8,18] (Socio-Technical Security- modeling language), an actor and goal-oriented security requirements modelling language for socio-technical systems. STS-ml was chosen because: (1) it is specifically thought for socio-technical systems, relating security to interaction, (2) it supports a rich set of security requirements, while providing a clearer ontological foundation than existing approaches [11,16]. Moreover, STS-ml is fully supported by the STS-Tool [19] on modelling, analysing, and deriving a consistent set of security requirements.

In STS-ml, requirements models are created through three views: (i) the *social view*—represents the main stakeholders (in terms of actors) together with their objectives (via goals) and the interactions they enter in the socio-technical system; (ii) the *information view*—represents stakeholders' informational assets and their representation via documents; and (iii) the *authorization view*—represents the authorizations that actors grant to others over their information. Figure 2 shows a partial STS-ml model of the motivating example.

Social view. Actors in STS-ml are modeled in terms of (i) agents—concrete entities that are already known at design-time (e.g., *Immigration office*), and (ii) roles—abstract entities representing a class of participants (e.g., *Web-Service*). Roles can be adopted (played) by different agents at runtime. An actor's rationale captures actors' goals, and how they are achieved via AND/OR goal decompositions (e.g., the root goal of the *Immigration Office* is *Immigration monitored*). Moreover, to achieve their goals, actors might need to *read* or *modify* documents, as well as create (*produce*) new documents (e.g., *Immigration Office* reads document *Visa* to achieve goal *Visa checked*). Most importantly, the social view captures actors' social interactions via two social relationships: *goal delegation* and

---

[1] The System Wide Information Management (SWIM) [2].
[2] This scenario is a variant of Case Study *B* of the FP7 EU Funded Project Aniketos http://www.aniketos.eu.

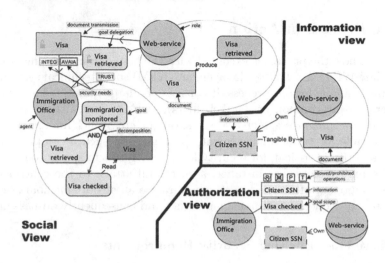

Fig. 2. STS-ml model of an ATM scenario

document transmission. STS-ml allows actors to express their concerns about security (security needs) over the interactions they enter to then derive security requirements with respect to confidentiality, integrity, availability, accountability, reliability, and authenticity.

Information view. STS-ml considers information a first class citizen, considering most security issues are concerned with the protection of information. Information owners are the ones concerned with the protection of information. Therefore, information ownership is a crucial aspect to model. In STS-ml, the relationship *own* relates an actor to the information that it owns.

But, information may be available in various forms. Thus, STS-ml distinguishes between information and its representation in form of *documents*. Documents become relevant from a security point of view because of the information they might represent. Thus, the purpose of the information view, apart from representing information entities and their respective owners, is to link together the documents actors use and exchange in the social view with their informational content. This link is drawn through "Tangible by" relationships, which indicate that an information entity is represented by a document. In Fig. 2, information *Citizen SSN* (Social Security Number) is made tangible by document *Visa*.

Authorization view. STS-ml allows capturing the permission and prohibition flow over information, on top of capturing information flow. An adequate representation of permissions and prohibitions is crucial to establishing whether information is used and exchanged in compliance with security requirements.

The authorisation view represents the permissions and/or prohibitions on information that actors grant one to another. An authorization relationship details: (i) the permissions/prohibitions on the operations actors can perform over information (Read, Modify, Produce, Transmit) while manipulating documents for the achievement of their goals; (ii) information entities for which permissions/prohibitions are specified; (iii) the scope of authorisation, referring to the goal(s) for the fulfillment of which permission/prohibition is specified; and finally, (iv) transferrability, specifying whether permissions can be further granted to others (not applicable to prohibitions). In Fig. 2, the *Web-Service* authorizes the *Immigration Office* to use *Citizen SSN* in the scope of goal *Visa checked.*

3.2   Phase Two: Generating Secure Procedures

In order to verify compliance with security requirements, we generate security policies, define the process that will be executed in the socio-technical system, and verify compliance of security policies against the business processes. We have chosen the SecBPMN (Secure BPMN) [25] framework, for it offers support throughout these activities. Indeed, SecBPMN is aimed at modeling business processes with security aspects, modeling security policies, and verifying if one or more business processes are compliant with these security policies. The language is composed of: SecBPMN-ml (SecBPMN- modeling language), a modeling language for business processes; SecBPMN-Q (SecBPMN - Query), a graphical query language for specifying security policies in terms of SecBPMN-ml elements; and a software component, which verifies compliance of business processes with security policies. Each SecBPMN component is used in an activity of the second phase of the process in Fig. 1. The rest of the section describes how SecBPMN is used in each activity of **Phase 2**[3].

Activity 2.2. Define/update processes. In this activity business processes of a socio-technical system are defined using SecBPMN-ml [25], which extends BPMN with security concepts about information assurance and security defined in [6]. There are many proposals that extend BPMN with security concepts, e.g., [20,28], but they are focused on a restricted set of security concepts. SecBPMN-ml, on the other hand, covers, as far as our knowledge goes, the most comprehensive set of security concepts.

The expressiveness of SecBPMN-ml permits security designers to define which are the security mechanisms that should be used in the implementation and execution of each activity. For example, it is possible to specify that the communication of a data object between two activities will be encrypted.

Figure 3 shows part of a SecBPMN-ml model of a business process used in the ATM socio-technical system, where users can use different web-interfaces to select the best option for a flight, buy tickets, and perform most of the bureaucratic processes required to take the flight.

Activity 2.1. Generate security policies. This activity consists in generating security policies from STS-ml security requirements, in a semi-automated fashion [27], using SecBPMN-Q. For example, the security requirement of integrity

---

[3] Note that we do not follow the flow of the process, but rather present the activities following a more natural description for SecBPMN, swapping activities 2.1. and 2.2.

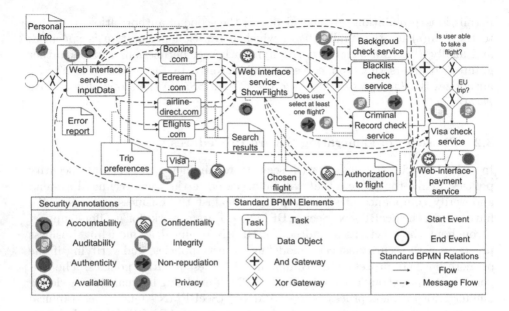

Fig. 3. Example of a business process modeled using SecBPMN-ml

attached to the "Visa" document in Fig. 2, can be transformed in the SecBPMN-Q security policy shown in Fig. 4.

The graphical security policy in Fig. 4 is composed of two activities labeled with "@X" and "@Y", while the "@" symbol is used to match any activities. The two activities are linked with a path relation (the arrow with two slashes in the middle), which matches all the business processes where the first activity, marked with "@X" is executed before the second activity, marked with "@Y". The security policy is enriched with a message flow (represented as a dashed arrow), which exchanges a data object called "Visa". When executed, this security policy will match any message flow between two activities that exchange the "Visa" data object. The confidentiality annotation requires the communication channel to assure the data object will be received only by authorized users. Similarly, the integrity security annotation attached to the "Visa" data object, imposes the data object to be protected by unauthorized modifications.

SecBPMN-Q is essential for the transformation of security requirements in security policies. In previous work [26], we have demonstrated that it is possible to transform the most used security requirements in SecBPMN-Q security policies.

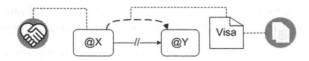

Fig. 4. Example of a security policy modeled using SecBPMN-Q

This activity uses the transformation rules we provided in [26] to support the generation of security policies.

Activity 2.3. Verify security policies. This activity consists in verifying if one or more business processes, modeled with SecBPMN-ml, comply with SecBPMN-Q security policies. This activity is straightforward for toy examples, as for the business process in Fig. 3 and the security policy in Fig. 4. However, in real-world scenarios, as the overall ATM case study [1], where business processes can contain hundreds of elements, it is infeasible to verify security policies manually. The software[4] provided with SecBPMN framework supports automated analysis to verify if a SecBPMN-Q security policy is satisfied by one or more SecBPMN-ml business processes.

Automated analysis allows to highlight the path that complies with the security policy, see Fig. 5 for the security policy in Fig. 4, where (i) the first activity of the path "Web interface service - inputData" is linked with a message flow to the last activity of the path "Visa check service"; (ii) the message flow is used to exchange the data object "Visa" and it assures confidentiality of the transferred data object; (iii) integrity and authenticity of the "Visa" data object are preserved. Assuming that the properties of the security annotations of the security policy are less restrictive than the properties of the business process, the path, and consequently the business process, complies with the security policy.

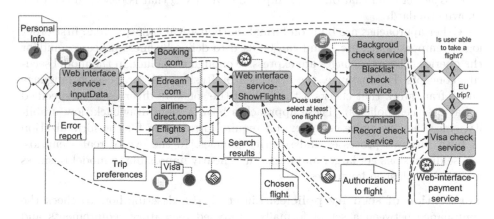

Fig. 5. Example of a path (highlighted in green) that satisfies the security policy showed in Fig. 4

4   Related Work

In the years past, several approaches have been proposed to address the verification of requirements in business processes [5,15,20,23,28]. However, as far

---

[4] http://www.secbpmn.disi.unitn.it

as our knowledge goes, there are no approaches that cover the overall security requirements engineering and verification process proposed in this paper.

In the following, we describe the most known approaches, while highlighting the differences with our approach considering the various phases.

Modeling BPMN with security concepts. As far as approaches dealing with security aspects are concerned, many graphical modeling languages extending BPMN [17] have been proposed. Ad-hoc notations are used in SecureBPMN [5] proposed by Brucker et al. to capture security and compliance requirements. Other extensions of BPMN also rely on security annotated business process modelling [15,20,23,28] similarly to our approach. However, differently from existing approaches, ours allows the definition of custom security policies. Instead, existing approaches employ software engines which use models created with the respective languages to check a fixed set of hard coded security policies. Examples of such engines include [22,24,28].

Modeling security policies. Graphical query languages have been proposed to check if a process satisfies a query, which can be interpreted as a policy. For instance, BP-QL (Business Process - Query Language) [4] and BPQL (Business Process Query Language) [9] allow to graphically define queries and check which business processes satisfy the queries. These two query languages are not based on BPMN, which makes their applicability and, most importantly, their learning process slower than that of, for example, SecBPMN-Q that is based on the well-known standard.

Other approaches are built on formal mathematical concepts (e.g. first order logic, temporal logic, etc.), and can be used to define business processes and/or the queries. These languages are expressive enough to include in the model security concepts. For instance, the approach of Rushby [21] proposes a language and a framework that checks if the code of the software diverges from specified behaviors (i.e., policies). These approaches have a main drawback: low usability, since they are quite complex and require lot of effort for the formalization of both business processes and security policies. In the eye of real scenarios, whose dimensions get larger and larger, it is nearly impossible to model business processes with such languages.

Verification of security policies. Liu et al. [14] describe how to check the compliance between a set of formally expressed regulatory requirements and business processes. The approach is accompanied by a software that allows verifying the business process against these compliance rules through the use of model-checking technologies. Their approach uses Business process Execution language (BPEL) instead of BPMN, and it is not focused on security, but rather focus on regulatory compliance.

Ghose and Koliadis [10] enrich BPMN with annotations, and they calculate how much a business process deviates from another business process. Differently from our approach, theirs focuses only on the structural difference between processes, again with no consideration of security requirements.

5 Conclusions

Security is quite a relevant aspect in the design of socio-technical systems, where a security leak in a single component may threaten the whole system, and security violations might have severe consequences. We have proposed a process intended to help security requirement engineers and security designers in verifying and maintaining the satisfaction of social and organizational security requirements through the procedural design of secure socio-technical systems. The proposed process is based on the STS-ml [8,18] for the elicitation of a consistent security requirements specification, and on SecBPMN [25] for the verification of the satisfaction of security requirements in a procedural way.

The need to follow the proposed process becomes particularly important in adaptive socio-technical systems, where the design of the business processes changes to adapt to external changes. We have shown how to capture security requirements through STS-ml models, map them to security policies, and verify their satisfaction by business processes of the socio-technical system using an example from the air traffic management domain. The proposed process builds on the assumption that the tasks (defined in the business process), and the security aspects will be enforced rightly.

Our ongoing and future work includes: (i) developing a software that integrates STS-Tool with the SecBPMN component in order to offer an integrated framework for the management of security requirements in socio-technical systems; (ii) conducting empirical evaluation with security experts, to validate the overall process, as well as the integration of STS-ml with SecBPMN.

Acknowledgment. The research leading to these results has received funding from the European Union Seventh Framework Programme (FP7/2007–2013) under grant no. 257930 (Aniketos).

References

1. Final report on aniketos on industrial case studies. Technical report (2014). http://aniketos.eu/sites/default/files/downloads/Aniketos%20D6.4%20-%20Final %20report%20on%20Aniketos%20%20applied%20to%20industrial%20case%20 studies.pdf
2. Federal Aviation Administration. SWIM ATM case study, Last visited, March 2014. http://www.faa.gov/about/office_org/headquarters_offices/ato/service_units/ techops/atc_comms_services/swim/
3. Anderson, R.: Security Engineering: A Guide to Building Dependable Distributed Systems. Wiley, New York (2008)
4. Beeri, C., Eyal, A., Kamenkovich, S., Milo, T.: Querying business processes with BP-QL. Inf. Syst. **33**(6), 477–507 (2008)
5. Brucker, A.D., Hang, I., Lückemeyer, G., Ruparel, R.: SecureBPMN: modeling and enforcing access control requirements in business processes. In: Proceedings of SACMAT'12, pp. 123–126 (2012)
6. Cherdantseva, Y., Hilton, J.: A reference model of information assurance and security. In: Proceedings of ARES '13, pp. 546–555 (2013)

7. Crook, R., Ince, D., Lin, L., Nuseibeh, B.: Security requirements engineering: when anti-requirements hit the fan. In: Proceedings of RE'02, pp. 203–205. IEEE (2002)
8. Dalpiaz, F., Paja, E., Giorgini, P.: Security requirements engineering via commitments. In: Proceedings of STAST'11, pp. 1–8 (2011)
9. Deutch, D., Milo, T.: Querying structural and behavioral properties of business processes. In: Arenas, M. (ed.) DBPL 2007. LNCS, vol. 4797, pp. 169–185. Springer, Heidelberg (2007)
10. Ghose, A.K., Koliadis, G.: Auditing business process compliance. In: Krämer, B.J., Lin, K.-J., Narasimhan, P. (eds.) ICSOC 2007. LNCS, vol. 4749, pp. 169–180. Springer, Heidelberg (2007)
11. Giorgini, P., Massacci, F., Mylopoulos, J., Zannone, N.: Modeling security requirements through ownership, permission and delegation. In: Proceedings of RE'05, pp. 167–176 (2005)
12. Johansson, H.J., McHugh, P., Pendlebury, A.J., Wheeler, W.A.: Business Process Reengineering: Breakpoint Strategies for Market Dominance. Wiley and Sons, Chichester (1993)
13. Johnstone, M.N.: Security requirements engineering-the reluctant oxymoron. In: Proceedings of Australian Information Security Management Conference, p. 5 (2009)
14. Liu, Y., Müller, S., Xu, K.: A static compliance-checking framework for business process models. IBM Syst. J. 46(2), 335–361 (2007)
15. Menzel, M., Thomas, I., Meinel, C.: Security requirements specification in service-oriented business process management. In: Proceedings of ARES '09, pp. 41–48 (2009)
16. Mouratidis, H., Giorgini, P.: Secure tropos: a security-oriented extension of the tropos methodology. IJSEKE 17(2), 285–309 (2007)
17. OMG. BPMN 2.0., Jan 2011. http://www.omg.org/spec/BPMN/2.0
18. Paja, E., Dalpiaz, F., Giorgini, P.: Managing security requirements conflicts in socio-technical systems. In: Proceedings of ER'13, pp. 270–283 (2013)
19. Paja, E., Dalpiaz, F., Poggianella, M., Roberti, P., Giorgini, P.: Specifying and reasoning over socio-technical security requirements with STS-tool. In: Ng, W., Storey, V.C., Trujillo, J.C. (eds.) ER 2013. LNCS, vol. 8217, pp. 504–507. Springer, Heidelberg (2013)
20. Rodríguez, A., Fernández-Medina, E., Piattini, M.: A BPMN extension for the modeling of security requirements in business processes. IEICE Trans. Inf. Syst. 90(4), 745–752 (2007)
21. Rushby, J.: Using model checking to help discover mode confusions and other automation surprises. Reliab. Eng. Syst. Saf. 75, 167–177 (2002)
22. Sadiq, W., Governatori, G., Namiri, K.: Modeling control objectives for business process compliance. In: Alonso, G., Dadam, P., Rosemann, M. (eds.) BPM 2007. LNCS, vol. 4714, pp. 149–164. Springer, Heidelberg (2007)
23. Saleem, M., Jaafar, J., Hassan, M.: A domain- specific language for modelling security objectives in a business process models of SOA applications. AISS 4(1), 353–362 (2012)
24. Salnitri, M., Dalpiaz, F., Giorgini, P.: Aligning service-oriented architectures with security requirements. In: Meersman, R., Panetto, H., Dillon, T., Rinderle-Ma, S., Dadam, P., Zhou, X., Pearson, S., Ferscha, A., Bergamaschi, S., Cruz, I.F. (eds.) OTM 2012, Part I. LNCS, vol. 7565, pp. 232–249. Springer, Heidelberg (2012)

25. Salnitri, M., Dalpiaz, F., Giorgini, P.: Modeling and verifying security policies in business processes. In: Bider, I., Gaaloul, K., Krogstie, J., Nurcan, S., Proper, H.A., Schmidt, R., Soffer, P. (eds.) BPMDS 2014 and EMMSAD 2014. LNBIP, vol. 175, pp. 200–214. Springer, Heidelberg (2014)
26. Salnitri, M., Giorgini, P.: Modeling and verification of ATM security policies with SecBPMN. In: Proceedings of SHPCS'14 (2014)
27. Salnitri, M., Giorgini, P.: Transforming socio-technical security requirements in SecBPMN security policies. In: Proceedings of IStar'14 (2014)
28. Wolter, C., Menzel, M., Schaad, A., Miseldine, P., Meinel, C.: Model-driven business process security requirement specification. JSA **55**(4), 211–223 (2009)

Accountability, Data Protection and Privacy

PRIPARE: A New Vision on Engineering Privacy and Security by Design

Nicolás Notario[1(✉)], Alberto Crespo[1], Antonio Kung[2], Inga Kroener[3],
Daniel Le Métayer[4], Carmela Troncoso[5], José M. del Álamo[6],
and Yod Samuel Martín[6]

[1] Atos Spain S.A., Madrid, Spain
{nicolas.notario, alberto.crespo}@atos.net
[2] Trialog, Paris, France
antonio.kung@trialog.com
[3] Trilateral, London, UK
inga.kroener@trilateralresearch.com
[4] Inria, Lyon, France
daniel.le-metayer@inria.fr
[5] Gradiant, Vigo, Pontevedra, Spain
ctroncoso@gradiant.org
[6] Universidad Politécnica de Madrid (UPM), Madrid, Spain
{jmdela, samuelm}@dit.upm.es

Abstract. The new EU Data Protection Directive (DPD), approved by the EU
Parliament acknowledges the need of Data Protection by Design and by Default
in order to protect the rights and freedoms of data subjects with regard to the
processing of personal data. PRIPARE confronts the lack of a truly engineering
approach for these concepts by providing a methodology that merges state-of-
the-art approaches (e.g. Privacy Impact Assessment and Risk management) and
complements them with new processes that cover the whole lifecycle of both,
personal data and development of ICT systems.

Keywords: Privacy by design · Security by design · Methodology · Privacy

1   Introduction

The Universal Declaration of Human Rights declares in Article 12 that "No one shall
be subjected to arbitrary interference with his privacy. ... Everyone has the right to
the protection of the law against such interference or attacks" [1]. Recent revelations
of mass surveillance have put privacy at the forefront of political and societal debate
and uncovered serious violations and lack of effective respect for this human right. As
it is impossible to think of a violation of human rights at such scale in the "offline
world" without international condemnation, the United Nations (UN) has reacted to
these events in the "digital world" by adopting a resolution that affirms "that the same
rights that people have offline must also be protected online, including the right to
privacy" [2]. The same resolution also calls on countries "To review their procedures, practices and legislation regarding the surveillance of communications, their

© Springer International Publishing Switzerland 2014
F. Cleary and M. Felici (Eds.): CSP Forum 2014, CCIS 470, pp. 65–76, 2014.
DOI: 10.1007/978-3-319-12574-9_6

interception and collection of personal data including mass surveillance, interception and collection" [2].

In the EU, the current legislative process to approve the EU General Data Protection Regulation (GDPR) can be seen to be in line with this UN request and is aimed to effectively strengthen European citizens' privacy, in particular in the area of personal data protection. As reality demonstrates, a strong and consistent legal framework on its own is not sufficient to guarantee that stakeholders will correctly adopt adequate privacy practices. The Privacy by Design (PbD) concept has been around since the 90's. Cavoukian's 7 Foundational Principles articulation [3] of PbD is widely acknowledged by data protection commissioners world-wide, and there is growing evidence that this truly transformative approach has the potential to create far-reaching impact and benefits for citizens, government and business, as well as in several economic, industrial and ICT domains (e.g. health, energy, cloud, mobile/communications, Near Field Communication (NFC)/Radio Frequency IDentification (RFID), geolocation, big data/data analytics, surveillance and authentication technologies). While there is a unanimous consensus on the benefit of the principles in terms of privacy awareness, unfortunately there is still a lack of a systematic approach that would help businesses and organizations to include privacy-supportive processes and practices in their products and services. The new European GDPR, in its Article 23, states that controllers shall follow the data protection by design and by default principle, following the opinion of data protection authorities such as:

- The European Data Protection Supervisor (EDPS): Opinion of the EDPS on Promoting Trust in the Information Society by Fostering Data Protection and Privacy [4],
- The Article 29 Data Protection Working Party: Opinion 01/2012 on the data protection reform proposals [5].

Whenever it is approved, compliance with the new Regulation on Data Protection will further spark interest in the need to follow PbD principles and approach. Some industries particularly vulnerable to privacy risks have anticipated proactively developing tools that address privacy concerns (i.e. the RFID industry and the EU RFID Privacy Impact Assessment (PIA) [6]).

PRIPARE (www.pripare.eu) project has two important missions:

- To design and facilitate the application of a PbD and Security-by-Design (SbD) methodology (PRIPARE methodology) in the ICT research community in preparation for industry practice.
- To foster a risk management culture within organizations by preparing best practices material, supporting FP7 and Horizon 2020 research projects, providing educational material on approaches to risk management of privacy, and by identifying gaps and providing recommendations on Privacy and Security-by-Design (PSbD) practices.

The PRIPARE methodology will allow forging sustainable links between the different privacy stakeholders (regulators, educators, engineers and standardization organisms) in order to set the necessary common grounds on which to build trustworthy and privacy-respectful systems. Increasing levels of public trust in ICT systems will:

- Facilitate faster adoption of new services and technologies that feature high and tangible levels of privacy and security embedded into their design and provided by default;
- Increase the speed of innovation and creation of added value for a more competitive European ICT industry;
- Contribute to the advent of unhindered usage of Internet against disruptions, censorship and surveillance.

In Sect. 2 we underscore the complexity involved in achieving a common understanding of privacy and security by design and what are the current approaches for addressing this complexity. In Sect. 3, we provide the rationale behind the need to agree on a common terminology for privacy among different stakeholders and approach followed for this in PRIPARE project. Section 4 outlines the identified security and privacy and security principles that will be embedded in the PRIPARE methodology. Section 5 presents an outline of the PSbD methodology which will address existing PSbD engineering problems, explaining (in Sect. 6) the relationship of PRIPARE's PSbD methodology with other existing methodologies. The paper concludes with some remarks and a draft of future work for PRIPARE methodology.

2 Taking Privacy by Design One Step Further

Very often privacy is (or seems to be) in tension with other requirements, and the design space of data minimization can be very wide, with different options providing different types of benefits and drawbacks. Therefore it is of prime importance to be able to make reasoned decisions and to be able to justify them. As far as privacy is concerned, these decisions must be based on a privacy risk analysis in which the privacy values at stake are clearly defined, as well as the sources of risks and their potential impact on these values. The result of this analysis should guide the choice of appropriate solutions (architecture and tools) and serve as justification for this choice. Sources like legislation, industry standards, and guidance produced by trade bodies, regulators, or other organizations working in their sector can be used to identify privacy and related risks that then can be minimized.

There is a strong and clear relationship between privacy and identity management. Identity management refers to the set of processes that administers the life cycle (collection, authentication, use, and deletion) of an identity, and the data linked to it, within an organization or system and across its boundaries. Identity management systems designed to follow privacy and security principles will provide their users with tools that allow them to manage their privacy in a reliable, trustable, and usable way. Failing to follow these principles can lead to flawed systems that pose serious privacy threats like identity theft or unintentional disclosure of personal data.

Identity management systems have evolved from silo-like approaches, where all the identity information is kept and used within a single organization, to federated, or network-centric, approaches where the underlying infrastructure enables a participating entity to share their users' personal data with others, e.g. by means of the OASIS (Organization for the Advancement of Structured Information Standards) Security Assertion Markup Language, Liberty's Identity Web Services Framework, or Open-Social technologies, among others.

Several solutions have been proposed to develop a privacy-enhancing identity management infrastructure including the use of pseudonyms and attribute-based (or zero-proof) credentials, privacy policies negotiation, development of usable interfaces and privacy metaphors, etc. [7]. In addition, the identity management domain has begun to consider user-centric architectural and usability aspects, and to support user control to different extents, which is called user-centric identity management. For example, URL-based systems such as OpenID[1] allow users to choose the entity storing their personal data, OAuth enables users to decide on what pieces of information to share, Kantara User Managed Access[2] (UMA) lets an individual control the authorization of data sharing and service access made between online services on the individual's behalf, and card-based systems further allow users to include the pieces of information to be shared with a third party.

At the start of the PRIPARE project, it was realized that stakeholders use PbD and Security by Design with different definitions. PRIPARE provides its own definition of a privacy and security by-design process: An approach to System Engineering which takes into account privacy as well as measures to protect ICT related assets throughout the whole engineering process.

PbD is hailed as the solution to the digital world's privacy problems. It is usually presented as a set of principles that can be applied from the onset of systems development to mitigate privacy concerns and ensure compliance with Data Protection legislation. However, these principles often remain vague and rely on ambiguous concepts, and are hence difficult to apply to engineering systems [25]. There are many open questions and challenges that need to be addressed at both the management and development levels in order to define effective methods to integrate privacy into systems [24]. A variety of approaches are being used to address these privacy concerns throughout the lifecycle of products or systems.

- PIA and risk management processes: these will be discussed in more detail within the PRIPARE PSbD Methodology section.
- OASIS standardization efforts. OASIS is as a non-profit consortium that drives the development, convergence, and adoption of open standards for the global information society. There are currently two Technical Committees (TC) related to PbD:
  - The PMRM [17] TC (Privacy Management Reference Model and Methodology). The objective of PMRM (pronounced pim-rim) is to provide a methodology for developing operational solutions to privacy issues. A first specification of PMRM was issued in July 2013.
  - The PbD Documentation for Software Engineers TC (PbD-SE TC) [29]. The TC objective is to provide privacy governance and documentation standards for software engineers.

---

[1] http://openid.net/

[2] https://kantarainitiative.org/confluence/display/uma/Home

3 Converging to a Common Terminology

To enable the development of a methodology addressed to multiple stakeholders from different countries and industries, it is necessary to define a common terminology that facilitates communication to be straightforward and without ambiguities. There are many sources of terminology for the domains of privacy, security, and risk management. The most relevant sources for terminology for PRIPARE are the ISO Standards [15, 16], the EU Data Protection Directive (DPD) [14], EU GDPR [13] (approved by the EU parliament) and PMRM [17].

Beyond the discussion of specific terminology, an initial decision was made in terms of terminology style. In the EU DPD [14], terminology is focused on the term "data" or "personal data". It defines, in its principles and articles, responsibilities of data controllers, and data processors. It also defines sensitive categories of data. The European Data Protection Supervisor (EDPS), as expected, also follows that naming convention that is also endorsed by the Article 29 Data Protection Working Party [19]. On the other hand, ISO talks about Personal Identifiable Information (PII). Looking at the definitions, both terms refer to the same concept but the wording is different. All concepts in the ISO standards are defined in terms of the PII: PII controller, PII processor, in the same way as the EU DPD does with "data". The OASIS PMRM [17] also makes use of the ISO wording.

Wording style had to be carefully chosen as only one style should be used within PRIPARE to avoid confusion. A survey among the participants of the consortium unanimously decided to adopt the EU wording style within PRIPARE.

A literature review conducted in the initial stages of the project revealed some terms that can be classified as elusive or controversial such as accountability, consent or informed consent, personal data, privacy or proportionality. Previous studies regarding these terms have been taken into account and discussed among project experts, after which a proposed definition was agreed upon by the project partners. The accepted definitions will be published and used within PRIPARE as a basis for further work.

4 PRIPARE's Principles

There are a variety of principles that are relevant for the PRIPARE project. The consortium has identified several sources such as the European DPD [14], the proposal for a new EU GDPR [13], OECD privacy principles [27] or Federal Trade Commission (FTC) FIPPs and had successful discussions regarding the most appropriate principles for the PRIPARE project. The focus on principles discussion was further refined towards discussing ideas and principles of data minimization, personal data, user-centricity, accountability, privacy and consent.

The security principles under discussion by the PRIPARE consortium included applying defense in depth, using a positive security model, avoiding security by obscurity, keeping security simple, and establishing secure defaults. The source for these principles is the Open Web Application Security Project (OWASP) [28]. The project consortium has accepted these principles preliminarily. The security principles may be further debated with stakeholders as the project progresses.

The principles of data protection included in the PRIPARE project for discussion came from the European DPD 95/46/EC [14] and from the Proposal for a new European GDPR [13] (discarding OECD and FTC's articulations). These principles include safeguarding personal data, proportionality and data minimization, compliance with the data subject's right to access and amend their personal data accountability, and the right to deletion. These principles are important in terms of the data lifecycle, from the collection of personal data (and an individual consenting to this collection of their personal data), to processing (and the right of the individual to object to this processing and the principle of proportionality), to the deletion of personal data (and the right of the individual to have his data retained only for a set time period and to have his data erased after this time). To date, the project consortium has agreed on the principles listed. However there may still be a need for the PRIPARE project to include a reference to the use of state-of-the-art technologies and the need for engineers to build in new technological solutions to minimize privacy risks. The data protection principles, including issues such as "what is meant by consent?" will be further discussed with stakeholders as the project progresses. The draft of the EU GDPR, among multiple other changes, modifies the notion of consent to define it as explicit and informed, rather than implicit. The PRIPARE project will take these new developments into account.

Besides security and privacy principles, the consortium has also discussed the notion of privacy itself within PRIPARE. Privacy is certainly not a universal concept that can be applied across all technologies and all situations. Finn et al. [20] argue that current attempts to capture the complexities of privacy issues in reactive frameworks are inadequate. They state that "Rights to privacy, such as those enshrined in the European Charter of Fundamental Human Rights, require a forward-looking privacy framework that positively outlines the parameters of privacy in order to prevent intrusions, infringements and problems." Finn et al. suggest that Clarke's taxonomy is no longer adequate for addressing the range of privacy issues that have arisen with regard to a new and emerging set of systems and technologies. They therefore suggest an approach that encompasses seven types of privacy: privacy of the person, privacy of behavior and action, privacy of communication, privacy of data and image, privacy of thoughts and feelings, privacy of location and space, and privacy of association. This approach is beneficial in terms of navigating the various definitions of privacy in the literature to date. Rather than focusing only on personal data and personal communications, as has been the case to date in data protection legislation, the taxonomy proposed ensures that different types of privacy are protected. This is important in relation to PIAs, which should take into account all seven types of privacy. With regard to the PRIPARE project, it would be beneficial to keep this taxonomy in mind when thinking about Privacy by Design. Rather than getting caught up in the myriad and diverse definitions of privacy, basing the PRIPARE methodology on this taxonomy of seven types of privacy will move the debate forward as opposed to reinventing the wheel.

Accountability, as one of the EU DPD principles, was largely discussed as it has become a widely debated topic in recent years (in relation to privacy and data protection). EU discussions on accountability suggest that current legal regulations for protecting privacy are inadequate and that without a change in the current direction, the problems of data protection are set to continue. Furthermore, commentators in the field have suggested that "Accountability can form the focus for dealing with issues of scale in regulation, privacy risk assessment, self-regulation through certification and seals and foster an environment for the development of new technologies for managing privacy" [26]. Finally, accountability is tied together with legal compliance and the idea that those who control data should, on request, be able to show compliance with data protection legislation. Although these discussions place accountability at center stage, the practicalities of achieving accountability in practice are left open to further debate. For the purpose of the PRIPARE project, the definition of accountability that will be used is the one that appears in the EDPS glossary: "The principle intended to ensure that controllers are more generally in control and in the position to ensure and demonstrate compliance with data protection principles in practice. Accountability requires that controllers put in place internal mechanisms and control systems that ensure compliance and provide evidence – such as audit reports – to demonstrate compliance to external stakeholders, including supervisory authorities" [18]. However, the consortium is aware that there is much more to accountability than that which is listed in the quote (as already outlined in this paragraph).

The starting point of PRIPARE's methodology is the idea of minimizing the trust that users need to place on the data controllers or data processor which will be collecting, storing and processing their personal data. This principle implicitly ensures that the data minimization principle is fulfilled, since the best approach to minimize trust is to minimize the amount of data that needs to be entrusted.[3] The methodology will seek to minimize the amount personal data distributed to potentially untrustworthy parties, which in turn minimizes the risk of privacy breaches.

5   PRIPARE PSbD Methodology

PRIPARE will adopt identified best practices on PIAs and risk management processes to provide an unobtrusive methodology that will complement existing system development and project management methodologies. This way PRIPARE's methodology or reference model will ensure and ease the process of building privacy-friendly systems, bridging the gap between the abstract notion of Privacy by Design and the concrete system designing and building process.

PRIPARE's PSbD methodology aims to be holistic. This means that it can be applied to systems or subsystems that compose it, even those being designed separately; it must be adaptable to the specific aspects of each domain specific standard; and it must also take into account the various types of systems, from the small to huge applications.

A recent PIA framework developed for RFID has been cited as being a "landmark PbD document" [8]. The framework is the first of its kind to be sector-specific and developed by industry. It provides guidelines on how to process data specifically

---

[3] "Protecting privacy by minimizing trust" is an on-going work from some of PRIPARE partners that will be published in the future.

related to RFID applications, and how to assess privacy and data protection issues through PIAs. In order to be effective, PIAs need to move beyond legal compliance checks in order to "offer a prospective identification of privacy risks before systems and programs are put in place," and that they "have to consider privacy risks in a wider framework which takes into account the broader set of community values and expectations about privacy" [9].

PIAs should not be considered as simply legal compliance checks, which ask: If we did X, would we be in compliance with the law and the fair information principles upon which the law is based? Nor should they be considered to be privacy audits used to assess existing technologies, although, as Wright argues, a PIA can enable an organization to demonstrate compliance with legislation in the case of a privacy audit or complaint. Undertaking a PIA can "provide evidence that the organization acted appropriately in attempting to prevent the occurrence. This can help to reduce or even eliminate any liability, negative publicity and loss of reputation" [10]. A 2007 Linden Consulting report [9] for the ICO states that they are most useful for new programs, services or technologies. However, they are not simply used to warn against potential risks but also to mitigate these risks, and to change the development process accordingly. PIAs, therefore, move beyond the legal compliance to assess and address the "moral and ethical issues posed by whatever is being proposed" [11]. The Ontario Data Protection guidance states that the "cyclical nature of the information life cycle must be supported by appropriate policies, practices, procedures, tools and contracts". With reference to this life cycle of information, the guidance states that "risk must be properly identified, minimized to the extent possible and appropriately managed where it can't be eliminated" and "a proper contemplation of the information life cycle includes these concepts". A privacy impact assessment is one of the ways that the information life cycle can be managed and privacy risks minimized [12].

Wright suggests that there is currently a "growing interest in Europe in privacy impact assessment" [10]. The UK introduced the first PIA methodology in 2007, although PIAs have been used in Australia, Canada, New Zealand and the United States since the mid-1990s. Conducting a PIA is now mandatory for government agencies in the UK, Canada and the US. It has been found that "unless they are mandatory, many organizations may not undertake them even though their projects, technologies or services have serious privacy impacts" [10]. In terms of best practice, Wright concludes that a PIA process should include:

- An assessment of privacy risks an organization might face in relation to a new project
- A process of engaging stakeholders (including external stakeholders);
- Examples of specific risks, recommendations and an action plan;
- Third party reviews and benchmarks that organizations could use to test how well they are following the process,
- Publication of the PIA report and PIA updates if there are changes in the project.

PRIPARE will embrace and incorporate this view of PIAs in its procedure and reference model approaches. Ideally, a PIA should include (or be complemented by) a privacy risk analysis. Inspiration can be drawn from the security area which has a long experience in risk analysis. Risk analyses in this area typically includes well identified steps such as the definition of assets, the identification of threats, vulnerabilities, attacks, etc., leading to a decision making phase (risk acceptance, mitigation, avoidance, etc.). In the case of privacy, the decision should involve the choice of specific architectures and technologies (Privacy Enhancing Technologies, PETs). However PIAs differ from traditional security analyses in several ways: privacy properties are not similar to security properties (even if related), privacy itself is more difficult to grasp than security, and the decision making phase should involve all stakeholders. So the transposition of security risk analysis to privacy analysis is not straightforward and warrants serious thought.

In terms of best practice, Wright also suggests that, in addition to a third party review, accountability mechanisms, such as mandatory reporting requirements, should be implemented. Finally, Wright argues that tying PIAs to budget submissions for new projects and programs can ensure that a greater number of PIAs are actually undertaken, as well as enhancing accountability.

6 Complementing Current Methodologies with PRIPARE

From the beginning of a system until its disposal there are several phases that are considered as the *System Lifecycle*. The management of the different phases of the lifecycle usually follows some methodology. Different methodology types can be used to manage this life cycle and often project management and system development methodologies are mixed to provide an ad hoc methodology that can be used through the entire system lifecycle. Usual stages that can be found in project development methodologies are: Initiating, Planning, Executing, Monitoring & Controlling and Closing.

PRIPARE will have to provide a way to integrate its methodology steps into existing and widely-adopted project management methodologies as it will involve a series of tasks that affect not only the engineering process itself but also resource allocation and organizational requirements. Special focus will be made on the most extended PM methodologies: PMBOK[4] and PRINCE2.[5]

By addressing the integration of the PSbD methodology with the most extended system development and project management methodologies, PRIPARE will embed its principles (from the EU DPD, the new EU Data Protection Regulation Draft, Cavoukian's PbD Foundational Principles, OWASP security principles, etc.) and best practices (in PIAs, risk assessment, Security by Design) into new to-be-developed ICT systems. As it is impossible to address integration with all existing system development methodologies, this integration will be focused on methodology families or similar methodologies. The integration of methodologies will be addressed by using the general description of a methodology family (e.g. waterfall, iterative, incremental, prototype), or by using a representative methodology of the family (scrum as representative of agile methodologies). Complementing some of the methodologies may be

---

[4] http://www.pmi.org/PMBOK-Guide-and-Standards.aspx
[5] http://www.prince-officialsite.com/

quite easy as they have similar stages that can be matched. However, others (i.e. scrum) pose great challenges, such as:

- How to implement PbD in a methodology that has no design stage?
- How to reflect privacy requirements in a methodology that only uses user stories?

These issues will have to be tackled during the methodology design in order to provide an effective and applicable privacy and security-by-design software and systems engineering methodology. PRIPARE's methodology will have to be as unobtrusive as possible to encourage adoption. This can be achieved by making some steps optional or by being less prescriptive in *how* things should be done (however, an idea or an example of "how" should always be provided to ease the adoption process).

7 Concluding Remarks and Future Work

PRIPARE will consider existing PETs, risk management methodologies, PIA frameworks and other approaches to engineer and operationalize PbD (i.e. OASIS PMRM [17]) with the objective of providing an easily applicable methodology suitable for different stakeholders (engineers, decision makers etc.). This will defuse some of the worst PbD critics regarding its chances of adoption [21] such as: "More aspirational than practical or operational" and "Difficult to be implemented into engineering practices". It will also ensure that systems developed with the methodology will follow PRIPARE's security (OWASP) and EU GDPR data protection principles and privacy best practices. PRIPARE will develop a truly positive-sum methodological approach for engineering privacy into ICT Systems software design and development lifecycles that will be:

- Short, easy-to-understand, and easy-to-use,
- Principles-based,
- Provisioned with risk assessment standards,
- Designed to cover the whole system lifecycle,
- Flexible so it can adapt depending on the nature of the project and the information collected,
- Useful for different stakeholders,
- Engaged with engineering practices.

To achieve this, PRIPARE's methodology will embrace current PIA practices, extending them with the best PIA practices as determined by different studies and projects (e.g. [22, 23]). It will include a complete and standard risk assessment process to minimize privacy and security risks. The methodology will be designed to provide tasks, inputs, outputs and best practices that will cover complete lifecycle of systems, from its inception to its disposal, by complementing existing system development methodologies. Later the proposed methodology will be consolidated with feedback from stakeholders during training, presentation, and dissemination events, seminars and workshops of the initially defined methodology. In order to ensure the success of PRIPARE's methodology, several other initiatives other than the methodology definition itself will be carried out in parallel:

- Liaison with other EU projects,
- Provision of information and reference material for the general public, ICT educators, policy makers, and governmental and non-governmental bodies acting for human rights protection.

References

1. United Nations General Assembly: The Universal Declaration of Human Rights, Paris (1948)
2. United Nations General Assembly: The right to privacy in the digital age. Resolution A/C.3/68/L.45/Rev.1
3. Cavoukian, A.: 7 Foundational Principles of Privacy by Design. Information & Privacy Commissioner, Ontario, Canada
4. European Data Protection Supervisor (EDPS): Opinion of the European Data Protection Supervisor on Promoting Trust in the Information Society by Fostering Data Protection and Privacy (2010)
5. Article 29 Data Protection Working Party: Opinion 01/2012 Opinion 01/2012 on the data protection reform proposals, March 2012
6. RFID Industry, Privacy and Data Protection Impact Assessment Framework for RFID Applications, January 2011
7. Camenisch, J., Leenes, R., Sommer, D.: Digital Privacy: PRIME-Privacy and Identity Management for Europe. Springer-Verlag New York Inc., New York (2011)
8. Privacy by Design: "PbD based RFID PIA". http://www.privacybydesign.ca/index.php/pbd-based-rfid-pia/
9. Linden Consulting Inc.: Privacy Impact Assessments: International Study of their Application and Effects, Information Commissioner's Office, UK (2007)
10. Wright, D.: The state of the art in privacy impact assessment. Comput. Law Secur. Rev. **28** (1), 54–61 (2011)
11. Flaherty, D.: Privacy Impact Assessments: An Essential Tool for Data Protection, Canada (2000)
12. Cavoukian, A.: Privacy risk management: building privacy protection into a risk management framework to ensure that privacy risks are managed by default. In: Information and Privacy Commissioner, Ontario, Canada, p. 12 (2010)
13. European Commission, INOFFICIAL CONSOLIDATED VERSION AFTER LIBE COMMITTEE VOTE PROVIDED BY THE RAPPORTEUR Proposal for a REGULATION OF THE EUROPEAN PARLIAMENT AND OF THE COUNCIL on the protection of individuals with regard to the processing of personal data and on the free movement of such data (General Data Protection Regulation), Brussels, 22 October 2013
14. European Parliament and the Council, Directive 95/46/EC of 24.10.1995 on the protection of individuals with regard to the processing of personal data and on the free movement of such data, OJ L 281, 23 November 1995
15. International Organization for Standardization (ISO): Information technology – Security techniques – Privacy framework, ISO/IEC 29100:2011, First edition, Geneva, 15 December 2011
16. International Organization for Standardization (ISO): Information technology – Security techniques – Evaluation criteria for IT security, ISO/IEC 15408-2, First edition, Geneva, 1 December 1999

17. Organization for the Advancement of Structured Information Standards (OASIS): Privacy Management Reference Model and Methodology (PMRM), Version 1.0. July 2013
18. European Data Protection Supervisor (EDPS): European Data Protection Supervisor Glossary. https://secure.edps.europa.eu/EDPSWEB/edps/EDPS/Dataprotection/Glossary
19. Article 29 Working Party. http://ec.europa.eu/justice/data-protection/article-29/
20. Finn, R., Wright, D., Friedewald, M.: Seven types of privacy. In: Gutwirth, S., Poullet, Y., et al. (eds.) European Data Protection: Coming of Age. Springer, Dordrecht (2013)
21. Rubinstein, I., Good, N.: Privacy by design: a counterfactual analysis of google and facebook privacy incidents. Berkeley Technol. Law J. **28**(2), 1333–1414 (2011)
22. Wright, D.: Making privacy impact assessment more effective. Inf. Soc. Int. J. **29**(5), 307–315 (2013)
23. European Commission - Directorate General Justice: Recommendations for a privacy impact assessment framework for the European Union, Brussels – London, November 2012
24. Spiekermann, S.: The challenges of privacy by design. Commun. ACM **55**(7), 38–40 (2012)
25. Gürses, S.F., Troncoso, C., Diaz, C.: Engineering privacy by design. In: Computers, Privacy & Data Protection (2011)
26. Guagnin, D., Hempel, L., Ilten, C., Kroener, I., Neyland, D., Postigo, H. (eds.): Managing Privacy through Accountability. Palgrave Macmillan, Basingstoke (2012)
27. OECD, OECD Guidelines on the Protection of Privacy and Transborder Flows of Personal Data
28. OWASP Application Security Principles. https://www.owasp.org/index.php/Category: Principle
29. Organization for the Advancement of Structured Information Standards (OASIS): Privacy by Design Documentation for Software Engineers

Interoperability Analysis of Accountable Data Governance in the Cloud

Vasilios Tountopoulos[1(✉)], Massimo Felici[2], Alain Pannetrat[3],
Daniele Catteddu[3], and Siani Pearson[2]

[1] Athens Technology Center S.A., Athens, Greece
v.tountopoulos@atc.gr
[2] HP Labs, Bristol, UK
{massimo.felici,siani.pearson}@hp.com
[3] Cloud Security Alliance, Edinburgh, Scotland, UK
{apannetrat,dcatteddu}@cloudsecurityalliance.org

Abstract. Cloud computing has emerged as a promising technology to drive innovation and leverage business development in various sectorial applications. Large scale enterprises and SMEs take advantage of cloud computing in order to benefit from cost-effective technological deployments allowing flexibility and scalability, and to offer added value solutions to their customers. However, customers' perceptions of the risks affecting data and IT governance, especially in complex service provision ecosystems, result in a lack of trust in the ability of the providers to handle their assets in a responsible way. This paper elaborates on the general aspects of an accountability-based approach, which can facilitate organisations dealing with the cloud to comply with applicable legislation and provide more evidence that confidential and/or personal data are handled in accordance with relevant data protection legislation.

Keywords: Accountability · Governance · Interoperability · Cloud computing

1 Introduction

Data governance in the cloud is of paramount importance. Unfortunately, cloud customers are faced with or perceive a loss of governance or lack of transparency about the way their data are processed in the cloud. Customers are clearly concerned about the loss of governance over their data in the cloud [1]. They worry about the possible uncontrolled replication or potential disclosure of their personal and/or confidential data to third parties. The uncertainty about who is able to access data stored in the cloud, and for what purposes, is aggravated by the complexity of cloud supply chains. This makes cloud customers feel uncomfortable about how their personal or confidential data are being managed. This concern is exacerbated as the legal framework is complex, failing to provide clarity around the rules that affect the cloud market. Thus, cloud deployments face two main barriers that have a direct impact on the adoption of cloud services for data-intensive business contexts: the uncertainty of the regulatory regimes regarding the processing of personal and/or confidential data, and the perception of emerging security threats [2, 3] in cloud service provisioning chains.

© Springer International Publishing Switzerland 2014
F. Cleary and M. Felici (Eds.): CSP Forum 2014, CCIS 470, pp. 77–88, 2014.
DOI: 10.1007/978-3-319-12574-9_7

This paper introduces an accountability-based governance framework as a means to complement existing data and IT governance practices and address privacy and data protection law compliance in complex cloud service provisioning ecosystems. We argue for an accountable cloud governance approach, which involves the ability to demonstrate, as appropriate, that the processing complies with data protection laws. The principle of accountability [4] addresses some important cloud customers' concerns regarding the use of cloud computing.[1] Accountability can be a valuable vehicle towards the implementation of improved mechanisms and procedures for data protection, efficient data stewardship and demonstration of compliance with regulatory regimes [4, 5]. The principle of accountability could be addressed across different levels, each of which relate to regulatory, organisational and technological aspects of a cloud service chain. From a regulatory perspective, various legal challenges arise from the current regulatory framework, which defines specific rules and introduces certain legal requirements in relation to data governance [6]. The organisational perspective includes the policies that implement cloud governance, raising responsibilities that should be, legally and ethically, accepted by all parties involved in the cloud business or cloud service supply chain. An ethical dimension of being accountable can also be considered as an inherent incentive to respect the rights of those placing their confidential and/or personal data in the cloud, which can, further, drive achieving a better position in the global market landscape, by implementing policy-driven cloud computing solutions [7]. From a technical perspective, accountability involves using mechanisms to protect personal and/or confidential data.

This paper presents an accountability-based approach for data stewardship in the cloud [8, 9]. The approach involves an accountability model (and related framework) for data governance in the cloud. The accountability-based approach supports an analysis of the interoperability requirements for cloud ecosystems. This paper is structured as follows. Section 2 describes the problem of data governance in the cloud. Section 3 introduces the accountability model underlying our accountability-based approach to cloud governance. Section 4 elaborates on the interoperability aspects of cloud governance. Finally, Sect. 5 highlights some concluding remarks.

2 Data Governance in the Cloud

The broad adoption of cloud services has driven different business models, which are based on complex service development and delivery supply chains, and, at the same time, have allowed cybercriminals to use reputable services to bypass many of the digital defences erected by companies [10]. Cloud data governance and management become highly challenging in order to overcome the problems, which set barriers in the wider adoption of cloud ecosystems. Such problems may relate to various cloud

---

[1] Note that accountability does not itself address important issues concerned with information security properties such as integrity, confidentiality and availability. However, this is only done indirectly by demonstrating that such properties are reflected within the designed system or service (which of course they might not be). Evidence supporting specific claims is necessary in order to assess how systems and services met specific requirements.

specific features and, in principle, they have a direct impact on building proper data governance policies for accountable approaches in the provision of cloud services.

Among the main concerns for prospective adopters of cloud services are loss of data control, compliance with laws and regulations, gaps in standards and specifications, the lack of simple mechanisms to assess the trustworthiness of potential partners and the effective implementation of incident response mechanisms [9]. These issues result in the lack of visibility and transparency within the service supply chain and the subsequent trust in data protection practices in the cloud. Accountability emerges as a cornerstone, where particular emphasis should be given to the proper definition of roles in the cloud service provisioning ecosystems and the subsequent allocation and enforcement of the responsibility for these, such as for data controller and data processors, and to facilitate the exercise of the rights of the data subjects.

Data governance in the cloud is not just effected by the complexity of the business and technical relationship between multiple parties and the increased sophistication of cyber-attacks, but also the legal uncertainty of the regulatory framework. More specifically, cloud governance is impacted by the cloud features, such as multi-tenancy of applications, where co-tenants may, for example, gain inappropriate access to the data of another application instance. Also, data duplication in the cloud creates problems in terms of compliance, since it can make the data lifecycle management difficult across various providers involved in a service provisioning chain. As a result, cloud customers are often sceptical about the cloud environment [11] due to a justifiable set of concerns, including how the ramification of any failures across the cloud provision chain can be discovered and mitigated, without losing control over data, and how compliance with established laws and regulations may be maintained.

When migrating to the cloud, data governance focuses increasingly on what security level the providers involved in the service chain can implement and guarantee. This means that of primary importance is the fact that critical privacy concerns are raised regarding the storage and processing (i.e. operations on data) of confidential or personal data in the cloud, any of which may be allocated to third parties. Given the technology-related challenges of building sustainable accountability-based cloud service chains [1], the legal requirements raise further barriers, which may affect the future of secure cloud computing. Indeed, a number of constraints have to be considered when designing and implementing accountability-based solutions for the cloud, which indicates that developing a perfect accountability solution is not feasible, and instead mechanisms for accountability should be evolved and improved over time.

3 An Accountability Model for Cloud Governance

We define a model of accountability (first introduced in [9]) that brings together different attributes, practices, and mechanisms. The accountability model consists of:

- **Accountability attributes** – conceptual elements of accountability applicable across different domains (i.e. the conceptual basis for our definition, and related taxonomic analysis), namely observability, verifiability, attributability, transparency, responsibility, liability and remediability.

- **Accountability practices** – emergent behaviour characterising accountable organisations (that is, how organisations operationalise accountability or put accountability into practice)
- **Accountability mechanisms** – diverse processes, non-technical mechanisms and tools that support accountability practices (that is, accountability practices use them).

Accountability attributes encompass the numerous elements and properties of accountability at the conceptual level. *Accountability practices* characterise organisational behaviour, and hence define what it means to be an accountable organisation. *Accountability mechanisms* are used in order to support such practices. Figure 1 illustrates how attributes, practices and mechanisms form a model of accountability.

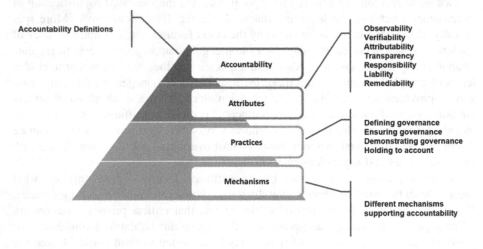

Fig. 1. Accountability attributes, practices and mechanisms

Accountability is interpreted in terms of accountability attributes. These accountability attributes are operationalised (that is, put into practice) by organisational accountability practices. Accountability practices need to comply with and mediate between external (drawn from relevant regulatory regimes and ethical attitudes) and internal (characterising organisational culture) criteria. In order to implement such practices, organisations use different accountability mechanisms tailored to their domains. The emerging relationships between accountability attributes, practices and mechanisms give rise to an operational interpretation of accountability (further descriptions of accountability attributes, mechanisms and practices is provided in [9]).

3.1   Accountability Framework

The relative lack of transparency in the cloud as to the providers and sub-providers that may be involved has given rise to concern regarding how risks and regulatory obligations may be assessed and managed – *"the lack of transparency of an out-sourcing chain consisting of multiple processors and subcontractors"* [5]. It is nec-essary to establish *chains of accountability*. Accountable organisations have to fulfil legal (as well as contractual and ethical) obligations for the usage or processing of personal and/or confidential data, and to ensure that contracted partners to whom they supply data enable themselves to remain compliant, wherever in the world the partners may be. We provide a definition of accountability tailored to the cloud:

> **Definition of Accountability for Data Stewardship in the Cloud:** *Accountability for an organisation consists of accepting responsibility for the stewardship of personal and/or confidential data with which it is entrusted in a cloud environment, for processing, storing, sharing, deleting and otherwise using the data according to contractual and legal requirements from the time it is collected until when the data are destroyed (including onward transfer to and from third parties). It involves committing to legal and ethical obligations, policies, procedures and mechanisms, explaining and demonstrating ethical implementation to internal and external stakeholders and remedying any failure to act properly.*

Our approach is to integrate legal, regulatory, socio-economic and technical approaches into a framework to provide accountability pre-emptively, to assess risk and avoid security and privacy threats and reactively to provide transparency, auditing and cor-rective measures for redress. This enables us to implement chains of accountability, including interdisciplinary mechanisms to ensure that obligations to protect data are observed by all who process the data, irrespective of where that processing occurs. To achieve this for the cloud a chain of responsibility needs to be built throughout the cloud service supply network starting from the cloud service customers, which can be overseen by regulators, auditors and business governance. Accountability is the result of complying with a combination of public (e.g. derived from regulatory regimes) and private (e.g. derived from organisational practices) accountability criteria in cloud ecosystems. Actors within cloud ecosystems can use mechanisms to support accountability practices, and thereby help them to comply with relevant regulatory regimes within specific application domains. Businesses need to meet these obligations, as well as obligations and requirements imposed by other stakeholders that include customers and data subjects. We provide a framework (Fig. 2) that embodies our accountability-based approach combining legal, governance and technical measures that may be used to support accountability in cloud service provision chains. The accountability framework involves different functional aspects of accountability: Pre-ventive (investigating and mitigating risk in order to form policies and determine appropriate mechanisms to put in place; putting in place appropriate policies, proce-dures and technical mechanisms), Detective (monitoring and identifying policy vio-lation; putting in place detection and traceability measures), and Corrective (managing incidents and providing notifications and redress).

New data governance models for accountability can serve as a basis for providing data protection when cloud computing is used. Accountability is becoming more integrated into self-regulatory programs as well as future privacy and data protection frameworks globally. It is an upcoming challenge to strengthen this approach and make it more workable by developing ways in which accountability and information stew-ardship can be provided. This goes beyond traditional approaches to protect data, in that it includes complying with and upholding values, obligations, and enhancing trust.

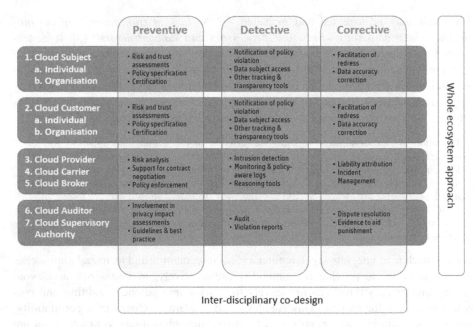

Fig. 2. Accountability framework

The framework based on the accountability definitions and concepts involves different mechanisms. These mechanisms form a reference architecture supporting accountable data governance, hence chains of accountability in the cloud.

3.2 Accountability Governance

A major driver for an accountability-based approach is to provide an incentive for organisations to 'do the right thing' with respect to relevant regulatory regimes. Various aspects of accountability as an evolving regulatory and enforcement approach (e.g. operationalization of accountability in Binding Corporate Rules,[2] provision of flexibility in terms of measures taken to support compliance etc.) can make things easier for organisations in terms of compliance and this, coupled with stronger penalties for non-compliance, can provide business incentives for organisations to use privacy data protection and security controls more effectively. For example, in response to the seemingly insufficient reflection of EU data protection principles and obligations in concrete measures and practices used by organisations, the Article 29 Data Protection Party advocated in their opinion on the principle of accountability that such a general principle could help move data protection 'from theory to practice', as well as provide a means for assisting data protection authorities in their supervision and assessment tasks [4]. There would be an associated requirement for data controllers to be able to

---

[2] Article 29 Data Protection Party has issued various documents on different aspects of Binding Corporate Rules, e.g. Explanatory Document on the Processor Binding Corporate Rules [12].

demonstrate their compliance to supervisory authorities upon request [13]. Hence, organisations would be allowed some increased control over aspects of compliance, e.g. which tools and mechanisms to use in order to achieve compliance, but at the expense of having to demonstrate on an ongoing basis that these mechanisms are appropriate for their business context, and operationally work as expected.

All actors involved (in particular, those directly involved in governance) have a role to play in making cloud services accountable for how data are used and managed in the cloud – *"Cloud governance encompasses two main areas: internal governance focuses on a provider's technical working of cloud services, its business operations, and the ways it manages its relationship with customers and other external stakeholders; and external governance consists of norms, rules, and regulations which define the relationships between members of the cloud community and attempt to solve disputes between them"* [14]. Both internal and external governance pertain to the collection, storage, processing operations on and dissemination of personal and/or confidential data, and other processing. Figure 3 shows the interaction between two organisations (as a continuous process) driven by accountability governance (constrained by external criteria and regulatory regimes but managed independently).

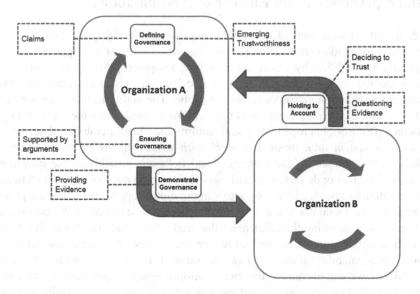

Fig. 3. Accountability governance

The legal and contractual context defines obligations, responsibilities and liabilities of actors in a given cloud ecosystem. Accountability entrusts organisations with the practical aspects of complying with data protection obligations. This involves clarification of requirements of the different actors within cloud ecosystems, as well as transparency and provisions of trustworthy accounts (in the sense of accountability) by organisations that collect or handle personal data. Accountable organisations need to define and implement appropriate governance mechanisms relating to the treatment of personal and/or confidential data in cloud environments.

Accountability governance then consists of taking responsibility for specific accountability criteria, with the aim of ensuring accountability by deploying suitable mechanisms and demonstrating them by compliance with such criteria through evidence. Organisations need to provide transparency regarding their systems and actions taken in order to show that stakeholders' expectations have been met and that organisational policies have been followed. They also need to remedy any failure to act properly (e.g. by notifications, remedies, sanctions), even in cloud-supply chains involving multiple service providers. Accountability governance redefines interactions between providers and customers/regulators as well as between providers themselves. The ethical nature of an accountability-based approach and the organisational obligations that result from taking this approach represent a shift from reactive to proactive governance of personal and/or confidential data. Organisations commit to the stewardship of personal and/or confidential data by accepting and addressing legal, contractual and ethical obligations. In order to do so, organisations deploy and use different mechanisms (e.g. policies, standards), take into account social norms, provide evidence to internal and external stakeholders, and remedy any failure to act properly.

4 Interoperability as an Enabler of Accountability

One of the attractive aspects of the cloud ecosystem is the ability to build new cloud services and applications from other pre-existing cloud services and applications. This is typically exemplified by cloud services like Dropbox [15], which builds upon Amazon storage, or more complex services like Netflix,[3] which combine IaaS, PaaS, and content distribution networks across the globe. The ability to make services work together seamlessly across complex supply chains is made possible by two largely intertwined features: interoperability and automation. Interoperability describes the *"ability of a system or a product to work with other systems or products without special effort on the part of the customer"* and is *"made possible by the adoption of standards"*.[4] Formal or de facto standards specify common data formats, semantics and communication protocols adopted by actors in the cloud supply chain. The adoption of standards in turn facilitates automation of the processes involved in the provision of cloud services, unleashing the efficiencies that make the cloud successful. We believe that, with adequate automation, we can reduce *real* or *perceived* costs associated with providing accountability in the cloud can be reduced. In turn, by reducing the cost of accountability we can encourage the greater adoption of best practices for data stewardship. In order to support automated mechanisms to enable accountability provision in the cloud, we first identified all actors typically involved in cloud accountability interactions. Next, we found that their accountability-related interactions could be classified in 4 general subgroups, which in turn could be used to shape requirements for interoperability for the purpose of accountability. In the A4Cloud project, we chose to extend the NIST cloud supply chain taxonomy [16] to create the following cloud accountability taxonomy composed of seven main roles:

---

[3] http://techblog.netflix.com/search/label/cloud%20architecture

[4] https://www.ieee.org/education_careers/education/standards/standards_glossary.html

1. **Cloud Subject:** An entity (individual or organisation) whose data are processed by a cloud provider, either directly or indirectly.
2. **Cloud Customer:** An entity (individual or organisation) that (1) maintains a business relationship with, and (2) uses services from a Cloud Provider.
3. **Cloud Provider:** An entity responsible for making a (cloud) service available to Cloud Customers.
4. **Cloud Carrier:** The intermediary entity that provides connectivity and transport of cloud services between Cloud Providers and Cloud Customers.
5. **Cloud Broker:** An entity that manages the use, performance and delivery of cloud services, and negotiates relationships between Cloud Providers and Cloud Customers.
6. **Cloud Auditor:** An entity that can conduct independent assessment of cloud services, information system operations, performance and security of the cloud implementation, with regards to a set of requirements, which may include security data protection, information system management, laws or regulations and ethics.
7. **Cloud Supervisory Authority:** An entity that oversees and enforces the application of a set of rules.

The NIST role taxonomy was chosen as a foundation because of its vast adoption. However, it has some shortcomings when used to describe accountability scenarios. For example, if we look at the data protection domain, which is central in this project, we can observe that the "data subject" is invisible in the NIST taxonomy, except when she/he is also a cloud customer. This was among the reasons that led us to extend and modify the NIST taxonomy as proposed above [17]. Next, we classify the accountability interactions between these seven cloud actors into four main subgroups:

1. **Agreement** covers all interactions that lead to one actor taking legal responsibility for the handling of certain data provided by another party according to a certain policy. These interactions may include a negotiation phase. A policy may *express* requirements that apply to all 7 core accountability attributes, and contributes to the *implementation* of the attributes of *responsibility* and *liability*.
2. **Reporting** covers all interactions related to the reporting by an actor about current data handling practices and policies (e.g. reporting security breaches or providing security/privacy level indictors). This type of interaction mainly supports the implementation of the accountability attributes of *transparency* and *observability*.
3. **Demonstration** covers all interactions that lead to one actor demonstrating the correct implementation of some data handling policies. This includes external verifications by auditors or cryptographic proofs of protocol executions, for example. This type of interaction mainly supports the *implementation* of the accountability attributes of *verifiability* and *attributability*. We emphasise that *Demonstration* differs from *Reporting* in that it implies some form of proof or provision of evidence.
4. **Remediation** covers all interactions that lead one actor to seek and receive or offer remediation for failures to follow data handling policies. This mainly supports the *implementation* of the accountability attribute of *remediability*.

By cross matching these four subgroups of interactions with the cloud account-ability roles above, we identified 31 key interoperability requirements for account-ability in the cloud. While we refer the reader to [18] for the details, we can highlight two key elements of this analysis. First and foremost, an essential requirement for enabling interoperability for the purpose of accountability in the cloud is the ability of two communicating parties to share a common understanding of security and data protection policy semantics and their associated metrics, be it for the purpose of agreement, reporting, demonstration and/or remediation. Unfortunately, this common ground for semantics hardly exists today [19]. For example, all major cloud providers use different semantics and metrics for availability [20]. The same can be said if two interacting actors use different technical standards to interpret properties such as "consent", "confidentiality level" or "user information" (independently of their legal meaning), just to give a few examples. Second, interoperable accountability mecha-nisms have to be interoperable across the cloud supply chain. For example, if a cloud provider needs to report data stewardship information to a customer, it may need itself to obtain information from other providers acting as its sub-providers, while still preserving a common understanding of policy semantics.

With so many actors and interactions, we need to set priorities in attempting to automate accountability interactions in the cloud. The logical step is to focus first on the most frequent and necessary interactions and later on the most uncommon ones. In this respect, *Information* and *Agreement* are the two subgroups of interactions we should start with, focusing in particular on Cloud Customers, Cloud Providers, and Cloud Subjects (*data subjects*). At the other end of the spectrum, we expect *remedi-ation* interactions and more generally interactions with supervisory authorities and auditors to be rarer and therefore less of a priority for automation.

There are currently some significant initiatives that could provide interoperability and automation supporting accountability in the cloud. To begin with, the A4Cloud project itself is proposing a policy language A-PPL, which is an extension of the PPL language [21], itself based on XACML [22]. More broadly, the A4Cloud project will produce a set of novel tools that will aim to tackle the interoperability issues high-lighted above. The Cloud Security Alliance is developing two relevant RESTful APIs: CloudAudit[5] to access audit data from cloud provider, and the Cloud Trust Protocol[6] for constant monitoring of security properties of cloud services, both contributing to automated *Information* and *Demonstration* interactions. Similarly, the NIST has begun examining how to define metrics applicable to the monitoring of security properties described in an SLA.[7] The European Commission is also investigating model terms for cloud SLAs [1], while ISO in [23] is developing a new standard for cloud SLAs. As these initiatives mature, we hope to see *accountability as a service* become a reality in the cloud in the next few years.

---

[5] http://www.cloudaudit.org/
[6] https://blog.cloudsecurityalliance.org/ctp/
[7] http://www.nist.gov/itl/cloud/

5 Concluding Remarks

This paper presented an accountability-based approach for cloud data governance, as a means for addressing interoperability requirements relating to the protection of personal and confidential data involved in complex service provision chains in the cloud. Through the description of an accountability model and the related framework, we emphasised the need to integrate together legal, regulatory, and technical aspects as an effective way to build sustainable chains of accountability. We then elaborated on the interoperability aspects, which can be identified across the interactions that happen between stakeholders involved in cloud data governance practices. As an extension to this work, the interoperability requirements can be aligned to legal requirements for cloud data governance, as they arise from the analysis of the implications of the established regulatory framework on the data protection in the cloud service provision ecosystem. An initial analysis of some data governance challenges in the cloud from a data protection regulatory perspective has been made in [6].

As future steps, we will be focusing on the implementation of algorithms and tools, which will enable realisation of the accountability framework and respective technical functions, which will be implemented by software components to provide technical support for the adoption of accountability mechanisms by the parties involved in complex service provision chains. In order to better illustrate the business benefits of accountability-based cloud data governance, prototype use case examples will be developed. These examples will showcase different aspects of the data and IT governance problem in the cloud and how accountability can practically work with the deployed security and privacy controls to foster higher levels of cloud consumers and providers' trust in both the cloud environments and the privacy and data protection mechanisms followed in them.

Acknowledgments. This work has been partly funded from the European Commission's Seventh Framework Programme (FP7/2007-2013) under grant agreement no: 317550 (A4CLOUD – http://www.a4cloud.eu/) Cloud Accountability Project. We would like to thank our project partners and colleagues who provided valuable comments to early drafts of this paper.

References

1. European Commission: Unleashing the potential of cloud computing in Europe. COM529 (2012)
2. Cloud Security Alliance: The notorious nine: cloud computing top threats in 2013. CSA Top Threats Working Group (2013)
3. European Network and Information Security Agency: Cloud computing: benefits, risks and recommendations for information security. ENISA report (2009)
4. Article 29 Data Protection Working Party: Opinion 3/2010 on the principle of accountability. 00062/10/EN WP 173 (2010)
5. Article 29 Data Protection Working Party: Opinion 05/2012 on Cloud Computing. 01037/12/EN WP 196 (2012)
6. Kuan Hon, W., Kosta, E., Christopher, M., Stefanatou, D.: Cloud accountability: the likely impact of the proposed EU data protection regulation. Queen Mary School of Law Legal Studies, Research Paper No. 172/2014; Tilburg Law School, Research Paper No. 07/2014

7. International Data Corporation (IDC): Quantitative estimates of the demand for cloud computing in Europe and the likely barriers to up-take, July (2012)
8. Felici, M., Jaatun, M.G., Kosta, E., Wainwright, N.: Bringing accountability to the cloud: addressing emerging threats and legal perspectives. In: Felici, M. (ed.) CSP EU FORUM 2013. CCIS, vol. 182, pp. 28–40. Springer, Heidelberg (2013)
9. Felici, M., Koulouris, T., Pearson, S.: Accountability for data governance in cloud ecosystems. In: 2013 IEEE International Conference on Cloud Computing Technology and Science (CloudCom 2013), Proceedings, pp. 327–332. IEEE Computer Society (2013)
10. Georgia Tech Information Security Center (GTISC) and Georgia Tech Research Institute (GTRI): Emerging cyber threats report 2014. Georgia Institute of Technology, Georgia Tech Cyber Security Summit (2013)
11. Organisation of Economic Cooperation and Development (OECD): The future of internet economy: a statistical profile. OECD Report, June 2011
12. Article 29 Data Protection Working Party: Explanatory document on the processor binding corporate rules. 00658/13/EN WP 204 (2013)
13. Article 29 Data Protection Working Party: Opinion 01/2012 on the data protection reform proposals. 00530/12/EN WP 191 (2012)
14. Reed, C.: Cloud governance: the way forward. In: Millard, C. (ed.) Cloud Computing Law. Oxford University Press, Oxford (2013)
15. Drago I., Mellia M., Munafo M.M., Sperotto A., Sadre R., Pras A.: Inside dropbox: understanding personal cloud storage services. In: Proceedings of the 2012 ACM Conference on Internet Measurement Conference (IMC'12), pp. 481–494. ACM, New York (2012)
16. Liu, F., Tong, J., Mao, J., Bohn, R., Messina, J., Badger, L., Leaf, D.: NIST cloud computing reference architecture. NIST special publication, 500-292 (2011)
17. A4Cloud: MS:C-2.3 conceptual framework. Milestone Report, May 2014
18. A4Cloud: D:C-3.1 requirements for cloud interoperability. Public Deliverable, November (2013)
19. Hogben G., Dekker M.: Procure secure, a guide to monitoring of security service levels in cloud contracts. European Network and Information Security Agency (ENISA) Report (2012)
20. Hogben G., Pannetrat A.: Mutant apples: a critical examination of cloud SLA availability definitions. In: IEEE 5th International Conference Cloud Computing Technology and Science (CloudCom), December 2013
21. Ardagna A.C., et al.: Primelife policy language (2009). http://www.w3.org/2009/policy-ws/papers/Trabelisi.pdf
22. OASIS: eXtensible Access Control Markup Language (XACML) Version 3.0 (2013)
23. ISO/IEC NP 19086, Information technology - Distributed application platforms and services - Cloud computing - Service level agreement (SLA) framework and terminology. Under development, November (2013)

Smart Grid Data Anonymization
for Smart Grid Privacy

Shahidul Hoque[1], Aneel Rahim[1], and Francesco Di Cerbo[2(✉)]

[1] Telecommunications Software and Systems Group,
Waterford Institute of Technology, Waterford, Ireland
{shoque,arahim}@tssg.org
[2] SAP Labs, Mougins, France
francesco.di.cerbo@sap.com

Abstract. We present an approach to adopt the DB Anonymizer (Database Anonymizer) GE (Generic Enabler) in the context of a case study relating to a Smart Grid Charging Optimization System (COS) that has been developed using real time Electric Vehicle (EV) and Wind energy data. The paper takes consideration of DB Anonymizer GE software for data anonymization with Smart Grid data use case and without Smart Grid data. In addition, the implementation of EV data anonymization and robustness of its anonymization strategy set is evaluated and described in the paper, along with the lessons learned and the potential for future improvements to the data anonymization strategy determination. The novelty of the mechanism itself stems from the effective evaluation of the GE for Smart Grid environment and hence, enhances the privacy preservation capabilities of the Charging Optimization System.

1 Introduction

The Smart Grid is changing the traditional electricity network paradigm by facilitating grid connections to millions of households with a cost effective, sustainable power system with low losses and high level of quality; maintaining the security of supply and safety. In order to fulfill the security and privacy requirements from different stakeholders within the Smart Grid, it is necessary to ensure that their data within the grid network is secure and preserves their privacy requirements.

The FINESCE project organizes and runs user trials in different European countries and one of the trials is building an energy management system named Charging Optimization System (COS), based on self-organizing technologies that monitor energy usage in a network, and suggest and implement efficiencies. The solution utilizes interruptible loads e.g. EV charging, to gain greater advantage of demand side management, thus providing grid operators with the real-time ability to stabilize any fluctuations in the grid supply by controlling the demand.

The research leading to these results has received funding from the European Union Seventh Framework Programme (FP7/FI-PPP Phase 2) under named on FINESCE & FI-WARE.

F. Cleary and M. Felici (Eds.): CSP Forum 2014, CCIS 470, pp. 89–96, 2014.
DOI: 10.1007/978-3-319-12574-9_8

For maintaining security and privacy of the demand side management application, it is necessary to maintain controlled sharing of information (data consumption, traffic profiling, determining usage patterns, etc.). Hence, anonimization of user information is crucial so that individuals cannot be determined.

The FI-WARE project offers the DB Anonymizer Generic Enabler (GE) software that helps in data disclosure activities by determining robustness of the anonymization strategies so that, before data anonymization, it is possible to determine the possibility to reconstruct the anonymized data by an attacker.

This paper takes consideration of DB Anonymizer GE implementation for data anonymization with Smart Grid case study and the reminder of the paper will consider the DB Anonymizer and its role in ensuring robust data anonymization in Smart Grid environment and evaluation of data anonymization strategies.

2 Data Anonymization and DB Anonymizer

Large organizations held datasets about their customers or their activities that from time to time have to be disclosed with third-parties for business reasons. Such datasets can contain personal information of individuals (more precisely, Personal Identifiable Information or PII), therefore to comply with personal data protection regulations (like EU Directive 95/46/EC [1] and its reform as stated in MEMO/14/186) [2] often datasets have to be anonymized before disclosure to preserve individuals' privacy.

However, two different problems may arise: first to decide if a piece of information has to be considered personal data or not, and second, to assess whether the exposure of non-personal data could be used by correlation algorithms to infer hidden (or anonymized) private data.

DB Anonymizer addresses the latter aspect, providing data anonymization functionalities centered on the estimation of the re-identification risk associated to information disclosure operations. The re-identification risk is defined as the risk that an attacker can reconstruct exactly a (anonymized) dataset's original content. DB Anonymizer computes the re-identification risk using a methodology validated by Trabelsi et al. [3] applying an algorithm proposed by Bezzi [4]; the methodology has the advantage of being applicable to virtually any use case dealing with personal information, as it combines *k-anonymity* with the Shannon entropy uncertainty estimation. DB Anonymizer exploits this characteristic to propose data anonymization functionalities ready to be plugged-in any scenario, by means of a REST API simple to integrate in any application. DB Anonymizer can be used as depicted in Fig. 1: a Data Manager in charge of a dataset disclosure operation can estimate the re-identification risk associated to an anonymization policy by means of DB Anonymizer GE, also obtaining propositions on how to change it to lower the associated risk. Data Manager then is empowered to alter or choose the appropriate anonymization policy considering both business needs and re-identification risk. DB Anonymizer can then be used to compute the anonymized dataset.

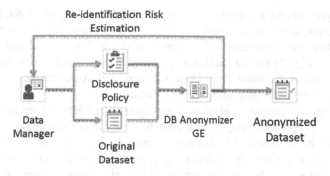

Fig. 1. DB Anonymizer in action

3 Smart Grid Data Privacy and DB Anonymizer

Traditional electricity grid is reforming due to infrastructural aging point of view and to address latest environmental and societal challenges. European Union Directive 2009/72/EC [5] states that within the condition of positive initial pilots' outcomes, by the year 2020, almost 80 % of EU consumers shall be equipped with smart grid. However, to effectively address this transition from electricity grid to smart grid, it's crucial that the security and privacy concerns from different stakeholders are resolved properly.

The FINESCE project addresses a lot security and privacy concerns in relation to smart grid such as data ownership, policy violations, insecure data disclosure, data transfer security, identity theft and inappropriate release of personal data to non-intender receiver and data loss due to link failure.

The DB Anonymizer GE will be used in the trail site of the project due to its offerings of handling insecure data disclosure and reconstruction of a dataset from an anonymized dataset content. In smart grid environment, the GE will be useful for anonymizing data from different sources such as EVSE (Electricity Vehicle Supply Equipment) and TS (Transmission System) data and define a fine scalable anonymization policy so that it is possible to keep the data secure and become tough for attackers to take control of user PII data. Getting control of PII data by attackers can lead to take out more personal data such as data consumption, traffic profiling, usage patterns etc.

4 DB Anonymizer Implementation

DB Anonymizer is an Open Source Software [6] provided by the FI-WARE project. It is designed to be used as-a-Service by any application that needs data anonymization capabilities. To this extent, a simple HTTP REST API can be used to integrate conveniently the anonymization functionalities with third-party applications. It is possible to use DB Anonymizer functionalities through the FI-LAB cloud facilities [7] offered by the FI-WARE consortium, or by setting up a private instance by means of the publicly available source code.

Figure 2 presents the main operations offered by DB Anonymizer. Such operations essentially permit to a Data Manager in charge of the dataset disclosure operation, to analyze a dataset anonymization policy (from right, the first, second and third operations shown in Fig. 2) and to maximize its business relevance and minimize its re-identification risk at the same time. Once satisfied, DB Anonymizer can produce an anonymized dataset according to the chosen policy.

DB Anonymizer considers identifiers and quasi-identifiers [4] in dataset analysis operations and supports natively a very generic anonymization technique called attribute suppression; it consists of eliminating specific attributes for all elements in a dataset. This technique does not require any specification with respect to the attribute semantics, therefore can be applied in many different scenarios. More anonymization techniques can be added to DB Anonymizer, for instance considering specific use case characteristics.

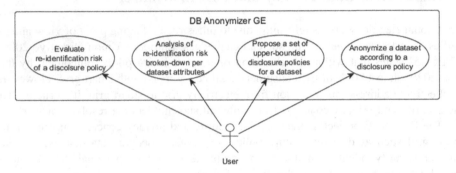

Fig. 2. DB Anonymizer main functionalities in UML Use Case Diagram

5   Case Study

To demonstrate use of the DB Anonymizer GE within the FINESCE platform, we consider a case study relating to an attack resolve mechanism through smart grid data anonymization. It involves component of FINESCE named Charge Point Optimization system (COS), several EVs' data taken by EVSE and renewable energy transmission data from Transmission System Operator (TSO).

The Fig. 3 shows that the COS is collecting data from different EVSEs and TSO and managing the data for getting data consumption, traffic profiling, usage patterns etc. While the data is stored in the COS without taking considerations of anonymizing the data and kept without removing the EVSE's PII, it is possible for malicious users to get access to the EVSE's PII data and later on, getting most sensitive information from the system and making vulnerable of the user privacy requirements. In addition, the malicious user can make turn on/off a TS by getting access to its PII data stored in the COS.

Hence, DB Anonymizer GE is used in the COS environment to anonymize data collected from EVSEs and TSO. The deployed GE facilitates data anonymization and later on, evaluation of the anonymization policy set to get better anonymization capabilities.

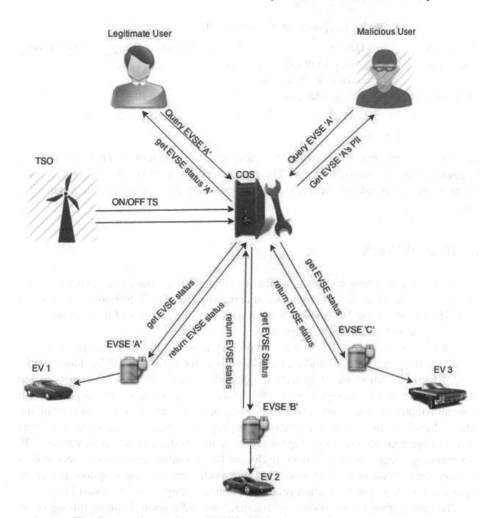

Fig. 3. Attack to pull out EVSE's PII in absence of anonymized data

We have taken account separate databases for the COS data, one is from EVSE and another from TS. The databases consist of several fields containing EVSE and TS data such as MPRN (Metering Point Reference Number), EVSE ID (identity), IP address, customer name, customer address, customer phone and TS ID, TS location, TS activation time etc. After the use of GE, the databases outcome with only MPRN and ESVE ID for EVSE data and TS ID and TS activation time for TSO data.

However, for the case study result, we have presented the anonymization policy evaluation result for Smart Grid data and without Smart Grid data in the following Table 1.

The result shows that the GE facilitates the data anonymization and the anonymized dataset policy is represented with the policy set file (.xml). The policy evaluation results signify that in the worst case an attacker can re-identify 45 % of the hidden/

Table 1. The policy set evaluation with DB Anonymizer GE

Data source	Dataset	Anonymization	Policy evaluation result
Smart grid	Policy_COS.xml dataApr-18-2014.sql	Done	0.45
Without smart grid	policy_safer.xml census_small-dump	Done	0.63

anonymized data. Hence, it needs for the same dataset to use more restrictive policy set to attenuate the re-construction risk. The gradual restriction of the policy set decreases the re-construction risk and hence, increases the privacy preservation of the Smart Grid data.

6 Related Work

The work proposed here crosses a number of areas such as smart grid, cyber security, privacy in smart grid, data anonymization and adoption of ICT technologies in smart grid. The FI-PPP Phase 1 FINSENY project addresses the baseline of ICT requirements of smart grid and Smart Energy Systems.

There has been a great deal of work on privacy concerns in smart grid, most notably looking at the privacy issues and proposed solutions for smart grid [8, 9]. These works mostly focus on smart metering technology and privacy concerns in relation to the collection and use of energy consumption data with a focus on privacy-by-design concept adoption to the smart grid. There has been a substantial work on surveying the attacks based on monitoring the electricity supply and privacy technologies for smart grid data aggregation and reviewing most commonly used smart grid policy tools [10]. For ensuring secure smart grid data disclosure by presenting protocols to secure data aggregation is done in another work [11]. For secure energy consumption data management, a data pseudonynization protocol has been design and evaluated [12].

The most relevant work is done with a mechanism for securely anonymizing smart metering data by attributing authenticated anonymous meter readings data with a specific smart meter or customer [13].

The anonymization algorithm proposed by Bezzi [4] combines two of the main anonymization approaches, namingly *k-anonymity* and *l-diversity*. The former aims at capturing on a dataset a combination of values of quasi-identifiers (i.e. elements in a dataset that can indirectly lead to the identification of a person like birth date or postal code) that can be indistinctly matched to at least k respondents. A limitation of k-anonymity is represented by the lack of consideration for the diversity in identifiers data that can lead to the identification of subjects with attribute values very different from others. The l-diversity approach fills this gap, requiring that each equivalence class has at least l well-represented values for each sensitive attribute [14]. Bezzi's algorithm combines k-anonymity indications and an estimation of the rareness of an element type to compute the probability of re-identification using the Shannon entropy uncertainty estimation.

7 Conclusion

In this paper, we have discussed about data anonymization and DB Anonymizer GE that has been adopted in a Smart Grid environment as part of a number of measures for ensuring consumer privacy. A complete discussion of the privacy preserving measures proposed by FINESCE for protecting Smart Grid environments goes beyond the scope of this paper; however, a number of FINESCE resources provide [15] additional information, to be integrated in the future. The practical tool has facilitated data anonymization operations and evaluation of the anonymization policy. The scalability issues of the DB Anonymizer with multiple sources of data in real-time environment are future challenges and can be considered as future research. In addition, the optimization of the anonymization policy set for large-scale datasets is also a crucial point that needs further work to be done, as well as considering scenario-specific anonymization strategies. The DB Anonymizer GE's support in Smart Grid data anonymization and hence, by evaluating the anonymized data against a particular policy and then evaluating the policy to make better policy set, enables the Smart Grid data controller to handle consumer data through effective privacy preservation.

References

1. Directive 95/46/EC of the European Parliament and of the Council of 24 October 1995 on the protection of individuals with regard to the processing of personal data and on the free movement of such data. http://eur-lex.europa.eu/legal-content/en/ALL/?uri=CELEX:31995 L0046. Accessed 14th May 2014
2. Progress on EU data protection reform now irreversible following European Parliament vote - MEMO/14/186 12/03/2014. http://europa.eu/rapid/press-release_MEMO-14-186_en. htm. Accessed 14th May 2014
3. Trabelsi, S., Salzgeber, V., Bezzi, M., Montagnon, G.: Data disclosure risk evaluation. In: 2009 Fourth International Conference on Risks and Security of Internet and Systems (CRiSIS), pp. 35–72, 19–22 Oct 2009. doi:10.1109/CRISIS.2009.5411979
4. Bezzi, M.: An entropy-based method for measuring anonymity. In: IEEE/CreateNet SECOVAL Workshop on the Value of Security Through Collaboration, September 2007
5. Directive 2009/72/EC of the European Parliament and of the Council of 13th July 2009 concerning common rules for the internal market in electricity and repealing Directive 2003/54/EC. http://eur-lex.europa.eu/LexUriServ/LexUriServ.do?uri=OJ:L:2009:211:0055:0093: EN:PDF. Accessed 14th May 2014
6. The source code of DB Anonymizer. https://github.com/fi-ware-security-sap/fiware-dba
7. A more detailed description of FI-LAB. http://www.fi-ware.org/lab/
8. Siddiqui, F., Zeadally, S., Alcaraz, C., Galvao, S.: Smart grid privacy: issues and solutions. In: 2012 21st International Conference on Computer Communications and Networks (ICCCN), pp. 1–5 (2012). doi:10.1109/ICCCN.2012.6289304
9. Skopik, F.: Security is not enough! On privacy challenges in smart grids. Int. J. Smart Grid Clean Energy 1, 7–14 (2012). doi:10.12720/sgce.1.1.7-14
10. Jawurek, M., Kerschbaum, F., Danezis, G.: SoK: Privacy Technologies for Smart Grids – A Survey of Options (n.d.)

11. Kursawe, K., Danezis, G., Kohlweiss, M.: Privacy-friendly Aggregation for the Smart-grid (n.d.)
12. Rottondi, C., Mauri, G., Verticale, G., Milano, P., Leonardo, P.: A Data Pseudonymization Protocol for Smart Grids (n.d.)
13. Efthymiou, C., Kalogridis, G.: Smart grid privacy via anonymization of smart metering data. In: First IEEE International Conference on Smart Grid Communications, pp. 238–243 (2010). doi:10.1109/SMARTGRID.2010.5622050
14. Machanavajjhala, A., Gehrke, J., Kifer, D., Venkitasubramaniam, M.: l-diversity: privacy beyond kanonymity. In: Proceedings of 22nd International Conference of Data Engineering. (ICDE), 3–8 April 2006, Atlanta, GA, USA, p. 24 (2006)
15. See for example. http://finesce.eu/global/images/cms/Results/D7.2_FINESCE_Consolidated_Trial_Description.pdf

Mobile Agents Based on Virtual Machines to Protect Sensitive Information

Bernhard Katzmarski[1]([✉]), Gunnar Schomaker[1], and Wolfgang Nebel[2]

[1] R&D Division Energy, OFFIS, Oldenburg, Germany
{katzmarski,schomaker}@offis.de
[2] Department for Computer Science, C.v.O. University of Oldenburg,
Oldenburg, Germany
nebel@informatik.uni-oldenburg.de

Abstract. Virtual machine technology is the principal reason for efficient provisioning of IT resources and infrastructure services. The mobile agent concept, similar to VM migration, allows software agents to change their computing platform. It appears likely to combine both, where a VM itself becomes a mobile agent. Currently VM migration is broadly used within data centers or classical cloud eco system. This work addresses its extension to external devices in local environments of end users as migration target. Technology attributes like strong isolation, platform independence and the ongoing effort to enable hybrid migration between heterogeneous computing architectures are delivering a promising and sophisticated basis. Here we give first insights into this approach, realizing a layer of abstraction which makes use of VM migration to separate sensitive information by migration and making use of advantages like isolation and location-aware functionality. Eventually we believe such cloud architectures will result into an overall higher level of security and trust!

1 Introduction

Cloud computing offers an attractive model to obtain processing and storage capabilities at low cost. On-demand self-service, scalability and a pay-per-use accounting are the most attractive benefits. However, these are still overshadowed by security concerns. Users don't know what the actual location of their data is and are justifiably concerned about their private data. In a multi-vendor driven architecture, it is hard to reveal who can gain access to data outsourced to the cloud and legal issues are also often unclear. Recent revelations about mass-surveillance programs demonstrate that especially communication data in networks and backbones are intercepted. The only countermeasure would consist of not transmitting sensitive data without encryption, or simply don't transmit it at all. Even if end-to-end encryption is used, data leaves and is exposed to threats like leakage if it needs to be processed. Hence, our idea is to reduce the need to transmit data for processing as much as possible.

Our approach follows the question *if there is a way to combine virtualization with Mobile Agents to achieve an overall higher level of trust.*

© Springer International Publishing Switzerland 2014
F. Cleary and M. Felici (Eds.): CSP Forum 2014, CCIS 470, pp. 97–107, 2014.
DOI: 10.1007/978-3-319-12574-9_9

We report on ongoing work in the context of TRESCCA under the European 7th Framework (FP7) and describe our concept for an active VM migration architecture currently under development.

2   State of the Art

Data encryption is the only reasonable way to protect confidentiality and integrity. However, if data is processed, it has to be decrypted. This simple fact limits the security potential of cloud solutions. Homomorphic encryption targets to enable processing on encrypted data, closing this gap [8]. However, the computational overhead is not yet acceptable for practical use, now.

These shortcomings can be addressed by the development of hardware-based solutions like the Trusted Platform Module (TPM), which is a dedicated chip that can serve as a root of trust to meet security requirements. It provides cryptographic primitives and a secure storage location for encryption keys. Because the TPM is an isolated chip, there are no software based attack vectors. Indeed, the TPM is not completely tamper resistant against hardware attacks but its cost efficiency and widespread availability makes it a sufficient solution for improving security. However, the TPM falls short on several aspects and was not designed with a virtual multi-tenant architecture in mind, which today's cloud providers are offering. It is not able to attest runtime behavior and stored data on a broken TPM will be forever lost.

Strong assumptions like hardware-based security extensions will transform local devices into a root of trust. Recent work has shown the effort to improve isolation of virtual machines by Network on Chip Firewalls, protecting against logical attacks [5]. Other approaches involve the confidentiality and integrity protection of external memories [14]. Both extensions combined would provide a higher level of trust on devices.

2.1   Virtualization

With server virtualization, multiple VMs are executable on one physical host. A hypervisor is responsible for their execution and the resource assignment. Eventually, sharing available resources increases their efficient use. Moreover, virtualization introduces benefits to provisioning, maintenance and availability. Failing physical machines do not endanger the execution of virtual ones. The migration of VMs is a key technology for cloud service providers. Besides disaster recovery, it is used to balance applications among physical servers, according to performance or energy consumptions [9]. On its essence, virtualization allows to suspend/resume and move machines between hosts. This describes the requirements of Mobile Agent Systems. Previous MAS were always struggling to choose or create such execution layer able to offer strong migration. Additionally, virtual machines offer a strong isolation property and are location-agnostic, meaning a VM is not aware of being executed on a virtualization host.

2.2 Mobile Agents

Mobile Agents describes a concept where software agents can move between different computing platforms. It was originally inspired by the idea to reduce network traffic in communication intensive applications. As only agents have to be transferred, network dependency is reduced, which leads to lower bandwidth demand and overcomes latency problems. Thereby, it is offering a reasonable alternative to the classical client-server model. A Mobile Agent can *decide actively* when and where it wants to be transferred.

Security concerns prevented Mobile Agent Systems to be adopted into real world applications. Vigna et al. [17] stated 10 reasons against Mobile Agent Systems and 4 of them are related to security issues. Without a reasonable level of trust between platforms and agents, they will not be considered to operate on sensitive data. To protect agents against malicious platforms is still a challenging topic. The underlying problem is that agents are always executed within the environment of the foreign platform. There is no way for the agent to determine if the platform is acting correctly. From a software vendor view, there is no point in trusting processing results of remote client devices.

Many existing MAS use Java as a platform due to its platform independence. A byte code virtual machine introduces an additional software layer for application execution. Application partitioning on that level usually has a much smaller footprint compared to VMs. It introduces more granularity for migration as for example whole applications, threads or even single methods are becoming candidates. It is even possible to take device dependent functionalities like cameras into account and only transfer independent application parts. The great benefit of this method is the ability to be analyzed. The approach allows to attest runtime behavior and to check security compliance by static analysis.

Java offers the possibility to have multiple threads within an application. These threads are reasonable candidates for migration between platforms. However, the runtime environment does not offer any method to suspend or resume Java threads. Existing methods are deprecated due to possible deadlock problems. This functionality has to be modelled by the programmer himself, caring manually for inconsistent states and race conditions. Same goes for serialization: indeed, Java offers object serialization but this mechanism is incompatible with threads. Threads depend on local state which is not in the scope of the serialization process. In another computing environment a deserialized object will never be the same object: It will always be a new object with same properties. Furthermore, within pure Java, it is not possible to access the instruction pointer to store at which point execution should be continued. Instead, it is only feasible to model a state machine: Transitions can mark fix points where migration can be done. The current state stored in a custom attribute is serializable and execution can continue in the next state.

These shortcomings limit the applicability of pure Java approaches. Sure, existing JVM could also be extended to support thread serialization and previous work has already addressed this [2,12,15]. Unfortunately, existing extensions are rather old and most likely incompatible with current versions of the JVM.

However, all thread serialization approaches are facing the same problems: related local state, like e.g. file descriptor, open database or network connections are living outside of the JVM and are usually hard to serialize.

2.3 Software to Data Paradigm

Software to data paradigm recently introduced by Thuemmler et al. [16] is a concept, where software comes to data. Our approach supports this idea and previous work already addressed issues like partitioning, distribution and offloading of application logic to remote parts. Osman et al. [11] use whole process migration while making use of operating systems' support. Other approaches are splitting a program at method level and migrate independent threads. Cuervo et al. [6] implemented MAUI in .NET to enable energy-aware code offloading but their approach require programmers to annotate methods as *remotable*. A similar approach called CloneCloud by Chun et al. [4] is based on the JVM and uses static analysis to avoid the need of annotations. Both approaches use a high level runtime environment which brings the benefit of being platform independent, on the other hand this makes them language dependent. Satyanarayanan et al. [13] present Kimberly for migrating VMs to nearby cloudlets by creating overlays based on virtual box. With the idea of cloudlets, they want to overcome WAN latency problems in mobile computing. The idea of overlays is to move only change sets of the virtual hard disk to save resources, while still being able to transfer entire OS-level VMs. Systems like the Internet Suspend/Resume System [10] or Soulpad [3] are following a similar idea. Due to VM migration technology, any device could be used to access the personal desktop. In contrast to *thin client vnc solutions*, these systems store and execute VMs on local devices directly, gaining some performance benefits. Spectra [7] and Chroma [1] rely on execution plans or specified tactics to determine how to partition an application, which can be seen as additional annotations. Protium [19] follows a static approach by separating the application into logic and view parts beforehand.

It can also be distinguished between different levels and partition approaches like static analysis and annotation-based solutions. Application layer solutions generally tend to have smaller footprints, but are restricted to certain languages or runtime environments. Whereas fully fledged OS-level VMs are more general and capable of running legacy code. On the other hand an *OS-level VM* cannot be easily partitioned like applications running in a runtime environment.

3   Concept

We combine the concept of Mobile Agents with the benefits of virtual machines. Virtualization offers a generic execution layer that provides *isolation* and *strong migration*. Hence, we consider the virtual machine itself being the agent, able to move between platforms.

3.1   Virtual Machine is Becoming the Agent

We are dealing with virtual machines as they offer the strongest possible isolation. Unlike previous work in this area, we present a *full os level virtualization* based approach where a VM will be able to trigger migration processes actively to meet security requirements. A vm-based approach is also more general and has no programming language restrictions, which makes it possible to even use legacy systems. To build a Mobile Agent System on top of virtual machines can create new possibilities, as well as introduce distinct challenges. In this model the virtual machine is becoming the agent, with the ability to move actively between systems. Due to its strong isolation property, it may overcome known issues in existing MAS. Within a partly trusted domain, this approach could create some security advantages, as data does not have to leave anymore, but software is coming as a visitor. On the other hand, this approach allows the integration into Infrastructure as a Service (IaaS) platforms that are based on VMs as well. As it is the most generic solution in todays cloud layer model, this allows the development of a flexible architecture with maximum synergy.

Location-Awareness. A hypervisor is responsible for execution and migration of virtual machines. It provides a full virtualized hardware interface, where VMs shouldn't even notice they are not running on physical hardware; they are *location-agnostic*. In our model, we have to soften the location-agnostic property of virtual machines and provide them with certain location information for decision-making. This is important, because our concept focuses security in a sense that a program only gets access to sensitive data or services if it resides in the respective environment - we call this *location-aware functionality*.

Strong Migration. As pointed out, the JVM does not support snapshots of execution states, indispensable for application-based migration. Means, Java does not offer *strong migration*. Thus, there is no serialization for execution state build-in inherently. This is where virtual machines can play their most prominent feature: the ability to stop execution at any point in time.

Active Migration. Active migration allows VMs to change their physical location dynamically at runtime. This is a very unique feature allowing application parts to decide *actively* to migrate to other locations, depending on the use case. In this aspect, the concept is very similar to that of Mobile Agent Systems: It's imaginable to have separated information and functionality and an actor part as a visitor moving around to fulfill a process. Existing approaches use migration to automatically balance applications according to performance or energy consumptions. They migrate transparently without applications' notice. The unique feature of our method is that an application can *actively request* the migration to a remote location. However, we need to study the impact on Infrastructure as a Service providers, as they are currently not prepared for VMs dynamically joining and leaving their environment. The generality introduced by VMs could make active migration also applicable in context of Big Data where it is obvious that moving the application towards data is much cheaper.

Overhead. Virtual machines usually need disk images and memory of several giga bytes to operate. The additional overhead of full operating systems limits the possible granularity of application partitioning. However, this approach is more general and has no programming language restrictions, a benefit for legacy applications. Although we are aware of the introduced overhead, we are taking this approach to study its feasibility. Moreover, a vm-based approach still offers the highest possible isolation. Clearly, with this approach we are addressing Infrastructure as a Service (IaaS) providers and trying to develop a compatible approach to existing open-source IaaS solutions like for example OpenStack. We can also expect that bandwidth is still increasing which makes our approach increasingly feasible in the future for home environments. Nevertheless, we try to keep VMs tiny and therefore the introduced overhead as low as possible.

3.2   Technical Challenges

Our goal is to make as much use of existing technology as possible to increase adoption rate. We currently focus host systems running linux and rely on KVM virtualization technology and its ecosystem of related tools:

- *kvm+qemu* as virtualization layer
- *libvirt* as an api for controlling VMs
- *virsh* as a command line tool for managing libvirt
- *qcow2* virtual disk format providing encryption, snapshots and overlays
- *iptables+dnsmasq* to manage connectivity of VMs

Inter-VM Communication. Any distributed system has to define its communication with all involved components. For classical virtual machines this is usually done via the network stack. This approach introduces some additional overhead especially if two VMs on the same host have to communicate with each other, but it provides reasonable amount of decoupling, separation and portability. Applications relying on network communication are also completely independent of virtualization and can also be run on bare metal machines. Inter-vm communication could also be done via specialized drivers, sockets or shared memory techniques [18]. However, these approaches always require manual adaptation to software components and infiltrate the isolation principle of the hypervisor.

Today's cloud computing IaaS providers do have a complex networking environment. From a VMs point of view, it can be distinguished between public and private IP addresses. Private IPs are typically assigned during the creation of a VM and never change. Private IPs are also never routed to the outside world. A provider might offer different pools to pick addresses from. Public IPs on the other hand, are world wide reachable and can be dynamically assigned or removed. In a scenario where VMs can move seamlessly between clouds and client devices, this networking concept creates some issues.

Although it might be possible to overcome addressing conflicts at least for client devices with IP-Tables rules, to rely on never changing private IP addresses will most likely not work. Public IP addresses face similar problems combined with migration: Public IP addresses cannot easily be transferred to other providers. One possible solution to overcome this might be the use of DNS. Instead of addressing services by IP addresses, a domain name must be used. In this way, a VM can migrate and even change its IP addresses. It is only necessary that related services renew their domain name information as soon as possible. However, this issue will vanish, as distribution of IPv6 continues.

Stop-Copy Migration. Live migration as used in data centers to guarantee service availability, is not necessary. In our context, the user has to wait until transfer of VM has finished, anyway. Moreover, live migration in WAN environments will most likely not be practical due to latency problems [6]. Additionally, the classical Mobile Agent Model doesn't even require the agents to be responsive while they are being transferred. In that sense, it will be enough to use a stop-and-copy migration strategy.

No Shared Storage. Compared to cloud computing environments, we cannot assume to have a shared storage pool available. Thus, the entire virtual hard disk of a VM has to be transferred! Obviously a bottleneck, because modern operating systems depend on several gigabytes of hard disk space. However, this problem can be solved by standard technology as well. Modern virtual disk formats like qcow2 support overlays in terms of a base image. The base image always remains static and the used disk image only contains change sets. Multiple VMs can even share the same base image. This approach reduces the needed disk space enormously. To transfer only overlays is much more efficient than it would be the case with normal migration. This approach can be called *dynamic VM synthesis* like described by Satyanarayanan et al. [13]. Overall, it is essential to keep the resource consumption of VMs as low as possible.

3.3 Usage Scenarios

We are envisioning multiple scenarios where our approach of vm-based agents can help to improve security and privacy. Within all described scenarios we assume the presence of trustable devices that are attestable and able to protect VMs at runtime. Of course, the problem of malicious platforms brainwashing agents does not completely vanish just by using virtual machines, as the hypervisor itself could be compromised as well. As previously described, certain hardware-based security extensions could help to harden VMs by making use of memory encryption and hardware-supported isolation. Furthermore, before sending a VM to a remote platform it's essential to attest the integrity of the target which clearly lies in the focus of future work.

E-Commerce. Sensitive payment information is still threatened through leakages and hackers. Online Shopping has become popular but in digital world there are particular needs, especially for commercial transactions. Online shop vendors build large databases of their customers and hence becoming attractive targets for malicious attacks. Although classical cash transfer is a secure variant, it suffers from a long period until the recipient notices. Usually, this model is not acceptable because the customer does not want to wait several days for his package only to send off. Payment with credit card is much faster but includes providing card number and validation code to a potentially untrusted shop. Third party payment providers evolved offering several benefits like reliable confirmations about transactions, buyer protection and they hide bank account information. However, having only a few payment vendors storing bank account information only shifts the problem towards them, building up centralized sensitive information pools which might become attractive targets.

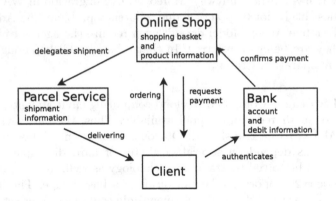

Fig. 1. Separation of sensitive information in an online shopping scenario

This approach is meant to protect sensitive payment data like bank account information. After purchasing goods, address information and email are delivered to the shop. This information is needed for shipment purpose, but no technical mechanism provides the protection and its exclusive usage. Transactions could be modelled such that the gathered information for each party is reduced. The goal is not to replace third party payment providers with new technologies, but to reduce the amount of personal and sensitive information they are collecting. Especially shop vendors or payment providers should be prevented to create coherent personal customers profiles.

Figure 1 illustrates this concept. A vm-based agent could move into the trusted location of the shop vendor to confirm the payment and come back to its owner and thereby reducing the collectable amount of information. This agent could be responsible for the whole process and travel around to fulfill the required task at every location. Every party only gets access granted to aggregated or anonymized information that is necessary for the current step. The agent would be the one having the coherent view on the whole process. Sometimes plaintext data is needed for a process step and will not be protected anymore, for instance when printing labels for shipment, but this should be acceptable as it is not linkable to related data of the process. Certainly, this assumes that locations are trustable, attestable and during migration no compromise can happen by man-in-the-middle attackers extracting related information from the VM.

Unique Digital Content. Our model includes that code and data is tightly coupled and can be handled as one single piece. By adding the possibility to migrate residing application and data, it could seamlessly be used on different devices while still being seen as a unique object. This approach could have enormous impact on digital assets and related legal issues. It would be possible to enforce uniqueness of digital assets tightly coupled together with needed application code. An E-book would be a virtual machine containing the content together with needed reader application and could be lend to a friend transparently.

Applications that are currently not in use could be offloaded and stored in the cloud to save resources. State of the application, all its data and changed configurations would still be available and no new installation would be necessary. Moreover, legacy versions of applications that otherwise wouldn't be available anymore, could be used transparently.

DRM. Digital Rights Management is always a challenge for vendors who want to protect their intellectual property. It is often done by a combination of proprietary hard- and software. Selected hardware enhancements on client devices have the potential to protect virtual machines containing sensitive information while the platform itself still being open. Trusted and untrusted VMs could run side by side on the same platform, reducing the walled garden approach by allowing users to install untrusted third-party software encapsulated in VMs. In this scenario, due to hardware-supported isolation and protection mechanisms, VMs cannot interfere with each other and the vendor can trust his content inside the VM if it is only executable on a protected device. On the other hand this approach would allow to protect the privacy of the customer as she does not have to offer which concrete device she is using to consume the content.

4   Conclusion and Future Work

This paper has presented an innovative approach for protecting privacy and enhancing security between edge devices and clouds. With the raising effort to allow hybrid migration between heterogeneous computing architectures, seamless migration of VMs between clouds and smart devices is conceivable. Being able to migrate applications enveloped by micro VMs enriches exciting possibilities with respect to interoperability, security and availability. Virtual Machines on light devices introduce strong isolation and their migration ability builds the enabling technology for our framework to be developed. We will improve privacy by *location-aware functionality*. This allows to separate sensitive information among devices and actors. This gives the potential to reduce the need of big vendor-driven databases of customer information. A program only gets access to sensitive data or services if it resides on the local device.

As future work, we plan to fully investigate especially the introduced overhead of full OS-level migration and to develop the service and an application model. Thereby, we are also studying the software to data paradigm [16] as a novel pattern to model applications. Furthermore, we plan to integrate the proposed service into the IaaS platform OpenStack as a plugin.

Acknowledgment. This work has received funding from the European Communitys Seventh Framework Programme (FP7/2007–2013) under grant agreement TRESCCA no 318036.

References

1. Balan, R.K., Satyanarayanan, M., Park, S.Y., Okoshi, T.: Tactics-based remote execution for mobile computing. In: Proceedings of the 1st International Conference on Mobile Systems, Applications and Services, MobiSys '03, pp. 273–286. ACM, New York (2003)
2. Bouchenak, S., Hagimont, D., De Palma, N.: Efficient java thread serialization. In: Proceedings of the 2nd International Conference on Principles and Practice of Programming in Java, PPPJ '03, pp. 35–39. Computer Science Press Inc., New York (2003)
3. Caceres, R., Carter, C., Narayanaswami, C., Raghunath, M.: Reincarnating pcs with portable soulpads. In: Proceedings of the 3rd International Conference on Mobile Systems, Applications, and Services, MobiSys '05, pp. 65–78. ACM, New York (2005)
4. Chun, B.-G., Ihm, S., Maniatis, P., Naik, M., Patti, A.: Clonecloud: elastic execution between mobile device and cloud. In: Proceedings of the Sixth Conference on Computer Systems, EuroSys '11, pp. 301–314. ACM, New York (2011)
5. Coppola, M., Grammatikakis, M., Kornaros, G., Spyridakis, A.: Trusted computing on heterogeneous embedded systems-on-chip with virtualization and memory protection. In: The Fourth International Conference on Cloud Computing, GRIDs, and Virtualization, CLOUD COMPUTING 2013, pp. 225–229 (2013)
6. Cuervo, E., Balasubramanian, A., Cho, D.-K., Wolman, A., Saroiu, S., Chandra, R., Bahl, P.: Maui: making smartphones last longer with code offload. In: Proceedings of the 8th International Conference on Mobile Systems, Applications, and Services, MobiSys '10, pp. 49–62. ACM, New York (2010)
7. Flinn, J., Park, S., Satyanarayanan, M.: Balancing performance, energy, and quality in pervasive computing. In: Proceedings of the 22nd International Conference on Distributed Computing Systems, ICDCS '02, pp. 217–226. IEEE Computer Society, Washington, DC (2002)
8. Gentry, C., Halevi, S.: Implementing gentry's fully-homomorphic encryption scheme. In: Paterson, K.G. (ed.) EUROCRYPT 2011. LNCS, vol. 6632, pp. 129–148. Springer, Heidelberg (2011)
9. Hoyer, M., Schröder, K., Schlitt, D., Nebel, W.: Proactive dynamic resource management in virtualized data centers. In: Proceedings of the 2nd International Conference on Energy-Efficient Computing and Networking, e-Energy '11, pp. 11–20. ACM, New York (2011)

10. Kozuch, M., Satyanarayanan, M.: Internet suspend/resume. In: Proceedings Fourth IEEE Workshop on Mobile Computing Systems and Applications, pp. 40–46. IEEE (2002)

11. Osman, S., Subhraveti, D., Su, G., Nieh, J.: The design and implementation of zap: a system for migrating computing environments. SIGOPS Oper. Syst. Rev. **36**(SI), 361–376 (2002)

12. Quitadamo, R., Cabri, G., Leonardi, L.: Mobile jikesrvm: a framework to support transparent java thread migration. Sci. Comput. Program. **70**(23), 221–240 (2008). Special Issue on Principles and Practices of Programming in Java (PPPJ 2006)

13. Satyanarayanan, M., Bahl, P., Caceres, R., Davies, N.: The case for vm-based cloudlets in mobile computing. IEEE Pervasive Comput. **8**(4), 14–23 (2009)

14. Su, L., Courcambeck, S., Guillemin, P., Schwarz, C., Pacalet, R.: Secbus: operating system controlled hierarchical page-based memory bus protection. In: Proceedings of the Conference on Design, Automation and Test in Europe, DATE '09, pp. 570–573. European Design and Automation Association, Leuven (2009)

15. Suezawa, T.: Persistent execution state of a java virtual machine. In: Proceedings of the ACM 2000 Conference on Java Grande, JAVA '00, pp. 160–167. ACM, New York (2000)

16. Thuemmler, C., Mueller, J., Covaci, S., Magedanz, T., de Panfilis, S., Jell, T., Gavras, A.: Applying the software-to-data paradigm in next generation e-health hybrid clouds. In: 2013 Tenth International Conference on Information Technology: New Generations (ITNG), pp. 459–463 (2013)

17. Vigna, G.: Mobile agents: ten reasons for failure. In: Proceedings of the 2004 IEEE International Conference on Mobile Data Management, pp. 298–299. IEEE (2004)

18. Wang, J.: Survey of state-of-the-art in inter-vm communication mechanisms (2009)

19. Young, C., Lakshman, Y.N., Szymanski, T., Reppy, J., Presotto, D., Pike, R., Narlikar, G., Mullender, S., Grosse, E.: Protium, an infrastructure for partitioned applications. In: Proceedings of the Eighth Workshop on Hot Topics in Operating Systems, pp. 47–52 (2001)

Privacy-Respecting School Community Interaction Platform

Ahmad Sabouri[1]([✉]), Souheil Bcheri[2], and Kai Rannenberg[1]

[1] Deutsche Telekom Chair of Mobile Business and Multilateral Security,
Goethe University Frankfurt, Grueneburgplatz 1, 60323 Frankfurt, Germany
{ahmad.sabouri,kai.rannenberg}@m-chair.de
[2] Eurodocs AB, Söderhamn, Sweden
sosso@eurodocs.net

Abstract. Privacy-preserving Attribute-based Credentials (Privacy-ABCs) are powerful techniques to provide secure privacy-respecting access control and cope with minimal disclosure of attributes as well as partial identities. The ABC4Trust EU Project has designed a generic architecture model that abstracts away the cryptographic details of Privacy-ABC technologies and provides well-defined APIs to the application developers. To further demonstrate the applicability of Privacy-ABCs and also verify the implementation of the proposed architecture, the ABC4Trust Project launched two pilots in Greece and Sweden.

In this paper, we report on the design of the School Community Interaction Platform as the pilot application in Sweden. The platform was developed as a web-based application to be used for chat communication, counseling, political discussions and the exchange of authentic sensitive, personal data between pupils, parents, and such school personnel as teachers, nurses, and so on, in a privacy-respecting way.

Keywords: Privacy-preserving attribute-based credentials · School community interaction platform · ABC4Trust · Privacy-respecting access control

1 Introduction

Nowadays, due to the faster and more convenient access to electronic services, many users would prefer to perform their transactions online rather than follow the traditional procedures. Hence, organizations and service providers need to employ some mechanisms to authenticate the online users before granting access to the resources and the service.

Even though most of the commonly used strong authentication techniques offer a suitable level of security, they are not appropriately designed to protect

The research leading to these results has received funding from the European Community's Seventh Framework Programme (FP7/2007–2013) under Grant Agreement no. 257782 for the project Attribute-based Credentials for Trust (ABC4Trust).

F. Cleary and M. Felici (Eds.): CSP Forum 2014, CCIS 470, pp. 108–119, 2014.
DOI: 10.1007/978-3-319-12574-9_10

the privacy of the users. For instance, use of X509 certificates causes "Over Identification" and mandates the users to reveal all the attested attributes in the certificate to preserve the validity of the digital signature even if only a subset of attributes is required for the authentication purpose. Apart from this, the online users also have to be able to compartmentalize their activities in different domains and prevent profiling by both service providers and identity service providers (IdSP), as it is not very trivial in the offline world to recognize and link various actions of a user in different contexts. Evidently, the static representation of X509 certificates fails to address the problem and makes it possible to trace users' online activities.

Using online authentication and authorization techniques such as OpenID, SAML, Facebook Connect, and OAuth could support the minimal disclosure principal, as they enable the user to provide the service provider with only the requested information rather than the whole user's profile stored at the IdSP. However, all these protocols suffer from a so-called "Calling Home" problem, meaning that for every authentication transaction the user is required to contact the IdSP (e.g., Facebook, OpenID Provider). This potentially introduces privacy risks to both users and service providers. More specifically, it would not be difficult for the IdSP to trace the user and profile her online activities due to the knowledge it gains about the service providers she visits. Moreover, the IdSP can collect a considerable amount of information about a service provider by analysing the profile of the users who request to authenticate to that specific service.

Conversely, Privacy-preserving Attribute-based Credentials emancipates users by providing solutions to cope with minimal disclosure of attributes as well as supporting partial identities. Privacy-ABC users can obtain credentials from their IdSP, and when authenticating to different service providers, they can produce unlinkable Privacy-ABC presentation tokens containing only the required subset of information available in the credentials without involving the IdSP or any third party in the process. Therefore, they can help overcome the risks of Over Identification and Calling Home problems. As prominent instantiations of such Privacy-ABC technologies one could mention Microsoft's U-Prove [1] and IBM's Idemix [2]. Both of these systems are studied in depth by the EU project ABC4Trust [3], where their differences are abstracted away to build a common architecture for Privacy-ABCs and tested it with real-world, large-scale user trials.

In this work, we report on one of the ABC4Trust pilots and elaborate on the scenarios and the design decisions. In the rest of this paper, we start with an overview of the pilot environment. Then, we briefly introduce Privacy-ABCs and their life-cycle in Sect. 3. Next, we continue with the design of the trial and the key scenarios in Sect. 4 and Sect. 5 respectively, and describe its high level architecture in Sect. 6. In the end, we conclude the paper in Sect. 7.

2   About the Pilot

One of the ABC4Trust pilots concerns a privacy-respecting School Community Interaction Platform among the pupils. According to the 2013 statistics [4], 86 to

97 percent of children between the ages of 12 to 15 years in Sweden are accessing the Internet on a daily basis. At the same time, the use of the Internet has become much more common in Swedish schools in recent years. More specifically, the daily Internet use in schoolwork has increased from 11 % in 2009 to 53 % in 2013 among the students in the previously referenced age group. The observed growth in use of the Internet and social networks among Swedish teenagers confirms the choice of the pilot environment by ABC4Trust.

The Norrtullskolan school of Söderhamn, Sweden, hosted the school trial of ABC4Trust, where a privacy friendly platform, built upon Privacy-ABCs, was deployed to boost the communication between the pupils, their parents and school personnel. On the one hand, pupils were able to authenticate themselves to access restricted online activities and restricted information. On the other hand, they would be able to remain anonymous when asking private and sensitive questions to school personnel, while assuring the school personnel that they communicated with the authorised pupils of the respective school or class.

3   Privacy Preserving Attribute-Based Credentials

Privacy-preserving Attribute-based Credentials can offer strong authentication and a high level of security to service providers with user privacy preserved, so that it follows the paradigm of Multilateral Security [5]. Users can obtain certified attributes in the form of Privacy-ABCs, and later derive unlinkable tokens that only reveal the necessary subset of information needed by the service providers.

A Credential is defined to be "a certified container of attributes issued by an Issuer to a User" [6]. An Issuer vouches for the correctness of the attribute values for a User when issuing a credential for her. For example, a school can issue an "Enrolment Credential" for a pupil, which contains several attested attributes such as firstname, lastname, studentid and the enrolment year.

A typical authentication scenario using Privacy-ABCs is shown in Fig. 1 where a User seeks to access an online service offered by a Service Provider. The Service Provider performs a so-called Verifier role and expresses its requirement for granting access to the service in the form of a Presentation Policy. In the next step, the User needs to come up with a combination of her credentials to derive an acceptable authentication token that satisfies the given policy. When the Verifier confirms the authenticity and credibility of the Presentation Token, the User gains access to the corresponding service. It is worth noting that the human User is represented by her UserAgent, a software component

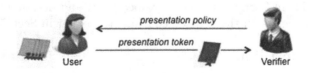

Fig. 1. A sample presentation scenario

running either on a local device (e.g., on the User's computer or mobile phone) or remotely on a trusted cloud service. In addition, the User may also possess special hardware tokens, e.g. smart cards, to which credentials can be bound to improve security.

Presentation tokens based on Privacy-ABCs are cryptographically proven to be unlinkable and untraceable, meaning that Verifiers cannot tell whether two presentation tokens were derived from the same or from different credentials, and that Issuers cannot trace a presentation token back to the issuance of the underlying credentials. Furthermore, since the User is actively involved in the generation of Presentation Tokens, there is no risk of user impersonation introduced by the other parties.

As Fig. 2 shows, in addition to *User*, *Issuer*, and *Verifier*, two other (optional) entities are involved during the life-cycle of Privacy-ABCs [6]. The Revocation Authority is responsible for revoking issued credentials. Both the User and the Verifier must obtain the most recent revocation information from the Revocation Authority to generate presentation tokens and respectively, verify them. The Inspector is an entity who can de-anonymize presentation tokens under specific circumstances. To make use of this feature, the Verifier must specify in the presentation policy the conditions, i.e., which Inspector should be able to recover which attribute(s) and under which circumstances. The User is informed about the de-anonymization options at the time that the presentation token is generated and she has to be involved actively to make this possible.

It is important to elaborate on the assumptions that are required for Privacy-ABCs to work. Privacy-ABCs are not effective in cases where tracking and profiling methods that work based on network level identifiers such as IP addresses or the ones in the lower levels. Therefore, in order to benefit from the full set of features offered by Privacy-ABCs, the underlying infrastructure must be privacy-friendly as well. The recommendation for the users would be to employ network

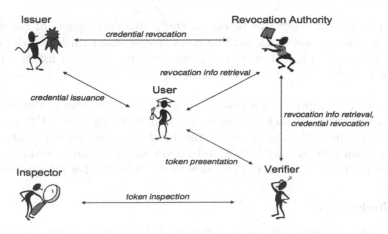

Fig. 2. Entities and relations in the Privacy-ABC's architecture [6]

anonymizer tools to deal with this issue. Furthermore, greedy verifiers have the chance to demand for any kind of information they are interested in and avoid offering the service if the user is not willing to disclose these information. Therefore, the assumption is that the verifiers reduce the amount of requested information to the minimum level possible either by regulation or any other mechanism in place [7].

4   The Design of the School Community Interaction Platform

In this section, we introduce the design of the pilot application at a glance. In particular, the four key elements in the design of the application that will be further elaborated upon include: the involved actors, the structure of the credentials, the abstract model for the Community Interaction Platform, and management of identities. Due to the space limitation, many details are not reported in this paper, however, [8–10] describe the earlier version of the design and implementation decisions in details.

4.1   Involved Actors

The analysis conducted in the early phases led in the identification of several types of actors within the context of the pilot. Here we briefly describe which actors were involved in the operation of the School Community Platform:

Administrator: A major effort had to be taken during the setup and initialisation phase as well as the running period of the pilot to administer the processes and manage the operation of the pilot. The administrators were responsible for setting up the system, provisioning of the users, rolling-out the smart cards and coordinating all the technical support in the operation phase.

User: A user is considered to be one of the active participants of the School Community Interaction Platform. The users receive smart cards and the necessary credentials enabling them to access the system. The final list of roles for the users includes: *Pupil, Counsellor, Teacher,* and *Guardian.*

Inspector: The Inspector is a trusted entity in the pilot who is able to assist the school in extraordinary circumstances and de-anonymize a Privacy-ABC presentation token, thereby revealing the identity of the corresponding user. The inspection process must have well-defined conditions and procedure and be known to the users in advance. Please see Sect. 5.5 for further information.

4.2   Credentials

In this section, we report on the final design of the credential formats employed in the trial. Designing Privacy-ABCs requires a deep understanding of the scenarios, the infrastructure and the environment. In the case of the ABC4Trust

Söderhamn pilot, the credentials' structure had to change with the lessons learnt from the tests until they reached a stable state. There had been several factors impacting the design of the credentials. Apart from the scenarios and the requirement analysis, limitations on computation and storage of smart cards affected the design of the credentials. As a side note, smart cards are very challenging when it comes to practice. Here we point out some of the decisions imposed by the smart card limitations but more details on such challenges can be found in [11]. It is worth noting that smartphones can offer better performance and usability than smart cards, therefore ABC4Trust is currently conducting some feasibility study on smartphone implementation. Nevertheless, in order to achieve a comparable level of security, smartphones need to be equipped with Secure Elements for storing the cryptographic keys.

The most important credential used in the pilot was named *CredSchool* and contained the personal information of the users. This credential included the first name, last name, Pilot User Number (PUN), gender, and the school name of the users as well as a so-called revocation handle used for revocation purposes. The PUN was introduced with the same format as the Swedish Civic Registration Number (birthdate + 4 digit random number). This credential was the key to access the Community Interaction Platform in the first step. Due to the storage and computation overhead of the revocation process, it was decided to have only this credential revocable and use it as a master credential whenever a revocation check was desired.

One of the other points where the storage limitation of the smart card impacted the credential design was in the case of *CredSubject*, which was designed to attest pupils' enrolment in different courses. The credentials could have been implemented as separate instances for each course. However, considering the overhead of each new credential on the smart card, the decision was made to have only one credential containing all the subjects as Boolean values. Therefore, whoever is enrolled in a subject will have the corresponding attribute set to "True", otherwise to "False".

Investigation of the pilot scenarios required us to consider another credential to attest enrolment of the pupils in a certain class or a grade. Therefore, the so-called *CredClass* came to address this requirement. This credential includes the class number (e.g. 9A), the class group (e.g. A) and the class year (e.g. 2014).

In addition to the aforementioned credentials, *CredRole* was designed to distinguish between the different types of users in the pilot introduced in Sect. 4.1. Similar to the case of *credSubject*, it would have been possible to consider one credential per each role a person has, but due to the storage limitation, all the roles were integrated in one credential with Boolean attributes for each role.

The relationship between the pupils and their guardians were modelled using *CredGuardian* and *CredChild*. Each pupil received one or more *CredGuardian* containing the Pilot User Number of her parents/guardians, and identically, each guardian received one *CredChild* for each child participating in the pilot as a pupil.

4.3   The Concept of Restricted Area

The Community Interaction Platform uses an abstract model called *Restricted Area* that provides the virtual environment for several types of activities. Restricted Areas are the functionality building blocks in the Community Interaction Platform and all the scenarios, which we will briefly describe in Sect. 5, are conducted within the RAs.

Every user in the pilot can initiate such a private space and define access policies in order to restrict the participation to her desired target group. More specifically, the access policies are defined with the help of a Graphical User Interface which offers the possibility to specify rules based on the attributes and the credentials that exist in the pilot. For instance, a teacher can create an RA with "Chat" functionality to collect the opinions of the pupils about his teaching methods and limit the access to this chat room to participants of a specific class. In this case the pupils of that class can join the discussion and stay anonymous under an *Alias* (read more in Sect. 4.4) while the other students from the school are prohibited from entering this chat room.

4.4   Partial Identity with "Alias"

The concept of partial identity is realized by aliases in this pilot. In general, the participants can choose to appear in the system under different aliases. They can use the same alias to visit multiple RAs and thus build a reputation based on their contributions. At the same time, they have the possibility to pick another alias whenever they like, which makes them unlinkable to all their previous activities.

It is important to mention that the aliases are unique globally in the system and they are mapped to cryptographic pseudonym values behind the scenes. Therefore, nobody can impersonate another alias without having the smart card (the secret key) of the person who first picked the alias. Furthermore, only the smart card contains a database of all the aliases owned by the user. As a result, nobody else would be able to associate different aliases of the same user.

In addition to the user selected alias names, every user receives a *Default Alias* that is the full name of the user and is generated at the first login to the system. Consequently, the platform also supports the cases where the identification of users is desired and they can interact with the system using their real identity when the Default Alias is selected.

5   Pilot Key Scenarios

The Söderhamn pilot of ABC4Trust aimed at providing a School Community Interaction Platform. The precise definition of the use-case scenarios in this pilot evolved through several forms prior to the deployment phase. In this regard, having introduced the key design elements in Sect. 4, we provide the latest scenario definitions in relation with their actual implementation. Figure 3 demonstrates an abstract overview of the scenarios and types of activities in the School Community Interaction Platform.

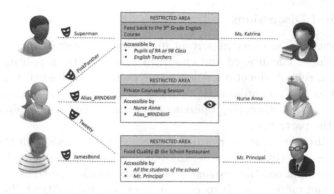

Fig. 3. School Community Interaction Platform

5.1   Counselling

In this scenario, a pupil who needs counselling would be able to contact the authorised professionals regarding various social or health related problems in addition to school and educational issues. In this case, the pupil is the one who initiates such a counselling communication. The counselling session begins immediately if the school personnel are available online. Otherwise, the communication can be performed asynchronously (send a message and receive the answer later).

Due to the fact that the school should be able to rescue the pupil in extreme circumstances such as a case of depression where the pupil threatens to commit suicide, the Inspection functionality is enabled for the counselling session by default (read more about Inspection in Sect. 5.5). As it is shown in Fig. 3, upon entering a counselling RA, the pupil receives a new alias generated randomly by the system to avoid linkability to any other activity of the pupil in case of an Inspection.

5.2   Restricted Chat Rooms

The live chat feature was expected to be one of the widely used services in the platform. The users had the possibility to create Restricted Areas with chat functionality and limit the access to their desired target group. For example, a pupil could initiate a chat room to discuss the quality of the English Language course for the 9th grade and make it accessible by the English teachers and the pupils of the class 9A and 9B (see Fig. 3).

In addition to the group chat, it would be possible to create private chat rooms and limit the participant to specific persons by using their Aliases in the policy. For example the pupil *Superman* enjoys the discussion with *PinkPanther* in a public chat room and therefore invites her to a private chat room accessible only by these two to better express and exchange opinions, without actually knowing who the other person is.

5.3 Political Discussions

Political discussions are very important in modern, democratic societies. Young citizens should be encouraged and enabled to participate in political discourse as part of their school education. Anonymous political discussions can encourage some pupils to freely express their opinions. This can, e.g., be useful to allow for the expression of dissenting opinions on sensitive subjects against a settled majority of the participants.

Political discussions are performed using restricted areas with the chat and wall functionality activated. In order to overcome the fear of being identified and accused for an opinion, the restricted area configuration settings do not allow Inspection (read more about Inspection in Sect. 5.5) for political discussions.

5.4 Document Sharing

The school produces many documents (exam results, grades, individual development plans, etc.) that need to be shared with or distributed to the pupils and their parents/guardians. Furthermore, the users communicating in an RA (e.g. a Chat Room) might need to share some documents such as photos to boost their discussions. To accommodate these needs, document sharing is possible at any Restricted Area that has the "Document Sharing" functionality activated. Every user, entitled to access a Restricted Area, will be able to upload documents there. The uploaded documents are then available and accessible by all users who have access to that RA.

By default a Personal Restricted Area exists for every user in the system and important documents will be uploaded to this RA to be picked up by the user. Personal Restricted Areas are set to be accessible by the *Default Alias (real identity)* of the users only.

5.5 De-Anonymization Under Special Circumstances

In exceptional situations such as the protection from immediate danger to life or health, the *inspection board* of the school may decide to request the *inspector* to reveal the identity of a user. However, the conditions to initiate an inspection process shall be clearly defined in the contractual relationship beforehand and announced in advance. The inspection board consists of the schoolmaster and a combination of the teachers, nurses, pupils and parents.

In the context of the Community Interaction Platform, the special circumstances of inspection were defined at the beginning of the trial and known to the users as the *inspection grounds*. All the RAs in the system that have the inspection features enabled are visibly marked and the users would be informed about the inspection grounds before entering the RA. Therefore, the users were completely aware of the condition and could decide to join or abandon the activity. Nevertheless, to alleviate the concern relating to the political discussions, the system does not allow any RA made for political discussion to be inspectable.

To further assist the users, upon entering an inspectable RA, the system automatically checks whether the current alias has been used in an inspectable RA before or not, and warns the user about the possibility of being linked to her previous activities under this alias in case of an inspection.

6   High Level Architecture

In this section, we provide an overview of the components in the Söderhamn pilot deployment architecture and briefly introduce its subsystems. Figure 4 depicts the high level view of the pilot deployment architecture.

ABC System: The reference implementation of the ABC4Trust project delivers the modules to support operations by each of the entities in the Privacy-ABCs' ecosystem. The so-called ABC System component represents these modules integrated into the corresponding applications in the pilot either as libraries or via webservice wrappers. As it is demonstrated in the Fig. 4, the ABC System exists in every subsystem of the deployed architecture.

School Registration System: The School Registration System performs as the Identity Service Provider in the pilot scenarios. It is responsible for the provisioning of the participants, managing their attributes and issuing credentials for them. The School Registration System also provides the administrators with tools that facilitate the initialization and the roll-out processes.

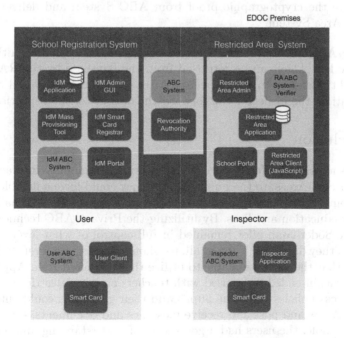

Fig. 4. Söderhamn pilot deployment architecture

Restricted Area System: The actual functionalities of the School Community Platform have been implemented within the Restricted Area System. More specifically, the Restricted Area System is comprised of the followings: *School Portal* as an entry point to the pilot sub-system; *Restricted Area Application* that is where the designed scenarios of the pilot are implemented; *Restricted Area Admin* for administrative purposes; and the *Restricted Area Client* that most importantly provides the functionality of an *Alias Selector* and a *Dashboard*. The Alias Selector handles the list of aliases owned by the user while the Dashboard allows the user to see a personalised view of the Restricted Areas for the selected alias.

Revocation Authority: Situations may arise when a user might lose control over her smart card, the role of a user changes, a user is no longer part of the system, or a user has not followed certain rules associated with a credential. In any of these cases the authority (the school administration) that issued the credential should be able to revoke it in a way that does not interfere with the privacy properties of the ABC technology.

User Client (Identity Selector): The Identity Selector component provided by the reference implementation has been used in the pilot to enable the users to manage their credentials and interact with the ABC System during the issuance and presentation sessions. For example, when a user requests to enter a restricted area, it is the Identity Selector that pops up and guides the user through the steps of the protocol to view the different possible policies, select the preferred one, retrieve the cryptographic proof from ABC System and deliver it to the Restricted Area System.

Inspector Application: The inspection tokens are encrypted with the inspector's public key. They can be retrieved from the database by the RA administrators and transferred to the Inspector. After getting the decrypted reply from the application, the inspector can forward the output to the inspection board.

7   Conclusion

This pilot successfully offered a privacy-respecting Community Interaction Platform, Restricted Areas, to the pupils so that they could have a flexible means of not only communicating with each other, but with key adults who had an interest in their education and lives. By utilizing the Privacy-ABC technologies, the users of the Söderhamn pilot remained in full control of what level of personal information they disclosed, if any at all, to whomever and whenever. In hindsight, we can see that the users were able to utilize the Restricted Area Application in the way it was intended to be used with teachers creating Restricted Areas and defining access policies while the pupils and their guardians could enter defined Restricted Areas and post and receive messages and documents, etc.

On the whole, the users had a good level of understanding and appreciated the overall concept of the Privacy-ABC technology. As part of the pilot's success evaluation, at the end of the pilot duration ABC4Trust incorporated methodological survey questions to determine how the pupils react to the importance of the Privacy-ABC system in enhancing their privacy. A well-established model called the Technology Acceptance Model (TAM) was used as a basis to build the questionnaire concepts. The over all statistical analysis show that the pupils understood and trusted the system that it improves their privacy when performing different activities such as anonymous chatting with other peers, parents or school teachers. Other measurement concepts also showed that many pupils would use the system if it were to continue operating.

References

1. Microsoft U-Prove. http://www.microsoft.com/uprove
2. Identity Mixer. http://idemix.wordpress.com/
3. Attribute-based Crednetials for Trust (ABC4Trust) EU Project. https://abc4trust.eu/
4. Findahl, O.: Digital identities and the open business (2013). https://www.iis.se/docs/Swedes_and_the_internet-2013.pdf,
5. Rannenberg, K.: Multilateral security a concept and examples for balanced security. In: Proceedings of the 2000 Workshop on New Security Paradigms, pp. 151–162. ACM (2001)
6. D2.1 Architecture for Attribute-based Credential Technologies Version 1. https://abc4trust.eu/download/ABC4Trust-D2.1-Architecture-V1.pdf
7. Sabouri, A., Krontiris, I., Rannenberg, K.: Trust relationships in privacy-ABCs' ecosystems. In: Eckert, C., Katsikas, S.K., Pernul, G. (eds.) TrustBus 2014. LNCS, vol. 8647, pp. 13–23. Springer, Heidelberg (2014)
8. D5.1 Scenario Definition for both Pilots. https://abc4trust.eu/download/ABC4Trust-D5.1-Scenario-Definition.pdf
9. D6.1 Application Description for the School Deployment. https://abc4trust.eu/download/ABC4Trust-D6.1-Application-Description-School.pdf
10. D6.2 Necessary hardware and software package for the school pilot deployment. https://abc4trust.eu/download/ABC4Trust-D6.2.Hard-and-Software-Package-for-School-Pilot.pdf
11. Sabouri, A., Lindstrom Jensen, J., Lyneborg Damgrd, K., Dam Nielsen, J., Rannenberg, K.: Integrating and trialling attribute-based credentials on smartcards for building trust - the ABC4Trust project. In: 24 SmartCard Workshop. Fraunhofer Verlag, Stuttgart, pp. 8–21 (2014)

Teaching Privacy by Design
to Non-technical Audiences

Susan Perry[1] and Claudia Roda[2(✉)]

[1] International Politics Department, The American University of Paris,
Paris, France
sperry@aup.edu
[2] Computer Science Department, The American University of Paris,
Paris, France
croda@aup.edu

Abstract. As research in cyber security and privacy advances, privacy initiatives should be disseminated to the broader public. Education of this public is a
key tool in conveying the seminal importance of security and privacy in our use
of digital technology. This article presents a curriculum that, by targeting the
non-engineering public, provides an opportunity for rapid acceptance of the
innovative security and privacy research in which we are currently engaged.

Keywords: Privacy by design · Education · Curriculum

1 Introduction

When we speak of digital technology, our focus is often prohibitively narrow. Taking
our cues from scientific research models, we examine the parts, rather than the whole,
inadvertently isolating software from hardware, the technological frameworks from
their actual use, or the costs of the digital revolution from its benefits. This article
explores the practice of joining two disciplines – law and science – in a university
classroom in an attempt to understand more fully the dense, multidimensional nature of
digital privacy. We demonstrate how privacy by design may be effectively taught to a
combined group of undergraduate and graduate students in the social sciences whose
knowledge of technology is limited to their own user experience. Our curriculum aims
to explore a new educational space at the theoretical intersection of human rights and
digital technology, while integrating a practical component that allows students to
produce educational materials for stakeholder audiences; this merging of theory and
practice provides our students with the opportunity to reflect on the convergence of law
and science. We have designed our curriculum to address the salient need for privacy
protection education for all sectors of the general public, as well as practitioners,
regulators and students in related disciplines. The educational and reference material
generated by the project targets the socio-ethical, legal and technical issues that privacy
by design raises for these stakeholders across society.

The term "privacy by design" was coined by Ann Cavoukian, the Information and
Privacy Commissioner for Ontario since 1997, as a set of guiding principles in the
design of computer software. Our curriculum incorporates her seven principles as core

F. Cleary and M. Felici (Eds.): CSP Forum 2014, CCIS 470, pp. 120–132, 2014.
DOI: 10.1007/978-3-319-12574-9_11

learning goals that enable students to practice privacy-by-design as they learn about it and produce knowledge materials for other stakeholder groups. As will become clear in our paper, we believe that some of Cavoukian's principles are not limited to the context of privacy by design and can be effectively applied to other contexts at the interface of human rights and digital technology. Moreover, these principles have been used to support security by design [1]. Privacy-by-design principles include (1) proactive measures, (2) privacy as a default setting, (3) privacy embedded into design architecture, (4) transparency, (5) user-centric privacy measures, (6) functionality, and (7) end-to-end privacy implementation [2]. Although the definition of privacy by design through its seven principles has been, at times, challenged both for being difficult to operationalize and unclear [3, 4], we found that the seven principles form an excellent pedagogical tool for blending the technological and social aspects of privacy.[1] We will argue, however, that Cavoukian's functionality principle is somehow problematic, from a human rights standpoint, because human rights law stipulates a hierarchy of rights ranging from non-derogable to progressive that challenges Cavoukian's notion of win-win privacy, with no political or legal trade-offs. Our curriculum thus incorporates discussion of Cavoukian's principles into the teaching of a theoretical human rights framework for digital technology, along with the practical design of educational materials to raise awareness of privacy for stakeholder communities. The first part of this article explores the use of a human rights framework for understanding privacy by design, incorporating recent theory on participatory action research (PAR) as it applies to the university classroom [5]. The second part of this article presents our curriculum for the teaching of privacy by design, highlighting the originality of its combined focus on theory and practice. Part Three of this paper analyses the educational material produced by our students, the potential impact of this material on the broader stakeholder public, and how we may further develop privacy-by-design initiatives by the non-specialist community.

2 The Theoretical Framework for Privacy by Design

When Commissioner Ann Cavoukian and John Borking (representing then Commissioner Peter Hustinx) of the Dutch Data Protection Authority first presented their joint paper on Privacy-Enhancing Technologies in Brussels in 1995, they said "it was met with silence by the Commissioners in attendance" [6]. Since then, discussion has replaced silence and a range of scholarly literature has appeared to reinforce the principle of privacy by design in law and in practice. But, how were the theoretical underpinnings of Cavoukian's idea constructed? And what is the most effective method to foster a risk management culture that incorporates stakeholder concerns about privacy?

---

[1] Note that the Office of the Information and Privacy Commissioner offers PbD educational material organized in two sets of slides aimed at introducing the concept to a large audience including "chief privacy officers, engineering instructors, social scientists, and privacy leaders". See http://www. privacybydesign.ca/index.php/publications/curriculum/.

Privacy, as a right, is a relative late-comer to the pantheon of civil and political rights enshrined in the International Covenant on Civil and Political Rights (ICCPR). Warren and Brandeis' seminal article of 1890 treated privacy as a critical right, related to the full protection of person and property [7]. As the age of photography weakened control over one's personal image, the protection of intangible property and the right to prevent publication required legal protection that extended beyond intellectual property protection and protection from libel or slander [7]. The "right to be let alone" was thus linked from its inception with the right to prevent publication, an important factor when we consider the development of privacy by design as it relates to digital technology. The Universal Declaration of Human Rights, promulgated by the UN General Assembly in 1948, includes specific privacy protections in Article 12, taking up the ideas first expressed by Warren and Brandeis on the special protection of an individual's "honour and reputation" [8]. The ICCPR renders privacy protection legally binding in international law. General Comment 16, drafted by the UN Committee on Human Rights, focuses on the obligation of States to use legislative tools to protect their citizens' privacy: "this right is required to be guaranteed against all ... interferences and attacks whether they emanate from State authorities or from natural or legal persons" [9]. Although the General Comment was promulgated in 1988, before the advent of the digital revolution, clearly the term "legal persons" is intended to mean businesses and consequently obliges States to guarantee the protection of user data by technology companies under their jurisdiction.

The ethical argument for privacy by design extends human rights law to the architecture and use of digital technology. Legal scholar Richard Posner argues that privacy is an overrated construct in a digital society [10], while sociologist Richard Harper views our trust in technology as an evolving paradigm [11]. We have argued that human rights can hardly be overrated, particularly when it comes to protection of the most vulnerable members of society [12]. Helen Nissenbaum's theory of privacy suggests that contextual integrity is at the core of what we consider privacy violations [13]. David Wright argues for a process of impact assessment that includes privacy and other human rights concerns [14]. Much of this scholarship addresses concerns that are also expressed by digital technology users, who indicated in a 2013 Pew survey a rising level of mistrust concerning data protection; according to the survey, "86 % of internet users have taken steps online to remove or mask their digital footprints—ranging from clearing cookies to encrypting their email" [15]. The impact of the Snowden revelations, along with a rich trove of user anecdotes concerning online privacy violations, have led users to demand greater control over their online data.

Regardless of whether this high level of user mistrust concerning privacy protection of digital information is justified, international human rights law and the fairly robust Data Protection Regulation proposed by the European Commission on 25 Jan 2012 require protection of online privacy. In guiding our students to produce educational materials for various types of stakeholders, we have focused on the practical problem of how best to implement the right to privacy on a day-to-day basis. Providing an already mistrustful population with privacy-enhancing knowledge and tools is a seminal example of the mis en oeuvre of participatory action research methods [5]. PAR is based on the ideas of engaged inquiry and democratization of knowledge, where research is done with the concerned subjects rather than on or for them. Our curriculum thus attempts to provide privacy-by-design constructs as part of the organizational basis for course activities, as well as the content focus of the actual materials produced – a way of engaged inquiry and knowledge democratization that echoes the founding discourses of the Internet itself – a free and open space for the development of people everywhere (see [16]).

3 Integrating Privacy by Design into a University Curriculum for the Social Sciences – The Seven Principles

Our curriculum is designed as an interdisciplinary study of the rich intersection between human rights and digital technology. Each of Cavoukian's seven principles is addressed through the lens of a case study, with issues selected on the basis of their cross-cutting impact. It should be noted that our curriculum does not address these principles in order, but proposes a slightly different arrangement that allows for greater pedagogical cohesiveness. Approximately two-thirds of classroom time is dedicated to lectures and discussion, with the professors and visiting lecturers, while one third is devoted to developing privacy-by-design educational materials for stakeholder communities. The interaction between theory and practice, or analysis and production, privileges participatory action research, enabling students to engage in meaningful inquiry and to model the dissemination of their own knowledge. Students evaluate the course qualitatively and quantitatively at the end of the semester, and these evaluations are an important tool for improving course content and delivery, as well as fine-tuning curricular details.

3.1 Full Functionality — Positive-Sum, not Zero-Sum

Our curriculum begins with an overview of the histories of human rights law and digital technology from 1945 to the present. In many respects, we are virtual tightrope walkers, precariously balancing two remarkable acquisitions of the post-Cold War period: the simultaneous development of the formal international human rights framework and the informal network of information technologies. The promulgation of binding treaty law for the implementation of human rights has accelerated since the end of the Cold War, alongside the proliferation of multiple channels of communication offered by the growth of information technology. This dual paradigm has created new tensions between individual citizens and their States, one that reinforces shifting political patterns. We encourage our students to reflect on how the human rights framework, on a national and international level, interacts with digitally-driven networks to provide citizens with leverage to safe guard their rights. And yet, as digital technology users learn to intervene in governance in a myriad of innovative ways, governments and companies are using the same technology to interfere with human lives on a brand new scale, both for better and for worse. It is the dense, contested nature of this interaction that creates the potential for greater democracy or more abject tyranny.

We take issue with the idea that human rights protection of digital technology users is a win-win equation for all concerned. On the one hand, rights protection may be expensive for governments or business to implement, but such protection reinforces the social contract that underpins democratic governance and provides an ethical legitimacy for political and corporate actors. On the other hand, discrimination, violence against women and environmental pollution are expensive to society, and could be mitigated through timely implementation of human rights law. Our curriculum encourages students to identify the trade-offs that occur as new technologies are regulated, or not regulated, by the public sector. We emphasize that no public or private actor is above the law or the general public interest, hence functionality may not apply in all circumstances.

We conclude by stressing how the issue of privacy has been, and will continue being, a multifaceted problem that both creates a variety of different expectations amongst stakeholders and affords multiple technical solutions. We explore the diversity of privacy paradigms that populate the online experience (e.g. control, confidentiality, practice [17]) highlighting the user perspective [18]; we compare the regulatory frameworks currently applied in various countries with a focus on Europe and US law (e.g., [19]) and introduce several privacy enhancing technologies, explaining their role in embedding privacy into digital systems [20, 21].

3.2   Proactive not Reactive; Preventative not Remedial

In addressing the issue of proactive measures, we examine a pervasive element of the digital revolution that suffers from a lack of proactive, or even remedial regulation: the hardware that makes the digital revolution possible. Fascination with wireless technology – the sleek design of smartphones and tablets, the dizzying range of applications and available information, the ability to be "connected" at all times – has blinded the general user to the potential costs of the hardware necessary to make the technology function. There are over five million mobile phone towers worldwide, for example, serving 96 % of the global population through the provision of electro-magnetic waves (EMF), a low-frequency form of radiation [22]. This "invisible" infrastructure constitutes one of the largest experiments with human biology and environmental capacity to date, and yet scientists are still debating how to measure its impact and how to evaluate the long-term consequences of electromagnetic wave exposure on the human organism [23]. Class discussions indicated the extent to which our students had never reflected on the levels of electricity required for the storage of digital data or the electromagnetic wave emissions necessary to make their smart phones function. This curricular unit is designed to provide students with a lay-person's understanding of EMF science, the controversies over EMF measurement and its impact on living organisms, and the human rights paradigm that requires proactive application of the precautionary principle. By applying Cavoukian's first principle to an often-ignored aspect of the digital revolution, we enrich the argument for proactive regulation and extend the case to protection of human health and the environment.

3.3   Privacy as a Default Setting

In "Integrating privacy and ethical impact assessments", David Wright and Michael Friedewald argue for an ethics of design, the application of a human rights framework to software production before the rollout of the final product [24]. This curricular unit provides students with an understanding of the potential ethical controversies surrounding software design. We invited David Wright into our classroom to discuss with students his evaluation of both the privacy enhancing technologies we use, as well as the application of binding human rights treaty law in the very design of every IT product. As his work makes clear, privacy would be a default setting if a privacy impact assessment were properly applied in all circumstances. Our students were particularly intrigued by the potential for cross-cultural and political application of Wright's system of ethics: who should determine the framework of a PIA – governments, companies or users? Is Wright's ethical impact assessment [25] a strictly Western construct, or could it be applied to protect privacy in an authoritarian state? Could a PIA be used for political or economic purposes to prevent the design or delivery of new IT products? How will freedom of expression be impacted if privacy is the default setting? These and other questions extended discussion of Cavoukian's principles to the larger realm of human rights and their universality.

3.4   Visibility and Transparency — Keep It Open

Our classroom discussions indicated that the issue of censorship strikes a chord with our students, all of them sensitive to the precarious balance between national security and citizen privacy, as disclosed by the Snowden revelations. Policy transparency, whether it be focused on spying or on censorship, is another lens through which to examine the idea of a free and open Internet. We use China as an example of the tensions between users determined to pursue online freedom of expression and a government bent on forestalling the possibility of organized street demonstrations facilitated through social media [26]. The closed system of the Chinese Internet, with copycat search engines (baidu), Twitter (weibo), and WhatsApp (We Chat or weixian), is an ideal laboratory in which to explore the contradictions inherent in the principle of Internet freedom versus the need for governments to monitor online citizen activity to prevent crime and terrorism. It is hardly a surprise that the Chinese Party-State has built a Great Firewall in an effort to keep online protest from spreading to the streets, a seminal concern in a nation that already experiences a significant number riots, or "mass incidents", per year.[2] Our curriculum encourages students to examine the reasons for government control of the Internet, and to weigh the importance of a series of violations ranging from freedom of expression to private property to privacy. We examine government censorship and user-driven self-censorship, as well as clever tools designed to circumvent censorship, such as the "grass mud horse" lexicon, a humorous

---

[2] The Chinese government last published the number of annual mass incidents in 2005. Anecdotal speculation brings the number to as high as 180,000 riots per year - see Freeman, Will (2010) The Accuracy of China's mass incidents. Financial Times, March 2.

set of character puns developed by Chinese netizens. Students are encouraged to think about the impact of censorship on privacy by design; privacy as a default setting is a weak concept unless bolstered by a visible and transparent privacy protection policy within a strong legal framework, such as the recently proposed Data Protection Regulation.

3.5 Privacy Embedded into Design

The Internet of Things (IoT), a diffuse concept that embraces the connection of objects to one another and to humans, is of particular importance to an audience of general users. We have structured this curricular unit to focus on the potential ubiquity of privacy violations in a world where things are more connected than people. Starting from a list of six European Union concerns regarding the IoT [27], we examine issues such as trust, agency and autonomy in the context of privacy and the Internet of Things. Both hardware and software violations come to the fore, as students analyse the advantages and disadvantages of a fully digitized world. Our curriculum encourages students to evaluate who would be most vulnerable to privacy violations – the poor who lack regular access to a digitized environment, employees whose work and physical presence may be assessed via digital monitoring, the elderly who rely on assisted living technologies – and how this might matter. Is it possible to successfully embed privacy protection into all design and how is the user to express the level of desired protection, or to know whether such options exist? Our students quickly took the discussion one step further to ask what other human rights protections are challenged by the Internet of Things?

3.6 End-to-End Security — Full Lifecycle Protection

This course unit asks the students to consider the different stages of design, implementation, deployment, maintenance, upgrading and disposal of both simple and complex systems. As users, our students rarely consider this whole lifecycle or the complexity associated with systems that integrate different components. The objective is to highlight that privacy can only be achieved by taking appropriate measures across system components and throughout the whole lifecycle. We draw on the example of privacy protection in the charging procedure for electronic vehicles. This procedure, if not appropriately designed, may reveal to charging station and mobility operators unnecessary information about users' locations and possibly other personal data. Our students were introduced to the design of a protocol addressing the communication between the charging station and the vehicle baptized 'Popcorn' by its creators [28]. This specific example is particularly interesting because the procedure followed by the authors of Popcorn clearly shows how privacy impact assessments may be used both to derive design requirements and to assess the level of privacy protection of the solution. We invited scholar and protocol team member Frank Kargl to illustrate the privacy issues addressed by the protocol and explain, to our non-technical audience, the privacy enhancing technologies (PETs) supporting the system. Professor Kargl argued that e-mobility through ad hoc, needs-based electric car rental, particularly in urban areas, is considered one of the next milestones for the automotive industry. But, connecting electric cars to a power grid without storing data on user identity, mobility or payment methods is a challenge. This curricular unit follows our work on privacy as a default setting and embedded privacy, allowing students to explore the practical implications of privacy protection in their daily lives. The success of Popcorn in protecting user privacy demonstrates that human rights protection is often an issue of creative thinking.

3.7   Respect for User Privacy — Keep It User-Centric

This principle is explained as "Respect and protect interests of the individual, above all" [1] and requires a clear identification of users and their needs. We encouraged our students to reflect on users and their needs by asking them to design educational materials on privacy for a variety of stakeholder communities. Few guidelines were issued to students. Thanks to the small class size typical of liberal arts institutions, we were able to establish groups of no more than five students, each with an assigned target audience: the general public; the digitally reluctant; children; EU regulators not working on privacy; national regulators not working on privacy; and human rights advocates. None of these audiences can be considered specialists on privacy issues. Students were given the option to make their final product available to the Creative Commons, following a discussion of copyright protection and whether the Creative Commons offered an opportunity to impact political discourse on the issue of privacy protection. They presented their projects to their classmates on two occasions in order to receive peer feedback, and submitted four drafts for our comments before handing in their final project in electronic form. In our determination to empower our students, we underestimated their initial sense of panic caused by the lack of detailed guidelines. Nonetheless, within three months, our students demonstrated, through their production of rich, yet streamlined educational material, a mature understanding of the theoretical convergence of human rights and digital technology as manifested in online privacy issues.

4   Student Production of Educational Materials for Privacy by Design

In this section, we provide two examples of student production of privacy-by-design educational material, one for the general public (produced by a group of graduate students) and one for children (produced by a group of undergraduates). Both samples represent patterns that we noted across student submissions: (1) the incorporation of their own user experiences into the design of educational materials; (2) a commitment to striking visual design; (3) a sophisticated awareness of the Internet as a public good, an online extension of their "heterogeneous and thickly integrated" social lives [13].

Figure 1 presents the first page of a two-page, student-produced infograph that synthesizes online and offline life in a realistic manner, visually demonstrating the blended characteristics of a typical student day. In addition to the visual sleekness of

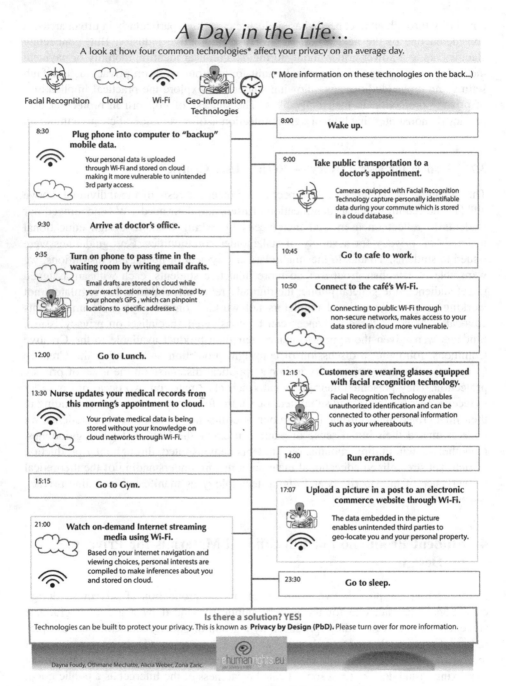

Fig. 1. First page of general public infographic.

the sample, we note the contextual integrity suggested by Nissenbaum, a seamless transfer of offline activities to online platforms [13]. This sample also demonstrates our students' understanding of the theoretical integration of individual human rights with

Fig. 2. Extract from information booklet for children.

the possibilities for privacy violations inherent in digital technology use, and the provision of recourse for privacy violations. It is possible that our choice of a participant action research methodology may have led our students to think in terms of PbD as a legal or technical recourse, to render more robust their assessment of commonly-occurring violations.

The second knowledge product (Fig. 2) is a cartoon that focuses on the protection of minors from cyber bullying; the cartoon was drawn from a student-produced magazine addressing children and their parents. According to the Australian government, the most vulnerable age for this form of harassment is 14–15 years old, the group targeted by this cartoon's school setting [29]. Again, participant action research methods may have encouraged our students to privilege their own personal experiences in a carefully constructed design that provides recourse, in this case reporting the incident to parents and the use of a hotline. The choice of a colorful design and two female characters was carefully thought through, as was the extreme simplification of the message and the pitch for privacy as a default setting. Both Figs. 1 and 2 are aimed at a general public that is unfamiliar with privacy by design as a concept, or the idea that privacy could be a default mechanism on social media sites. This should be the starting point for educational materials on privacy, since all sectors of society must be brought on board if privacy is to become the default setting expected by the general public when using the Internet, or purchasing digital objects and software.

5 Conclusions

By working closely with six student teams over the course of the semester, we were provided with a window on the thinking of the general user. Non-engineering students who spend an average of two-three hours a day online are ideally situated to design knowledge products that promote online security and privacy amongst the general public. The condensed analyses embedded in their knowledge products is a reflection of the curriculum's assigned readings, lectures and discussions that bring together law and science in an effort to explore the Internet as it impacts their lived experience. By transferring privacy principles to the larger domain of human rights and digital technology, our students were able to view security and privacy protection as part of a larger exploration of how we are going to live in a digitally connected society. Only by privileging the broader perspective can we deliver on the promise of digital technology to enhance democratic dialogue and facilitate human lifestyles, and make sure that it is safe to use for the generations to come.

References

1. Cavoukian, A., Dixon, M.: Privacy and Security by Design: An Enterprise Architecture Approach (2013). http://www.privacybydesign.ca/index.php/paper/privacy-security-design-enterprise-architecture-approach/. Accessed 10 May 2014
2. Cavoukian, A.: Foundational Principles (Privacy by design) (1997). http://www.privacybydesign.ca/index.php/about-pbd/7-foundational-principles/. Accessed 22 May 2014

3. Rubinstein, I., Good, N.: Privacy by design: A counterfactual analysis of Google and Facebook privacy incidents. Berkeley Technol. Law J. 4 (2011)
4. Gürses, S., Troncoso, C., Diaz, C.: Engineering privacy by design. In: International Conference on Privacy and Data Protection (CPDP), Belgium (2011)
5. Reason, P., Bradbury, H. (eds.): Handbook of Action Research. Sage Publications, London (2013)
6. Cavoukian, A.: Privacy by design: the definitive workshop. A foreword by Ann Cavoukian. Identity Inf. Soc. 3, 247–251 (2010)
7. Warren, S., Brandeis, L.: The Right to Privacy. Harvard Law Review IV (1890)
8. Universal Declaration of Human Rights: G.A. Res. 217 A(III), adopted by the U.N. Doc. A/810, 10 December 1948
9. Office of the High Commissioner for Human Rights: CCPR General Comment No. 16: Article 17 (Right to Privacy) The Right to Respect of Privacy, Family, Home and Correspondence, and Protection of Honour and Reputation. Adopted 8 April 1988
10. Posner, R.: Privacy is Overrated, New York Daily News, 28 April 2013
11. Harper, R. (ed.): Trust, Computing and Society. Cambridge University Press, Cambridge (2014)
12. Perry, S., Roda, C., Carlson, K.: Submission United Nations Committee on the Rights of the Child - General Comment on the Rights of the Child and the Business Sector (2012)
13. Nissenbaum, H.: A contextual approach to privacy online. Daedalus 140, 32–48 (2011)
14. Wright, D., Finn, R., Gellert, R., Gutwirth, S., Schütz, P., Friedewald, M., Venier, S., Mordini, E.: Ethical dilemma scenarios and emerging technologies. Technological Forecasting and Social Change forthcoming
15. Pew Research Internet Project: Anonymity, Privacy and Security Online (2013). http://www.pewinternet.org/2013/09/05/anonymity-privacy-and-security-online-2/
16. Internet Society: Internet Society Mission Statement (2014)
17. Diaz, C., Gürses, S.: Understanding the landscape of privacy technologies. Information Security Summit (2012). http://homes.esat.kuleuven.be/~cdiaz/activities.html. 1 May 14
18. Jutla, D.N.: Layering privacy on operating systems, social networks, and other platforms by design. Identity Inf. Soc. IDIS 3, 319–341 (2010)
19. Schwartz, P.M., Solove, D.J.: Reconciling Personal Information in the United States and European Union. California Law Review Forthcoming (2014)
20. European Commission: Communication on Promoting Data Protection by Privacy Enhancing Technologies (PETs), COM(2007) 228 final, Brussels, 2 May 2007
21. Goold, B.: Building it in: The role of privacy enhancing technologies in the regulation of surveillance and data collection. In: Goold, B., Neyland, D. (eds.) New Directions in Surveillance and Privacy. Willan, Devon (2009)
22. International Telecommunication Union: ICT Facts and Figures (2013). http://www.itu.int/en/ITU-D/Statistics/Documents/facts/ICTFactsFigures2013.pdf. Accessed 26 Sep 2013
23. Roda, C., Perry, S.: Mobile phone infrastructure regulation in Europe: Scientific challenges and human rights protection. Environ. Sci. Policy 37, 204–214 (2014)
24. Wright, D., Friedewald, M.: Integrating privacy and ethical impact assessments. Sci. Public Policy 40, 755–766 (2013)
25. Wright, D.: A framework for the ethical impact assessment of information technology. Ethics Inf. Technol. 13, 199–226 (2011)
26. Perry, S., Roda, C.: Conceptualizing and contextualizing the changing nature of internet usage in china. In: China and the New Internet World: The Eleventh Chinese Internet Research Conference (CIRC11). Oxford Internet Institute, Oxford (2013)

27. van der Hoven, J.: Fact Sheet – Ethics, IoT Expert Group. European Commission (2011). http://ec.europa.eu/information_society/newsroom/cf/dae/document.cfm?doc_id=1751. Accessed 10 May 2014

28. Höfer, C., Petit, J., Schmidt, R., Kargl, F.: POPCORN: Privacy-preserving charging for eMobility. In: First Workshop on Security, Privacy and Dependability for CyberVehicles (CyCar) at 20th ACM Conference on Computer and Communications Security (2013)

29. Australian Ministry of Education Safe Schools Hub: "What is cyberbullying?" http:// safeschoolshub.edu.au/for-parents/what-to-do-about-/staying-cybersafe/what-is-cyberbullying-. Accessed 22 May 2014

Research and Innovation

An Integrated Framework for Innovation Management in Cyber Security and Privacy

Dharm Kapletia[✉], Massimo Felici, and Nick Wainwright

Security and Cloud Lab, Hewlett-Packard Laboratories, Long Down Avenue,
Bristol BS34 8QZ, UK
dharmendra.kapletia@hp.com

Abstract. This paper is concerned with increasing the impact of publicly funded research and development (R&D) in cyber security and privacy. In the context of a high level of threat, there is a pressing need for firms and institutions to implement innovative and robust cyber security and privacy technologies. This particular challenge requires a systematic coordinated approach across both the public and private sectors. The innovation ecosystem involves complex interactions between key actors such as policy makers, incumbent service providers, and new innovators, each with their own view of how to increase the impact of R&D in cyber security and privacy. Drawing on R&D literature and roadmapping theory, this paper presents a framework and research tool for establishing an integrated view of innovation management in cyber security and privacy.

Keywords: Innovation management · Impact · Cyber security · Privacy

1 Introduction

Research in security and trust like other domains faces difficult transition from research into practice [1]. Recent work on cyber security research highlights the main factors (i.e. *"insufficient awareness of the complexity of cyber security transfer"*, *"a scatter-shot approach to R&D"* and *"mismatch between market and threat environment"* [2]) that jeopardise transferring security technology from research to practice – *"many research investments lead to security technologies that never see the light of the day"* [2]. This difficulty that research outcomes have to transition into real world applications and markets is often depicted as the "valley of death" [3]. That is, most of research outcomes will fail to have any industry impact. Whilst this usefully serves to filter out poorly conceived propositions, the challenge therein is to identify and support technologies that are valued by the market and of importance to end users [4].

This problem can be analysed from two different viewpoints: *technological* and *contextual*. On the one hand, research outcomes may not be ready or mature enough to be deployed into practice. On the other hand, application domains may not be ready to adopt new technological developments due to low levels of innovation intakes.

From a technological viewpoint of analysis, it is necessary to identify and understand the barriers that inhibit technology transitions to practice, and how to address them [5, 6]. Another technological aspect to be considered is the maturity of developments.

F. Cleary and M. Felici (Eds.): CSP Forum 2014, CCIS 470, pp. 135–147, 2014.
DOI: 10.1007/978-3-319-12574-9_12

The NASA Technology Readiness Levels (TRLs) are often used to assess the maturity of technology to be delivered in operational environments [7, 8]. Moving from one technology readiness level to the next one (and above TRL 3 and TLR 4) requires dealing with a *"research and development degree of difficulty"* (that is, probability of success of R&D objectives) [9]. Moreover, it also requires a commitment of resources beyond the affordability of many research and development contexts, in particular, of publicly funded research [10, 11]. The assessment by TLRs is now being adapted for use in European Horizon 2020 funded research. This represents a significant shift affecting how funding decisions are reached and how post-funding evaluations are carried out.

From a contextual viewpoint of analysis, it is necessary to understand whether specific domains are ready to adopt new technologies. Specific application domains have developed and adopted validation processes (collecting evidence) to assess the readiness of technology to be deployed in operational environments in order to mini-mise the risk of innovation (e.g. see the EUROCONTROL E-OCVM [12, 13]). At the national level, the innovation index is widely adopted as a measure to assess the level of innovation in different countries [14]. The Global Innovation Index (GII) takes into account composite indicators ranking innovation performances. The combination of these two perspectives, i.e. technological readiness (that is, how mature technology is) and contextual innovation (that is, how ready the innovation environment is), identifies a readiness-innovation space to discuss strategies to support research impact. It high-lights two critical situations: (1) high-readiness of technology and low-innovation context, (2) low-readiness of technology and high-innovation potential context. The former characterises situations where technology has been extensively developed and used, but the deployment context is unable to benefit from innovation for different reasons (e.g. lack of innovation culture, unsuitable supporting mechanisms). The latter characterises situations where technology is under-developed for an innovation ecosystem.

With the aim of supporting evidence-based policy making and increasing the impact of R&D decision-making, this paper sets out the method for conducting a comprehensive and systematic empirical investigation of stakeholder experiences in cyber security and privacy innovation. This includes both demand side views as well as technology and innovator views, across the end-to-end spectrum of innovation management. Insights generated are expected to capture authoritative snapshots of the health of innovation ecosystems. This paper is structured as follows. Section 2 introduces an integrated innovation management framework. Section 3 outlines a systematic procedural method for capturing the views and experiences of cyber security stakeholders. Section 4 applies the proposed framework on a case study based on a literature review. This is to further explain the framework itself and its application on a concrete example. Section 5 high-lights some concluding remarks and discusses the application of the proposed framework for roadmapping R&D initiatives in cyber security and privacy.

2   An Integrated Framework for Innovation Management

In order to support effectively the transition from publicly funded research to operation environments it is necessary to address different challenges, e.g. human resources, government regulations, deployment issues, and funding cycles [6]. Enhancing the readiness level of technologies requires not only dealing with such challenges but also using the suitable support at the right time. Different mechanisms may be suitable for early research developments but not so effective in supporting transition to operations. Other instruments may support effectively technology transfers and adoption. In order to increase the impact of R&D in cyber security and privacy, different instruments (e.g. research projects, pilot projects, pre-commercial procurements [15, 16]) can support innovation at various stages [17], from R&D initiatives enhancing the maturity and readiness of technology to the adoption of innovative technology. Similar consider-ations may arise in analysing the risk of technology (new or existing) with respect to market (new or existing) [18]. The European Commission, for instance, is supporting the adoption of pre-commercial procurement in order to deliver innovation in public sectors in Europe [19]. The pre-commercial procurement has been successfully adopted and used across different services [20, 21].

Initial findings from SecCord research [22] combined with insights drawn from critical aspects of R&D, as discussed, highlight three discrete primary areas of investigation: (I) R&D policy and market, (II) technology readiness, and (III) tech-nology transfer (also referred to as transition). Figure 1 illustrates these areas of investigations forming together the integrated framework for innovation management underpinning empirical investigations and roadmaps in cyber security and privacy.

Some stakeholders clearly operate within one particular area of investigation (e.g. regulators and funders within R&D Policy and Market, and Information Communi-cations Technology (ICT) service providers within Technology Transfer), whilst others

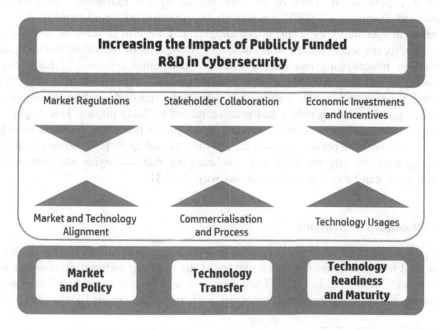

Fig. 1. An integrated framework for innovation management

can provide expert views and experiences across more than one process (e.g. innovators). The framework in Fig. 1 thus outlines the scope and focus for capturing, integrating and systematically analysing all stakeholder views of cyber security R&D impact.

3 Capturing Stakeholder Views and Experiences

There are a variety of tools available to capture stakeholder views and experiences. The use of roadmaps have been used for decades, offering a powerful visual representation of stakeholder views on where they want to go to achieve their desired objective [23]. In both academic and practitioner literature, they are reported as a recognised and proven tool, used extensively to ensure the right capabilities are in place at the right time. The process of roadmapping is said to require the simultaneous consideration of markets, products, technologies and interaction between them over time [24]. Much of the documented cases focus on the development and use of roadmaps at the firm-level, and advocates the importance of gaining cross functional views (across silos) and helping staff to see the impact they have on other parts of the organisation [25]. Roadmaps have also been used in similar fashion by governments looking at the industry level – bringing together a wide variety of stakeholder views from private and public sectors as well as other bodies such as educational institutions. The US government has developed such industry-based roadmaps for cyber security strategy and planning [26, 27].

Fellow colleagues and researchers across various European institutions, including other ICT projects[1] in Trust & Security funded by the European Commission's Framework Programme 7 (FP7), are actively investigating where investments need to be made in specific cyber security technologies and are also developing *technology roadmaps* for the security and privacy domains. At the level of individual technologies, technology roadmapping can offer a valuable stakeholder appraisal of early stage technologies and help strengthen value propositions and routes to market [28]. This research however will employ a *strategic roadmapping* approach – where the emphasis is more on characterising policy and practice related to R&D impact. This might for example include a focus on cross-boundary development processes, business models, security ecosystem dependencies, and involvement of end users [29]. While much has been reported recently on their use, roadmapping methodologies are continually evolving and can be customised in various ways [30, 31].

3.1 Roadmap Dimensions

The primary areas of investigation outlined in the integrated framework (Fig. 1) have been used to make up the three main layers of the roadmap architecture template for this research, as laid out in Fig. 2. They align well with typical layers found in generic roadmaps where the top is usually concerned with trends and drivers ('know why'); the

---

[1] http://cordis.europa.eu/fp7/ict/security/projects_en.html

middle contains products, services, systems, requirements ('know what'); and the bottom includes resources (includes technology) to be marshalled and integrated to develop the delivery mechanisms [32]. From an emerging typology of roadmaps, the proposed architecture for this research combines the 'strategic appraisal' and 'business reconfiguration' types [31]. This is based on the need to credibly establish and review evidence of the 'as-is' (current position in Fig. 2) in cyber security and privacy R&D. This can be compared and contrasted the desired 'to-be' end-state (vision in Fig. 2), which will lead to a gap analysis and initiate discussion of routes to address the gap.

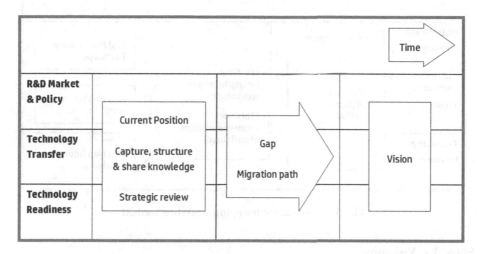

Fig. 2. Proposed roadmap architecture, incorporating the research framework

Following a robust and systematic method, this research project will develop an initial desk-based roadmap based on empirical data from semi-structured interviews and an online survey of cyber security stakeholders across stakeholders in Europe. The results will inform future activities towards a consolidated roadmap in cyber security and privacy. Future activities may include local and national roadmapping workshops. A judgement will be made as to when to best share the desk-based roadmap with other stakeholders. On the one hand, sharing the results after completion of all data gathering activities may help achieve triangulation using various sources of data. On the other hand sharing an emerging roadmap with stakeholders at key stages might validate key findings over time. Either way, a comparison of desk based and workshop based roadmaps at any stage in the research will provide interesting insights about the perceived reasons for similarities and differences.

3.2   Process for Building a Strategic Roadmap

The format and process of developing a strategic roadmap will adopt a customised approach based on extensive learning from practitioner and academic expertise and experience [29, 30]. Source materials have been modified slightly to fit the roadmap architecture in Fig. 2 and an industry-based level of analysis (rather than firm level).

The research will adopt a three stage process, moving from (1) *visioning key stakeholder end-states*, (2) *identifying problems and prioritising opportunities*, and (3) *establishing pathways forward*. Figure 3 outlines the specific empirical activities of mapping and analysis associated with each of the three stages.

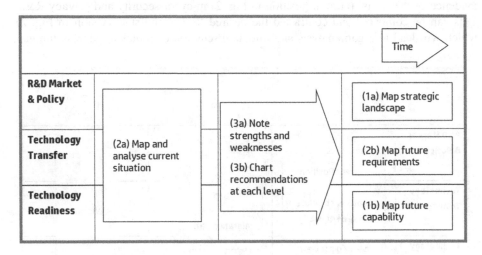

Fig. 3. Proposed roadmapping workshop method

Stage 1 – Visioning

(1a) Map strategic landscape – This involves developing a collective understanding of high level strategic goals related to R&D market and policy. This may include policy objectives, regulation, market maturity, national strategic initiatives, and future industry threats and challenges. Whilst there may be considerable differences in ideas between stakeholders, this activity can conclude by restating the common thread of increasing impact. This is an opportunity to create an appetite for change.

(1b) Map future capability – This relates to how future publicly funded R&D capability can be transformed at the operational level. Capability includes how organizations go about (individually or collectively) increasing the potential of their new security technologies. TRLs may be used in this context to frame how future capabilities relate to advancing through levels of maturity to a desired outcome.

Stage 2 – Opportunities

(2a) Map and analyse current situation – This will likely involve the greatest amount of time, whereby stakeholders involved in R&D market and policy, technology transfer and technology readiness articulate existing issues, challenges, enablers, and barriers associated with delivering impact. This will culminate with a process of ranking both problems and opportunities against Stage One findings.

(2b) Map future requirements – The focus at this point turns towards bridging the so-called 'valley of death' and may draw on problems and opportunities raised in 2a. Broadly speaking, this is likely to establish future positions related to business model choices, ecosystem needs, roles of intermediary entities, alternative/optimal forms of collaboration across boundaries, use of commercial vehicles, and different approaches to managing intellectual property rights.

Stage 3 – Pathways

(3a) Note strengths and weaknesses – This involves an in-depth collective discussion of the gaps identified from an analysis of Stage One and Stage Two. Gaps may be ranked against a scale to indicate the level of investment that is likely to be required to address them. If possible, broad indications of short, medium and long term timings associated with levels of investment may also be captured.

(3b) Chart recommendations at each level – This is the final activity of the workshop, which is designed to generate a final set of recommendations for increasing the impact of publicly funded R&D. The output of this activity may generate an execution roadmap to guide stakeholder decision-makers and research sponsors. This is where the importance of having participation from all stakeholder groups to help ensure recommendations have a greater chance of being implemented.

During roadmapping workshops, within each activity, stakeholder ideas will be captured using sticky notes against large wall charts, and then grouped into swim lanes (horizontal rows) where common themes exist, creating new categories. This may involve 'walking the wall' and critiquing ideas, filtering high-value trends via a voting process, and storytelling experiences through small group exercises [29].

3.3 Innovation Ecosystem

Past research also points out the importance of or securing committed and diverse stakeholders groups across disciplines, and ensuring their fully engagement with the process to avoid producing superficial roadmapping results [25]. Our research proposes the following stakeholder groupings and will seek participation from each one:

1. **Research and development** (individuals and organisations seeking to bring new technologies to market, e.g. University spin-outs and R&D labs in an enterprise)
2. **Security and privacy technology/service provider** (of ICT based systems, e.g. anti-virus security service provision)
3. **Technology owner or operator** (of ICT based systems, e.g. internal IT service within an organisation)
4. **Consultancy or industry support** (institutional associations, standards bodies, technology and market analysis, e.g. think tanks and incubators)
5. **Funders and Investors** (individual or entity responsible for sponsoring or investing in R&D, e.g. venture capitalist investment)

6. **Policy and regulation** (Government department, agency or appointed body, e.g. innovation policy development)
7. **Dependent third party** (those who might be compromised by a security breach, e.g. end user in an organisation).

This research incorporates learning from past roadmapping initiatives [31] to ensure a successful outcome. This includes a robust framework and roadmap architecture that is aligned with future developments of the European cybersecurity strategy [33], and a systematic process for empirical data collection and analysis through various sources, drawing on the support of a wide variety of stakeholders in cyber security and privacy.

4 Increasing the Impact of Cyber Security R&D in the US

This section assists in establishing proof of concept for the selected roadmap architecture (as set out in Sects. 2 and 3). Observations from industry leading developments in the United States presented an opportunity to conduct a desk-based roadmapping exercise. Various published US policy sources were analysed mainly from the 'regulator' stakeholder viewpoint [27, 34–40]. The US roadmap presented in Fig. 4 reflects data captured for activities 1a, 1b and 2b, which essentially outlines the future vision. It is possible to take this exercise further through desk-based research by investigating other documented stakeholder perspectives. This would help construct a more integrated view of innovation management in the US.

R&D Policy and Market	National Security Priorities	(3.1) Address critical weaknesses	(3.2) Solutions to emerging threats	(3.3) New, tested technologies	(6.1) Rapid adoption of R&T	(6.2) Define goals for standards bodies	(8.1) Departments report R&D requirements		
	Market incentives	(4.2) Shifting risk to the private sector	(A4.3) Create cross-agency forums	(4.5) Develop partnerships for mature technologies	(4.6) Rewards for program managers	(5.1) Incubators for radical R&D	(5.2) Seed funding for industry led R&D	(5.3) University and industry partnering	(7.4) Data protection for vulnerability data
	Exploiting the talent base	(5.4) Quality talent in public sector roles	(7.3) Focus funding on multi-disciplinary projects						
Technology Transfer	System of Systems approach	(1.1) Stakeholder collaboration	(8.2) Departments create scientific foundation						
	Intellectual property	(1.5) New ways of managing IPR	(7.1) Industry forum for commercialization						
Technology Readiness	Effective prototyping	(4.4) Leverage networked environments for test and evaluation	(1.2) Metrics and benefits (large scale systems)	(1.3) Proven demonstrations	(1.6) Committed to system trustworthiness				
	Deployment process		(1.4) Preparation for test evaluation	(1.7) Monitoring and accountability	(1.8) Critical areas for technology application	(2.1) Bridging new and legacy systems			
	Business case	(4.1) Early stage transition plan	(7.2) Industry need and evidence based investment						

Fig. 4. US example roadmapping exercise

A more detailed breakdown of the original data can be viewed in the appendix. As expected, common themes across source documents are represented by swim lanes and new category labels have been generated. For example, categories under technology readiness include: effective prototyping, deployment process and business case.

5   Discussion and Concluding Remarks

It is clear that measures must be taken to ensure that investments in promising cyber security and privacy technologies survive the valley of death and are given the opportunity to deliver high value impact. Given the complexity associated with cyber security research-to-practice transfer, it is vital to collect and analyse the views of key stakeholders (involved in the end-to-end process of innovation) when devising recommendations that could lead to future policies, strategies and interventions.

This paper has outlined a framework and research tool for developing an integrated view of innovation management in cyber security and privacy. Most importantly, it provides a robust and systematic approach for collecting and analysing industry-level stakeholder views using tried and tested strategic roadmapping methodology. This will be implemented to characterise views of the cyber security innovation ecosystem in the United Kingdom and Europe. The research tool also can be applied to conduct a historical desk-based roadmapping exercise. In this regard, other future applications might include an impact assessment of past European funded R&D projects, the findings of which could inform planning for future research programmes. It may also be possible to repeat the process for other industries, particularly where similar complexities exists.

Insights generated by the research tool may assist identifying a mismatch between stakeholder views and recommendations, and current R&D policies and strategies. Having stakeholder engagement across the groupings identified in Sect. 3 will allow for a greater understanding of connections and dependencies in the ecosystem. For instance 'regulators' and 'investors' can learn more about challenges faced by 'innovators' or the impact of their decisions on established 'ICT owners and operators'. The risks are that the quality of the insights will depend heavily on the commitment and expertise of selected stakeholders. The end product of the roadmapping process should be regarded as a snapshot in time, unless maintained and updated. All findings and analysis will be presented in a white paper to the European Commission and disseminated widely to stakeholders, networks and forums in cyber security and privacy.

Acknowledgments. This work has been partly funded by the Seventh Framework Programme (FP7) of the European Commission, Security and Trust Coordination and Enhanced Collaboration (SecCord) – http://www.seccord.eu/ – grant agreement 316622.

Appendix

Increasing the impact of publicly funded R&D in the United States – Desk-based roadmapping

Source	Roadmap label		Documented evidence
A roadmap for cybersecurity research [34]	1.1	Stakeholder collaboration	Public-private collaboration among government, industry, and academia, + extraordinary economic, social, and technological forcing functions
	1.2	Metrics and benefits (large scale systems)	Metrics need to be experimentally evaluated and benefits to large scale systems clearly demonstrated
	1.3	Proven demonstrations	Proven demonstrations of effectiveness are required, this would help roll-out adoption in practice
	1.4	Preparation for test evaluation	Design mechanisms, policies, and plans for test evaluation that can be incrementally deployed
	1.5	New ways of managing IPR (Intellectual Property Rights)	Innovative approaches to licensing and sharing intellectual properties for global scale technologies
	1.6	Committed to system trustworthiness	Overarching commitment to system trustworthiness, going beyond past approaches
	1.7	Monitoring and accountability	Recognition of the pervasive needs for monitoring and accountability
	1.8	Critical areas for technology application	Understanding critical areas suitable for technology application
Cross sector roadmap for cybersecurity of control systems [27]	2.1	Bridging new and legacy systems	Encourage R&D into tying legacy systems into upcoming security solutions
Homeland Security – cybersecurity R&D priorities [35]	3.1	Address critical weaknesses	Driving security improvements to address critical weaknesses
	3.2	Solutions to emerging threats	Discovering new solutions for emerging cyber security threats
	3.3	New, tested technologies	Delivering new, tested technologies to defend against cyber security threats
Trustworthy cyberspace: Strategic Plan for the Federal Cybersecurity R&D Program [36]	4.1	Early stage transition plan	Early stage transition plan in place, that includes commercialization pathways, tech transfer coordination, proactive program management, and resources to reward success in transitioning
	4.2	Shifting risk to the private sector	Private sector is willing to take on significant risk-taking and shepherd research through the commercialization process
	4.3	Create cross-agency forums	Participation in cross-agency security entrepreneur forums, PI meetings, laboratory expos, and defense venture catalyst initiative
	4.4	Leverage networked environments for test and evaluation	Cross-agency activities designed to leverage available operational and next generation networked environments to support experimental deployment, test and evaluation in public and private environments
	4.5	Develop partnerships for mature technologies	Cross-agency activities designed to develop partnerships for mature technologies, through open system integrator forums (VCs, SIs, government), and small business innovative research conferences
	4.6	Rewards for program managers	Government funded R&D to build-in rewards for government program managers and principal investigators for commercial success

(Continued)

(Continued)

Increasing the impact of publicly funded R&D in the United States – Desk-based roadmapping

Source	Roadmap label	Documented evidence
Cybersecurity game-change R&D recommendations [37]	5.1 Incubators for radical R&D	Support game-changing R&D using incubators and Federal start-up funding
	5.2 Seed funding for industry led R&D	Support industry-based research consortia to lead and direct focused R&D using seed funding
	5.3 University and industry partnering	Support universities to create industrial partner programs designed to stimulate pre-competitive cooperation among industrial partners
	5.4 Quality talent in public sector roles	Recruit experienced high quality talent into government program manager roles, supporting technology transfer
Cyberspace policy review: assuring a trusted and resilient information and communications infrastructure [38]	6.1 Rapid adoption of R&T (Research and Technology)	Federal government to work with industry to develop migration paths and incentives for rapid adoption of research and technology development, including collaboration between academic and industrial laboratories
	6.2 Define goals for standards bodies	Federal government, in collaboration with private sector and other stakeholders, should use the infrastructure objectives and R&D framework to help define goals for national and international standards bodies
Roadmap to achieve energy delivery systems cybersecurity [39]	7.1 Industry forum for commercialization	Develop a matchmaking forum to connect researchers, vendors, and asset owners to accelerate research from concept to commercialization
	7.2 Industry need and evidence based investment	Develop mechanisms for utility and vendor engagement for pilot research studies to address the business case up front. Create a forum for industry to detail and request R&D topics
	7.3 Focus funding on multi-disciplinary projects	Require diverse (academic, lab, industry) participation to receive funding
	7.4 Data protection for vulnerability data	Support legislation that protects entities who disclose vulnerabilities in good faith to the appropriate parties
Federal R&D strategic plan [40]	8.1 Departments report R&D requirements	Required to provide Congress with a strategic plan based on an assessment of cyber security risk to guide the overall direction of Federal cyber security and information assurance R&D for IT and networking systems
	8.2 Departments create scientific foundation	Through existing programs and activities, support research that will lead to the development of a scientific foundation for the field of cyber security, including research that increases understanding of the underlying principles of securing complex networked systems, enables repeatable experimentation, and creates quantifiable security metrics

References

1. Maughan, D., Balenson, D., Lindqvist, U., Tudor, Z.: Crossing the "Valley of Death": transitioning cybersecurity research into practice. IEEE Secur. Priv. **11**(2), 14–23 (2013)
2. Anderson, R., Boehme, R., Clayton, R. Moore, T.: Security Economics and the Internal Market. ENISA (2008)
3. Downey, F.: Bridging the "valley of death": Response to the House of Commons Science and Technology Select Committee Bridging the "valley of death": Improving the Commercialisation of Research Inquiry from Engineering the Future. The Royal Academy of Engineering, London (2012)
4. Auerswald, P.E., Branscomb, L.M.: Valleys of death and Darwinian seas: financing the invention to innovation transition in the United States. J. Technol. Transf. **28**(3–4), 227–239 (2003). (Kluwer Academic Publishers)
5. Benzel, T.V., Lipner, S.: Crossing the great divide: transferring security technology from research to the market. IEEE Secur. Priv. **11**(2), 12–13 (2013)
6. D'Amico, A., O'Brien, B., Larkin, M.: building a bridge across the transition chasm. IEEE Secur. Priv. **11**(2), 24–33 (2013)
7. Mankins, J.C.: Technology readiness levels: a white paper. NASA (1995)
8. NASA: HRST technology assessments technology readiness levels, chart
9. Mankins, J.C.: Research & Development degree of difficulty (R&D3): a white paper. NASA (1998)
10. ENISA: Security economics and the internal market: evaluation of stakeholder replies (2008)
11. ENISA: Security economics and the internal market: ENISA conclusions on follow-up activities (2008)
12. EUROCONTROL: European operational concept validation methodology, E-OCVM version 3.0, volume I (2010)
13. EUROCONTROL: European operational concept validation methodology, E-OCVM version 3.0, volume II annexes (2010)
14. INSEAD: The global innovation index 2012: stronger innovation linkages for global growth. INSEAD and WIPO (2012)
15. ENISA: EP3R 2012 activity report. European Public+Private Partnership for Resilience (2012)
16. ENISA: EP3R 2013 work objectives. European Public+Private Partnership for Resilience (2013)
17. NIST: Between invention and innovation: an analysis of funding for early-stage technology development. NIST GCR 02–841, November 2002
18. Hartmann, G.C., Myers, M.B.: Technical risk, product specifications, and market risk. In: Branscomb, L.M., Auerswald, P.E. (eds.) Taking Technical Risks: How Innovators, Executives, and Investors Manage High-Tech Risks. MIT Press, Cambridge (2003)
19. European Commission: Pre-commercial procurement: driving innovation to ensure high public services in Europe. European Communities (2008)
20. European Commission: Opportunities for public technology procurement in the ICT-related sectors in Europe, final report (2008)
21. European Commission: Communication from the Commission to the European Parliament, The Council, The European Economic and Social Committee and the Committee of the Regions, Pre-commercial Procurement: Driving innovation to ensure sustainable high quality public services in Europe, SEC(2007) 1668, COM(2007) 799 final, Brussels (2007)
22. Felici, M., Wainwright, N.: Deliverable 6.4 – Future Internet Initiatives Year 1. SecCord Project No. 316622, November 2013

23. Probert, D., Radnor, M.: Frontier experiences from industry-academia consortia. IEEE Eng. Manag. Rev. **31**(3), 28 (2003)
24. Groenveld, P.: Roadmapping integrates business and technology. Res. Technol. Manag. **50** (6), 49–58 (2007). (Industrial Research Institute)
25. Cosner, R.R., Hynds, E.J., Fusfeld, A.R., Loweth, C.V., Scouten, C., Albright, R.: Integrating roadmapping into technical planning. Res. Technol. Manag. **50**(6), 31–48 (2007). (Industrial Research Institute)
26. Department for Homeland Security: A roadmap for cybersecurity research. United States Government (2009)
27. Industrial Control Systems Joint Working Group: Cross-sector roadmap for cybersecurity of control systems. Department for Homeland Security, United States Government (2011)
28. Dissel, M.C., Phaal, R., Farrukh, C.J., Probert, D.R.: Value roadmapping. Res. Technol. Manag. **52**(6), 45–53 (2009). (Industrial Research Institute)
29. Petrick, I.J., Martinelli, R.: Driving disruptive innovation: problem finding and strategy setting in an uncertain world. Res. Technol. Manag. **55**(6), 49–57 (2012). (Industrial Research Institute)
30. Radnor, M., Probert, D.R.: Viewing the future. Res. Technol. Manag. **47**(2), 25–26 (2004). (Industrial Research Institute)
31. Phaal, R., Farrukh, C., Probert, D.: Customizing roadmapping. IEEE Eng. Manag. Rev. **32** (3), 80–91 (2004)
32. Phaal, R., Farrukh, C.J.P., Probert, D.R.: Developing a technology roadmapping system. In: Technology Management: A Unifying Discipline for Melting the Boundaries, Portland International Conference on Management of Engineering & Technology (PICMET), pp. 99–111 (2005)
33. European Commission: High Representative of the European Union for Foreign Affairs and Security Policy, Joint Communication to the European Parliament, The Council, The European Economic and Social Committee and the Committee of the Regions, Cybersecurity Strategy of the European Union: An Open, Safe and Secure Cyberspace, JOIN (2013) 1 final, Brussels (2013)
34. Department of Homeland Security, Science and Technology Directorate: A roadmap for cybersecurity research, November 2009
35. Cybersecurity R&D priorities, United States Homeland Security (2014)
36. Trustworthy cyberspace: strategic plan for the federal cybersecurity research and development program. Executive Office of the President National Science and Technology Council (2011)
37. NITRD: Cybersecurity game-change research & development recommendations. The Networking and Information Technology Research and Development (NITRD) Program (2010)
38. White House: cyberspace policy review: assuring a trusted and resilient information and communications infrastructure. United States Whitehouse publication (2009)
39. ESCSWG: Roadmap to achieve energy delivery systems cybersecurity. The Energy Sector Control Systems Working Group (ESCSWG), Sept (2011)
40. Space Foundation: U.S. non-military cybersecurity research & development and related policies, Cybersecurity, Federal Research and Development Strategic Plan. Space Foundation (2014)

IPACSO: Towards Developing an Innovation Framework for ICT Innovators in the Privacy and CyberSecurity Markets

Zeta Dooly[1], Seamus Galvin[2], Jamie Power[3(✉)], Bart Renard[4], and Ulrich Seldeslachts[5]

[1] TSSG, Waterford Institute of Technology, Waterford, Ireland
Zeta@ipacso.eu
[2] Espion Ltd., Dublin, Ireland
Seamus@ipacso.eu
[3] RIKON, Waterford Institute of Technology, Waterford, Ireland
Jamie@ipacso.eu
[4] Vasco Data Security, Wemmel, Belgium
Bart@ipacso.eu
[5] LSEC, Louvain, Belgium
Ulrich@ipacso.eu

Abstract. A pressing challenge facing the cybersecurity and privacy research community is transitioning technical R&D into commercial and marketplace ready products and services. Responding to the need to develop a better understanding of how Privacy and CyberSecurity (PACS) market needs and overall technology innovation best-practice can be harmonized more effectively the contribution of this paper is centred upon the development of a set of innovation guiding principles to inform the overarching IPACSO (Innovation Framework for Privacy and CyberSecurity Opportunities) innovation framework to be developed. These guiding principles have been developed from ongoing market and economic analyses and innovation modelling research in an effort to explore the identification of PACS specific deltas with respect to innovation. The development of the innovation guiding principles represent a pivotal component in meeting IPACSO's overall goals of supporting increased awareness of and engagement in innovation practices, in addition to supporting greater knowledge of market dynamics, barriers and solution potential for increased innovation activity in the domain.

Keywords: Innovation · Framework · Guiding principles · Privacy · Cybersecurity

1 Introduction

The publication of the EU CyberSecurity Strategy [1] and the progress in relation to the proposal for a Directive concerning measures to ensure a high common level of network and information security across the Union has and continues to impact the privacy and cybersecurity market. With clear objectives to encourage economic growth as people's confidence in buying things online and using the Internet is strengthened,

© Springer International Publishing Switzerland 2014
F. Cleary and M. Felici (Eds.): CSP Forum 2014, CCIS 470, pp. 148–158, 2014.
DOI: 10.1007/978-3-319-12574-9_13

opportunities for innovators in this domain is increasing. Nonetheless, a range of challenges including, but not limited to: pursuing a narrow innovation process failing to incorporate the internal and external ecosystem or customer needs, an overemphasis on technology-driven bottom-up innovation, in addition to unsupportive deployment channels for research output/commercialization's hamper the transitioning of technology related research developments and outputs to commercial deployment [2]. Compounding the above challenges, the privacy and cybersecurity (PACS) domain is deeply influenced from various themes driven by technical, human, societal, organizational, economic, legal, and regulatory concerns among others; these factors combine to create marketplace and innovation ecosystem with complex value chain relationships [3]. Mindful of this, this paper outlines IPACSO's methodological approach to develop a series of innovation guiding principles to inform a knowledge and decision-support framework for identifying, assessing and exploiting innovation opportunities across the PACS domain.

While a significant general body of information around innovation exists i.e. the set of rules, models and stages involved [4]; the contribution of this paper is centred upon the development of a set of innovation guiding principles to anchor the overarching innovation framework to be developed. These guiding principles are informed from ongoing market and economic analyses and innovation modelling research to explore the identification of PACS specific deltas with respect to innovation. Through a specific PACS lens, IPACSO therefore aims to support innovators in both industry and research communities with a responsive innovation framework to enhance their overall innovation engagement, management and deployment activities. Additionally, IAPCSO aims to support and provide relevance to academic, policy making and related innovation enabling and funding stakeholders in terms of providing guidance and support to innovation activities. In this vein, IPACSO seeks to refine generic innovation guidance to the PACS domain and stakeholder needs to support innovators via decision support guidance and toolkits to identify the potential and scope of opportunities in addition to highlighting innovation tactics specifically for this market.

Regarding the structure of this paper; firstly the rationale for an innovation framework is presented, followed by an overview of the IPACSO methodological approach, and culminates in the identification of the initial guiding principles which will anchor and inform the development of the IPACSO Framework.

2 Rationale for an Innovation Framework

A pressing challenge facing the cybersecurity and privacy research community is transitioning technical R&D into commercial and marketplace ready products and services – "New and innovative technologies will only make a difference if they are deployed and used. It does not matter how visionary a technology is unless it meets the needs and requirements of customers/users and it is available as a product via channels that are acceptable to the customers/users" [2]. While innovation is widely recognized by industry and academics as a sustainable and competitive enabler, nonetheless understanding of innovation management and practice remains fragmented, misunderstood and untamed by practitioners and researchers [4].

Innovators operate within complex and turbulent environments, and are increasingly confronted with escalating and rapid technology developments, competitive global market competition and shorter product life cycles meaning they must be reactive and flexible to organizational, technological and market shifts [5]. Indeed, the privacy and cybersecurity market is deeply influenced from various themes driven by technical, human, societal, organizational, economic, legal, and regulatory concerns among others; these factors combine to create marketplace and innovation ecosystem with complex value chain relationships [3]. Innovation therefore, cannot not occur within a vacuum and is impacted upon by a range of external contextual factors in addition to the following internal considerations, including but not limited to, strategy and culture, resources and skills, leadership, organizational structure and external linkages [6–8].

Reflective of the above, innovation practice is far from straightforward "...most innovation is messy, involving false starts, recycling between stages, dead ends and jumps out of sequence" [4]. Indeed, it is argued that the problem does not lie in the generation of innovative ideas, but more in the successful management of the innovation process from an idea to a successful product in the market [9]. As cited by [10], Booz Allen Hamilton found that a common denominator in terms of transitioning new products to market is the utilization of a defined process for managing innovation incorporating stage approval and measurement processes across critical components. In a similar vein, the 2013 iteration of The Global Innovation 1000 Survey [11] identified that the level of R&D investment is not exclusively what determines innovation success; as how R&D funds and efforts are invested in capabilities, talent, processes and tools significantly impacts upon innovation development efficiencies and success.

3 Methodology

In pursuit of the development of a knowledge and decision-support innovation framework in the privacy and cybersecurity technology space, the IPACSO project is guided by an overarching three-staged methodological approach, as synopsized below.

IPACSO is an EU-funded Coordination and Support Action (CSA) project aimed at supporting Privacy and CyberSecurity innovations in Europe. IPACSO is focused on adapting existing innovation methodologies available in other domains, both general and specific; optimizing these approaches for the Privacy and CyberSecurity (PACS) market domains. Ultimately, IPACSO will combine innovation support modules based on established Methods (both generic and technology-specific), with new innovation support approaches geared towards the specific needs of the European PACs marketplace.

Stage 1: Development of a PACS innovation knowledgebase that will provide a detailed, yet intuitive understanding of the cybersecurity and privacy innovation space industry, market and value chain assessments, product and industry taxonomies, PACS (economic insights and considerations, innovation model overviews).

Stage 2: Development an analytical and decision-support framework for innovation management, macro analysis and product and ideation to enable innovators to identify, assess, prioritize and execute product ideas in a rigorous, market-centric manner.

Stage 3: Proof of concept and validation of the developed framework on several levels, via iterative stakeholder engagement. IPACSO framework content will also be validated iteratively, via bootcamp events and through related dissemination and exploitation events and programmes.

For the purpose of this paper, Stage 1 takes centre stage and the methodological direction involves the triangulation of emerging findings from three parallel work-in-progress research streams to inform the identification of a series of guiding principles to anchor the overarching IPACSO innovation framework to be developed.

3.1 PACS Market Analysis

The PACS marketplace has experienced significant growth in recent years, with further overall growth anticipated on both EU and global levels between now and 2020. Globally the market is presently valued at €62.4 bn per annum, with a 13.4 % global annual growth predicted between now and 2020, leaving an anticipated 2020 market of over €111 m [12]. The EU market is presently worth approximately one-quarter of the global market at €16.5 bn, with just under 10 % growth per annum predicted within the region, leaving a future potential EU market of €25.1 bn by 2020.

Existing and future growth in the PACS space is driven by a number of key trends, including an ever increasing number of threat vectors in which ICT infrastructure can be compromised, driven by more diverse and pervasive emerging technologies (e.g. mobile, Internet of Things and cloud infrastructures), increasing regulatory initiatives making security and data breach notifications mandatory (e.g. EU Data Protection Directive [13], NIS Directive [14], increased technology standardization leading to security exploit information being readily available to attackers, and via increased security spending both internally and via outsourcing. Many commercial organizations are also moving away from viewing security as just a "tick the box" initiative, increasingly purchasing security in response to genuine fears of data breaches and other security threats. Exponential data growth is also another security market driver as privacy risks increase in line with growing data volumes and ease at which datasets can be de-anonymized. Data growth is also a driver of security technology innovation, as effective security monitoring and mitigation increasingly becomes a "big data" problem.

Within the PACS domain several challenges exist around bringing new innovations effectively to market. Key solutions in the domain are of a technically complex nature, generally developed by highly technical individuals with significant experience in the industry, many staying in the industry for long periods as serial entrepreneurs [15]. In addition, while the military and government space demands one-off bespoke solutions, the marketplace for PACS solutions serving general commercial requirements is highly saturated, with an ever growing array of PACS technology options. This is reflected in the year-on-year growth in attendees at key industry conferences such as RSA (this year's conference had 340 vendors exhibiting in the data security category alone) [16].

Such product saturation makes it difficult for PACS innovators to differentiate products from other offerings, to accurately evaluate their own product features versus those of competitors due to the vast competitive knowledge necessary, and ultimately for customers to find time to understand differences between products, especially when product benefits sound similar at the marketing level. This often leads to poor product decision making, and the cheapest alternative being purchased as opposed to the most effective one.

Other challenges relate to the reality that security is purchased as a risk mitigation measure rather than providing any direct return on investment value itself – making value justification arguments more difficult for PACS vendors to make, when the solution's value is related to some future security event whose timeline is unknown in advance [17]. Effective security ultimately involves people, process and technology elements, so consultancy and service expertise is also necessary to sell security products effectively. This is reflected in some of the high-profile M&A activity in the space where key product vendors (e.g. FireEye) are acquiring outside service and consultancy expertise (ala Mandiant) [18]. Challenges of moving PACS innovations from prototype to adoption and integration in real world environments can also pose barriers and challenges.

Aside from strong internal capabilities in technology product management and innovation models and processes, PACS innovators with appropriate access to the best innovation ecosystems and environments are also at a key advantage. Key ingredients supporting such optimal environments include sustained access to the hardest cyber security and privacy problems (i.e. within military and large organization settings), a strong cyber-academic base, access to a sustained skill and talent flow of scientists and engineers, appropriate funding and mentoring supports from venture capitalists and similar commercial investors, backed up by strong government leverage around commercially backed investments. Flexible tech-transfer terms and appropriate logistics and ease of human interaction within the innovation hub are also ideal ingredients [19].

3.2   Innovation Models

Innovation models are important because they assist management teams in framing, understanding, and acting on the issues which need managing [20]. For this reason a review of innovation models is presented to illustrate the interrelated stakeholders, processes and issues which need to be factored into an overarching innovation framework.

It is cautioned that if innovation models are limited the subsequent innovation management and delivery approach will also be hampered [4]. Understanding of the process of innovation at the firm-level has evolved throughout recent decades from simplistic linear and sequential models to increasingly complex models embodying a diverse range of inter and intra stakeholders and processes. Distinguishable by their management focus, strategic drivers, accommodation of external actors and internal and external processes and function level integration, Rothwell [6] documented five shifts or generations, as synopsized below [4, 6, 10, 20, 21], demonstrating that the complexity and integration of the models increases with each subsequent generation as new practices emerge to adapt to changing contexts and address the limitations of earlier generations [21].

The *first generation technology push era* of innovation models represents a simple linear structure which mapped innovation as a sequential process performed across discrete stages. Technology push is based on the assumption that new technological advances based on R&D and scientific discovery, preceded and 'pushed' technological innovation via applied research, engineering, manufacturing and marketing towards successful products or inventions as outputs. In the *second generation market pull* era a linear model depiction of innovation also applies, this time prioritizing the importance of market demand in driving innovation endeavors. What distinguishes this model from its predecessor is that rather than product development originating from scientific advances, new ideas originate in the marketplace, with R&D becoming reactive to these needs. The *third generation Interactive, Coupling or Chain-linked models* overcame many of the shortcomings of the previous linear atypical examples models, by incorporating interaction and feedback loops to recognize that innovation is characterized by a coupling of and interaction between science and technology and the marketplace. Consequently, the third generation models integrate multiple in-house functions and interdependent stages. While third generation models were non-linear with feedback loops, a sequential nature of the stages of innovation were characterized. In response, and aiming to reflect the high degree of cross functional integration within firms, *fourth generation integrated or parallel models* reflect significant functional overlaps between departments and/or activities. A further novel feature of this model is the concept of external integration in terms of alliances and linkages with suppliers, customers, universities and government agencies. Extending from the previous generation of innovation models, *fifth generation systems integration and networking models* emphasize that innovation is a distributed networking process requiring continuous change occurring within and between firms, characterized by a range of external inputs encompassing suppliers, customers, competitors and universities. Reflecting a systems thinking approach, the dominant characteristics are the integration of a firm's internal innovation ecosystem and practices with external factors in the National Innovation Environment. The fifth generation models are characterized by the introduction of ICT systems to accelerate the innovation processes and communications across the networking systems in terms of raising both development efficiency and speed-to-market through strategic alliances. More recently and following on from the seminal work of Rothwell's innovation generation model typology, researchers [22, 23] have suggested that Chesbrough's [23] open innovation model represent the latest wave of innovation models. Reflecting a dominant orientation to the preceding network models of innovation, the open innovation approach is not limited to internal idea generation and development, as internal and external ideas in addition to internal and external paths to market (licensing, insourcing etc.) are facilitated within the innovation development chain.

In addition to the overarching innovation models, an extensive corpus of literature [6, 7, 24, 25], has accumulated documenting the range of end to end phases relating to innovation processes: idea generation, selection, development, implementation and launch, and post launch in some cases (as synthesized by [21, 26]). A common thread emerging from the literature is that while there is logical order in these phases, the order is not necessarily linear. All models start with some form of idea generation or searching stage. Secondly, a selection phase follows to determine which projects are feasible and potentially lucrative enough to be pursued. Methodologies and practice of relevance to these initial stages include innovation management, market analysis and competitive intelligence, technology forecasting [25, 27–29]. The third step reflects the development phase where the idea is developed into a tangible product, process or service. This stage can be described differently where terminologies such as development, prototyping, manufacturing and realization are used interchangeably. Methodologies and practice of relevance to development stages include Agile, Lean Startup, Waterfall and Spiral [30–33]. The fourth phase represents implementation/launch and typically entails marketing, distribution, logistics and customer facing activities. Business modelling and product road testing [34, 35], methodologies and practices offer significant contribution for this key stage. Some authors also include a post launch phase to accommodate re-innovating, scaling and learning dimensions [8, 25].

3.3 PACS Economics

As stressed by [36] the main objective of cybersecurity investments is to reduce the risk of security breaches. However, a twin-goal might be the reduction in variability of potential losses from cybercrimes. It is a notoriously difficult matter to estimate the cost and benefit components in the area of increased IT security and privacy. In a nutshell, the Economics of CyberSecurity and Privacy models IT security and privacy as decisions by the players involved. Mindful of this, the principles of economics to the analysis of cybersecurity and privacy opportunities/problems can provide insights into cost-benefit trade-offs faced by different market participants, their strategic behavior and market outcomes (i.e. welfare effects). At the core of the economics of cybersecurity and privacy are security risks. Especially important are financial gains as motivation for cybercrime. Moreover, the field also covers the analysis of market mechanisms and market failures as well as the economic impact of government regulations of cybersecurity. This field of research not only uses economic theory for the explanation of cyber security and privacy opportunities/problems, but also increasingly employs approaches of behavioral economics. In this vain, cybersecurity and privacy issues can be evaluated using concepts such as asymmetric information problems (moral hazard, adverse selection) or externalities. The overview literatures typically concentrate on cybercrime statistics, market failures and instruments to improve market failures [37, 38].

The rationale for an economics perspective in this research is to surmount the difficulty of estimating tangible benefits leads to a problem of making a business case for spending on PACS. Often, companies only react with increased spending on IT security after a large-scale data breach has occurred. In such a situation, it is relatively easy for IT staff to make a business case. So timing is important for showing the value proposition of innovative PACS products and services. Moreover, as firms act under budget constraints, the option of spending more funds on improving IT security competes with other options that might improve revenues (such as spending more on marketing). If incentives are not aligned, they lead to suboptimal choices. For example, in order to obtain an economic incentive for the adoption of a new IT security system, the firm facing this decision needs to know (all) the costs and benefits involved in obtaining the system in order to make an optimal decision. There are a number of policy instruments that can impact on economic incentives of market players by changing cost-benefit categories and therefore the trade-offs of those participants. Mandatory instruments are implemented through legislation, regulations or mandatory Codes of Conduct encompassing: duty of care or diligence standards, Data breach notifications, property rights to personal information. Voluntary instruments include Trust marks and technical security seals i.e. TRUSTe, BBBOnline, EuroPrise; sharing of critical incidence information Computer Emergency Response Teams (CERTs) or Computer Security and Incident Response Team (CSIRTs). Other mechanisms are informal exchanges or community-driven Warning, Advice and Reporting Points (WARPs), the promotion of cyber insurance and security standards.

4   Guiding Principles for the IPACSO Framework

Responding to the challenge of transitioning technology related R&D into commercially viable innovations; the synthesis of the three aforementioned research streams signals a range of pertinent factors with reference to shaping the guiding innovation principles.

- Various market assessment techniques can support product development strategy at the "idea" level such as market hypothesis gathering, competitor and value chain assessments, product and technology roadmapping, business model generation and lean canvas techniques, and use case and persona development among others.
- Innovation process models involve a pattern of end-to-end stages and embody a diverse range of inter and intra stakeholders and processes. To offer tangible supports to PACS innovators, the proposed framework needs to accommodate each stage and support innovators in terms of their internal and external innovation ecosystems.
- Economic modelling of IT security and privacy purchasing decisions, market mechanisms and cost benefit trade-offs can inform business case, modelling and value propositioning supports.

Based on the foregoing triangulated desk research (discussed in Sect. 3 above) and as listed below in Table 1, six preliminary innovation guiding principles have been formulated as a precursor to the overarching IPACSO framework to be developed.

These principles, transcending innovation process and training, idea formulation, market analysis, legal/standards landscape and business modelling categories integrates key focal points of relevance to innovation engagement and management. These building blocks represent the culmination of the first stage of the overarching IPACSO methodology, providing a synthesized helicopter overview of key considerations and potential menus/modules for the knowledge and decision-support innovation framework for identifying, assessing and exploiting market opportunities in the privacy and cybersecurity technology space. These preliminary guiding principles will form the underpinning inputs to the design of the IPACSO framework in terms of responding to,

Table 1. Derivation of the guiding principles

Research themes		Guiding principles
PACS market analysis	1	Market Analysis: macro trends, technology SOTA, PESTEL, competitor analysis etc.
	2	Formulating Product/Service Idea: validation, scalability, value chain positioning, future proof etc.
Innovation models	3	Innovation Process: identify/refine /benchmark models, resourcing/ teaming/incentivizing
	4	Innovation Training: ideation, development approaches, portfolio management etc.
PACS economics	5	Legal/Regulatory/Standards Landscape: DP, CIO legislation, NIS Directive, CyberSecurity etc.
	6	Business Modelling: value propositioning, market validation, revenue sources, segmentation, channels etc.

and meeting target stakeholders' innovation requirements, pain-points and needs. Importantly, these six focal areas represent a platform to refine existing innovation and market knowledge methodologies, practices and tools to support innovators in identifying, assessing and exploiting innovation opportunities These guiding principles will subsequently be validated via the IPACSO Innovation Advisory Board and extended outreach and dissemination channels and will inform the second stage of the IPACSO process i.e. the development of the IPACSO Innovation Framework where knowledge paths and signposts to resources, tools and tactics will be provided to innovators to support their engagement, navigation and exploitation of their innovation endeavors.

5 Conclusions

The development of the proposed guiding principles represent a pivotal component in meeting IPACSO's overall goals of supporting increased awareness of innovation engagement and management practices, in addition to supporting greater awareness and knowledge of market dynamics, barriers and solution potential for increased innovation activity in the domain. The next phase in the IPACSO methodological process is to validate, and achieve consensus on these guiding principles through iterative stakeholder engagement in order to shape and inform the subsequent development criteria of the IPACSO framework. The actual components and content of the IPACSO framework will, in turn be developed into decision support modules and associated toolkits which will be equally iteratively developed, trialed and validated with target stakeholder engagement, primarily through validation training Bootcamps and wider dissemination and outreach channels.

Accordingly, the output of this initial phase of the IPACSO research project impacts and has implications at various levels, most notably in terms of framing both innovator and firm-level innovation requirements within the PACS domain, which has relevance to academic and policy making audiences also. Additionally, given that the research outputs form a pivotal component of the IPACSO project, they will actively contribute to ongoing debates and objectives around shaping support measures for PACS innovation awareness, competency building and innovation policy support developments in the domain. Furthermore, these insights, and the IPACSO project overall, will have relevance to the European trust and security Framework research programme portfolio which are increasingly charged with focusing on potential innovation arising from their activities, in terms of increasing project outputs for economic and societal benefit.

References

1. EC, Cyber Security Strategy of the European union: An Open Safe and Secure Cyberspace (2013)
2. Maughan, D., Baleson, D., Lindqvist, U., Tudor, Z.: Crossing the "Valley of Death": transitioning cybersecurity research into practice. J. IEES Secur. Priv. 11(2), 14–23 (2013)
3. OSMOSIS, D2.1 Report on the Identified Security's Market Potential/ D2.2 Report on Taxonomy Definition (2010). http://www.osmosisecurity.eu/system/files/OSMOSIS_D2.1% 20and%20D2.2_integrated.pdf
4. Tidd, J.: A review of innovation models discussion paper 1. Science and Technology Policy Research Unit, Tanaka Business School, University of Sussex (2006)
5. Garud, R., Kumaraswamy, A., Sambamurthy, V.: Emergent by design: performance and transformation at infosys technologies. Organ. Sci. 17, 277–286 (2006)
6. Rothwell, R.: Towards the fifth-generation innovation process. Int. Mark. Rev. 11(1), 7–31 (1994)
7. Cormican, K., O'Sullivan, D.: Auditing best practice for effective product innovation. Technovation 24(10), 819–829 (2004)
8. Jacobs, D., Snijders, H.: Innovation routine: how managers can support repeated innovation. Stitching Management Studies, Van Gorcum, Assen (2008)
9. Van der Panne, G., van Beers, C., Kleinknecht, A.: Success and failure of innovation: a review of the literature. Int. J. Innov. Manag. 7(3), 309–338 (2003)
10. du Preez, N., Louw, L.: A framework for managing the innovation process. In: PICMET Proceedings, CapeTown, South Africa (2008)
11. Jaruzelski, B., Loehr, J., Holman, R.: The global 1000 innovation survey: navigating the digital future. Strategy&PWC (2013). http://www.strategyand.pwc.com/global/home/what-we-think/reports-white-papers/article-display/2013-global-innovation-1000-study
12. Frost & Sullivan: Global Cyber Security Market Assessment, 17 February 2014
13. EC, EU Data Protection Directive. http://ec.europa.eu/justice/data-protection/document/index_en.htm
14. EC, NIS Directive (2013). http://europa.eu/rapid/press-release_IP-13-94_en.htm
15. ITSEF IT Security Entrepreneurs Forum, Discussion Roundtable (2013). http://www.security-innovation.org/ITSEF.htm
16. Forrester Tech Radar, Data Security, Q2 2014 (2014)
17. Benzel, T.V., O'Brien, E., Rodriguez, R., Arbaugh, W., Sebes, J.: Crossing the great divide: from research to market. IEEE Secur. Priv. 11(2), 42–46 (2013)
18. Forrester Quick Take, FireEye Acquires Mandiant, 7 January 2014
19. Tech Republic, How Israel is rewriting the Future of Cybersecurity and Creating the Next Silicon Valley (2013)

20. O'Raghallaigh, P., Sammon, D., Murphy, C.: A re-conceptualisation of innovation models to support decision design. J. Decis. Syst. **20**(4), 369 (2011)
21. Ortt, J., van der Duin, P.: The evolution of innovation management towards contextual innovation. Eur. J. Innov. Manage. **11**, 522–538 (2008)
22. Kotesmir, M., Meissner, D.: Conceptualizing the innovation process – trends and outloo. NRU HSE Working Paper Series Science, Technology, Innovation. No. 10/STI/2013 (2013)
23. Chesborough, H.: Open Innovation: The New Imperative for Creating and Profiting from Technology. Harvard Business School Press, Boston (2003)
24. Dooley, L., O'Sullivan, D.: Structuring innovation: a conceptual model and implementation methodology. Enterp. Innov. Manage. Stud. **2**(3), 177–194 (2001)
25. Tidd, J., Bessant, J.: Managing Innovation- Integrating Technology Market and Organizational Change. Wiley, Chicester (2005)
26. Eleveens, C.: Innovation Management: A Literature Review of Innovation Process Models and their Implications, Nijmegen, NL, pp. 1–16 (2010)
27. Phal, R., Farrukh, C., Probert, D.: Strategic roadmapping: a workshop-based approach for identifying and exploring innovation issues and opportunities. Eng. Manage. J. **19**, 3–12 (2007)
28. Cooper, R.: Perspective: the Stage-Gate® idea-to-launch process—update, what's New, and NexGen systems. J. Prod. Innov. Manage **25**(3), 213–232 (2008)
29. Fleischer, C.S., Benoussan, B.E.: Business and Competitive Analysis: Effective Application of New and Classic Methods. Financial Times Prentice Hall, New Jersey (2007)
30. Highsmith, J., Cockburn, A.: Agile software development: the business of innovation. Computer **34**, 120–122 (2001)
31. Reis, E.: The Lean Startup: How Today's Entrepreneurs use Continuous Innovation to Create Radically Successful Businesses. Crown Business, New York (2011)
32. Takeuchi, H., Nonanka, I.: The new new product development game. Harvard Bus. Rev. **64**, 137–146 (1986)
33. Boehm, B.: A spiral model of software development and enhancement. In: Proceedings of an International Workshop on Software Process and Software Environments, Coto de Caza, Trabuco Canyon, California, 27–29 March 1985
34. Osterwalder, A., Pigneur, Y.: Business Model Generation–A Handbook for Visionaires, Game Changers, and Challengers. Wiley, New York (2010)
35. Mullins, J.: The New Business Road Test. Financial Times/Prentice Hall, London (2010)
36. Gordon, L.: Incentives for Improving Cyber security in the Private Sector: A Cost-Benefit Analysis (2007). http://hsc-democrats.house.gov/SiteDocuments/20071031155020-22632.pdf
37. Moore, T.: The economics of cyber security: principles and policy options. In: Proceedings of a Workshop on Deterring Cyberattacks: Informing Strategies and Developing Options for U.S. Policy. The National Academies Press (2010)
38. Moore, T., Clayton, R., Anderson, R.: The economics of online crime. J. Econ. Perspect. **23**(3), 3–20 (2009)

An Empirical Study of the Technology Transfer Potential of EU Security and Trust R&D Projects

Martina de Gramatica$^{(\boxtimes)}$, Fabio Massacci$^{(\boxtimes)}$, and Olga Gadyatskaya

University of Trento, 38100 Trento, Italy
{deramatica,massacci,gadyatskaya}@disi.unitn.it

Abstract. European R&D Projects are characterised by a significant presence of industry and by heavy reports of exploitation plans. An intriguing question is therefore whether such projects actually delivered the technology transfer their funder is longing for. This report presents a comprehensive study on the innovation potential of FP7 projects funded by the ICT Call 1 for Trustworthy ICT and the Joint ICT and Security Call and is based on documental evidence and ethnographic research.

The analysis of the participants landscape reveals a connected community where few general software producers and integrators act as hubs between different interests groups (such as privacy and critical infrastructure protection) while specialised IT security companies play a minor role. In terms of innovation potential some projects have produced research results that are directly usable by citizens, but most projects have delivered tools and methods for ICT specialists. Most architectural results delivered look pretty hard to market. However, some projects have delivered results that are actually exploited. Such "success stories" exemplify tangible innovation outcomes from Trust and Security Programme.

Keywords: FP7 framework · Trust and security programme · R&D projects

1 Introduction

Trust and Security Programme in the FP7 ICT Framework has launched a significant number of joint R&D projects that aimed at finding solutions for critical security and trust gaps of ICT systems. While the selected projects have achieved a lot of impact in terms of scientific publications, the technology transfer potential of the delivered results often is not clear. The question remains, whether these projects have produced outcomes that might turn into new products interesting for the market.

In this study we have tried to assess the technology transfer potential for a significant subset of projects of Trust and Security Programme. We have classified the delivered technologies by the corresponding end-users. For each end-user category we identify the projects contributing to it, and assess the market potential.

© Springer International Publishing Switzerland 2014
F. Cleary and M. Felici (Eds.): CSP Forum 2014, CCIS 470, pp. 159–170, 2014.
DOI: 10.1007/978-3-319-12574-9_14

This study has been carried out by the University of Trento in cooperation with TSSG and HP Labs by combining documents analysis (projects publishable summary, deliverables and web sites) and personal focused interviews – with European project officers (currently or previously in charge of the project) and with project coordinators or technical leaders (see [1] for the full list of projects considered and more details of the study).

2   The Landscape of Partners, Industries and Collaborations

European R&D Projects are consortia built from academics, industrial and use case partners, funded in response to a competitive call on a pre-defined set of topics. For example Call 1 of the Framework Programme 7 listed for Security and Trust the following topics:

- Security and resilience in network infrastructures;
- Security and trust in dynamic and reconfigurable service architectures;
- Trusted computing infrastructures;
- Identity management and privacy enhancing tools;
- Longer term visions and research roadmaps; metrics and benchmarks.

These projects are roughly divided into STREPS (Specific targeted research Project focusing on technology) receiving around 2–3 M for 2/3 years and IP (Integrated Projects) that receive around 6–10 M for the same duration but have a substantial number of partners and should also deal with a broader range of issues than just technology; in both cases besides technical results the partners should also present their exploitation plans.

The projects considered in this study included more than 200 partners between industry, academia and research centres. In order to understand synergies and group dynamics, Fig. 1 shows the "social relationships" among the projects. To ease readability only the partners who participated in two or more projects are included. The size of a node is determined by the number of links - i.e. the number of projects - and not by the budget of the partner. Thus, a partner represented by a large node is not necessarily a well-funded organisation; rather it is a well-connected organisation in this community (obviously partners belonging to many IPs tend to be more funded than a partner doing a single STREP).

The structure of the network is a scale-free graph where few major hubs act as bridge between minor partners. There are no disconnected components, which would have meant separated communities each pursuing its own R&D activities.

On the bottom right one can recognise a "crypto-corner" (KUL, TU/e, Univ. of Bochum and Bristol, plus FT) and on the centre right a "privacy group" (KUL, Univ. Milano, Frankfurt, and Dresden, up to HP). KUL and Dresden universities act as bridges between the groups. On the far bottom left we find the partners working on "critical infrastructure protection" (SELEX, THALES, Alcatel, CINI), while Software Engineering partners are more scattered on the centre left (ETH, SINTEF, FHG, up to ATOS and TXT).

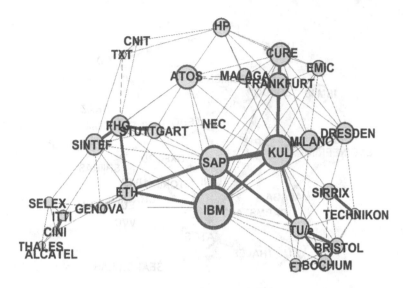

Fig. 1. Key partners in Call 1 and Joint Call projects

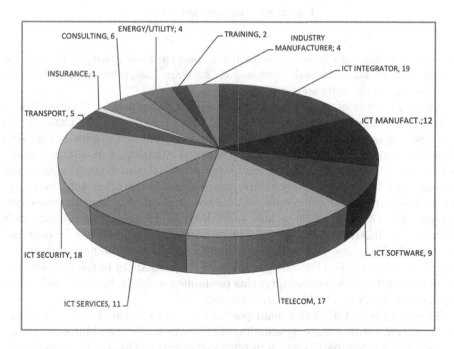

Fig. 2. Global Call 1 breakdown by industry sector

Moreover the core of the community is represented by few general software companies and IT integrators, while telecom and critical infrastructure operators

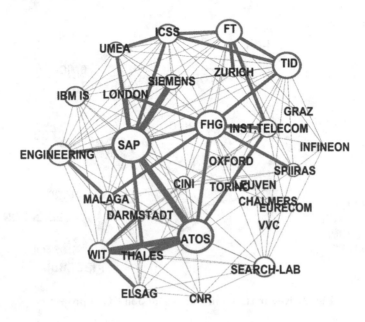

Fig. 3. Key partners in Call 5

play a minor role. This is only true for what concerns their ability of playing the role of research hubs. Indeed, later in Fig. 2 we see that telecom operators are as numerous as the software integrators.

The major role of some academic partners is explained by their ability to contribute to different fields (such as legal and IT experts). For example the University of Leuven (KUL) is a hub because very different groups participate: a law department, a crypto group of an electrical engineering department and a distributed system group from the computer science department. The same can be said of IT integrators and software companies. On the other side, no player has a significant social dominance and rather large players tend to cooperate. Interestingly, there is no large hub specialised in IT security company, only SIRRIX and SEARCH-LAB are present in both Call 1 and Call 5. In contrast, specialised IT security companies are a significant share of the participants (see Fig. 2). In other words, IT security companies do participate to the call but they are not the hubs of the community; this phenomenon might be explained by the fragmented nature of the IT security market.

The analysis of Call 5 (its main participants are presented in Fig. 3) shows the same trend with a large domination of software vendors and integrators and a significantly larger participation of telecom operator. This might be explained by the greater emphasis on critical infrastructure of Call 5 compared to Call 1 which had a greater emphasis on privacy. This is also reflected in the academic partnership: universities like Dresden and Milano focusing on privacy, faded from the picture.

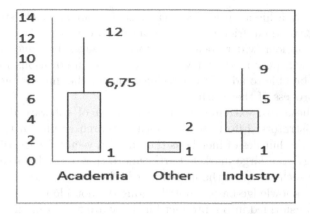

Fig. 4. Distribution of partners per project in Call 1

The graph in Fig. 4 shows the distribution of the different category of academic partners, large industries and SMEs for project.

The upper dash per category represents the maximum number of partners of that type per project, while the lower dash represent the minimum number. The solid box represents how the majority of projects (25–75 %) is distributed. The academia column is the aggregate value for research centres and universities. Since they are sometimes considered in different categories we also give the individual columns for both universities and research centres. From the picture it is clear that ICT Security is still a largely academic endeavour.

3   Classification of Project Results

The technical results with innovation potential have been divided into two major classes:

– at one end of the spectrum there are *results appealing to product innovation in ICT for citizens*;
– at the other end *results which address product or process innovation for ICT specialists*.

Illustrative examples of the extremes are a driver authentication module for a car (mass market) and a security protocol verification tool kit (niche market).

The innovation barriers to overcome depend on the position in the innovation spectrum. Advocate of the protocol verification toolkit must be able to tailor the toolkit to very specific customers needs and internal quality processes. They face a minor inertia as the adoption of a technology is essentially a single decision: proved that this technology saves money or improves product quality, the steps to adoptions are short. The major obstacle for results targeting innovation for citizens is the strong force of inertia: convincing tens of engineers from a company verification group to use a new tool is far different than convincing millions of customers to pay a higher price for a car that cannot be easily stolen but also cannot be lent to their friends by a simple hand-over of a key. Indeed, these results must consider wider societal acceptance issues but once accepted the law of inertia will play in their favour. In contrast, innovations for specialised markets must be able to adapt their technologies to the underlying dynamics of the product/process of their niche.

Between these two extremes is the wide area of software developers and system administrators. Efforts to transform research results in this area must also overcome the hurdles of inertia as they need a vector for the distribution of their technology to a large market. Furthermore they must be able to maintain and adapt the technology as the underlying IT languages and systems evolve.

Differently, knowledge-based contributions do not identify a specific result that can be transformed into a product but they are a tangible manifestation of an increased knowledge concretely used by the community, such as databases of information, attacks trends and vulnerabilities.

The variety of the innovation results achieved by the projects funded by the ICT Call 1 for Trustworthy ICT and the Joint ICT and Security Call is summarised in the following sections.

3.1   Product Innovation in ICT for Citizens

Among the results with the potential to reach a product innovation in ICT for citizens, we can list biometric technologies complementing traditional biometrics (such as fingerprints or iris recognition), which have already reached $250 million a year in sales[1].

This complementary biometric technology makes use of face dynamics, gait and activity-related actions to recognise the user on the move, to improve the results of traditional biometrics models, or to provide an alternative way to access to services by disabled people. In this domain the ACTIBIO project has developed and piloted a car driver authentication model.

A similar approach to complementary biometrics for mobile devices has been pursued by the MOBIO project. So far, most results of the latter are still at the research stage (e.g. a public database for research purposes project). Another wide market that can be affected by research results of security project is the domain of controller devices in critical infrastructures (SCADA networks). Some analysis from Frost & Sullivan finds that this market earned revenues of $4,584.5 million in 2009 and estimates to reach $6,902.4 million in 2016 [5]. Given the importance and the complexity of the context in which they are employed, the vulnerability of these systems exposes to serious threat a large number of vital infrastructures. The consequences of a successful cyber-attack on this

---

[1] Several banks around the world, e.g., Bank United (Houston, TX) and Nationwide Building Society (UK), have tested iris scanners as an alternative to personal identification number (PIN) codes for ATM access [3]

infrastructure of national significance are potentially dire (e.g. the Stuxnet attack in 2012)[2].

In this area the MICIE project has developed a tool that helps to increases the QoS in the supply of energy between the energy producers and customers. The validation activities of this project have demonstrated a considerable reduction in the time of unsupplied power The overall approach allows to better predict events and consequences of cascade failures on the system state. In the same area the INSPIRE and VIKING projects provided systems for assessment of the security state of the SCADA network by integrating suitable semantic information from intrusions, faults, attacks or other relevant societal information. Unfortunately, the performance of such systems is highly dependent on the presence of updated vulnerability and attack information, often not available. The lack of shared data about attacks and vulncrabilities has been raised by many project coordinators and it is one of the main hurdles to performance assessment for ICT security products.

The other domain with a deep potential is the realm of social networks and privacy protection.

3.2   Product Innovation for IT System Administrators

This class of users is significantly large. According a 2011 EURES survey the 5th and 6th top-most positions for requested professional job are respectively for IT programmers and IT administrators. They belong to the class of technical savvy users that could be easily targeted by owners of FP7 security and trust research results. In a Ernest & Young Survey [2]. it is reported that more than 66 % of respondents have not implemented any tool for DLP (Data Loss Prevention) and only 14 % claimed that the implementation has been a success. This shows the large potential of the market.

These results have the potential to improve the overall echo-system but it is unclear from the evidence supplied by the projects, whether there is enough economic margin for distributors (in the same way that RedHat and SuSe distribute variants of the Linux operating system).

For example, the PRISM project has produced specific probes for network monitoring. Those probes allow to reduce the data needed by telecom operators to process and store in order to be compliant with the conflicting claims of privacy protection and cyber-crime laws.

More specific results include the development of novel intrusion detection, tolerance or anyhow monitoring systems. (IDS for short). AWISSENET for instance has implemented an IDS that builds upon its results on service discovery and traffic analysis.

---

[2] Less known examples are the 2000 insider attack on the Australian water system that caused the spillage of 800,000 liters of sewage into rivers and parks in Queensland; the "Slammer worm" infecting the Davis Besse nuclear power plant in Ohio, causing a five-hour shutdown of computer systems in August 2003; and the Hatch nuke plant in Georgia shutting down for two days after an engineer loaded a software update for a business network that also rebooted the plant's power control system in June 2008.

3.3   Product Innovations for Software Developers

A frequent target of the projects involved are "Plug-and-play" security libraries and toolkit for mainstream software and Information Systems developers. The experts in the CACE project have provided a number of advanced crypto-libraries ranging from fast secure networking, including tools for automatically compiling zero-knowledge protocols, to secure multi-party computations. Secure multi-party computation libraries (applied to supply-chain information systems) are also among the results of the SECURESCM project. Other repositories of efficient implementations of secure system that cover both software and hardware implementations have been provided by the ECRYPT II project which has been able to achieve significant contributions from outside the consortium.

The TECOM project provided similar integrated packages for trusted operating systems, security layers and trusted protocols focusing for developers of embedded security-critical applications. In this case also some hardware solutions were considered and implemented. The WSAN4CIP project provided similar solutions for wireless sensors network for software attestation and secure execution environments.

3.4   Product and Process Innovation for ICT Specialists

Protocol designers can use the AVANTSSAR platform for protocol verification, based on the idea of Verification-as-a-Service. To facilitate interoperability the platform provides a translation services back-and-forth different protocol design languages into a core intermediate specification language that links the different verification services. The ability of the project to overcome the performance barriers has been demonstrated by the verification of a protocol by Google (not a member of the consortium). The AWISSENET project has directly produced some routing protocols based on geographical routing guides usable for location based services. In the latter case the evidence for the ability of providing those services outside the consortium is not clear yet.

Several projects focused on information system compliance covering the product/process innovation for ICT specialists market area of information system analysts, architects and auditors (for the design phase). The main result of such projects is typically a methodology supported by one or more tools. This market has a significant potential as it is at the high-end of the value chain of IT system development. Currently more than 200 firms offer risk-consulting services and this market is estimated for $36 billion and is expected to grow $50 billion in the next few years. Organisations require advice on GRC strategy, GRC organisation and process design and services to help develop and integrate GRC technology infrastructure [4]. However, this market is also very fragmented and reaching it out would require mayor dissemination effort.

An example is the MASTER methodology describing how to refine control objectives from high level regulations down to the specific protection activities. The methodology is supported by a design workbench that transforms policies at the level of business goals into low level policies for operation process used by the monitoring tool. Another example is the methodology for the development of security metrics proposed by the GEMOM project supported by a monitoring tool that produces output usable by decision makers such as CIOs, or CISOs. A similar audience can also be targeted by the supply chain risk simulator from SECURESCM which deals with the risks associated with supply chain information disclosure during the process of data sharing.

Projects focusing on embedded systems can produce brittle but directly marketable results: the UAN project produced a sensor network working on acoustic channels for underwater surveillance.

3.5   Knowledge-Based Contributions

A special category is represented by projects which research results cannot be easily transformed into products but that represent a significant contribution to some objectives of the Digital Agenda such as the development of databases of vulnerabilities (the INTERSECTION and the SHIELDS projects) or the models of reaction of the society under attacks (the VIKING project) or the world picture of current malware distribution (the WOMBAT project).

These contribution address the concern of lack of shared data, however it is not clear how to populate these data repositories with actual industry data after the project is over.

The only example of industry taken up among those projects is provided by Symantec that has extended the work of the WOMBAT project to a full-fledged experimental infrastructure with actual data (WINE).

4   Hard to Market Contributions

Many projects produced among their results security and privacy architectures and frameworks of different kind (e.g. CONSEQUENCE for the protection of shared data, GEMOM for the financial sector, INSPIRE for controller devices in critical infrastructures, INTERSECTION, PRISM and SWIFT for telecommunication networks, PRIMELIFE, PICOS and TAS3 for collaborative systems, TURBINE for pseudo-identities, etc.).

Those results are the most difficult ones to be transformed into innovative products: while an IDS system can be transformed and marketed into a product that third parties can buy, a security architecture can only be adopted within the main IT architecture. Therefore, the potential users are limited to the mainstream software integrators and producers (e.g. IBM, ATOS, SIEMENS, THALES, etc.) or public entities. Since IT integrators have their own security architectures and the benefit of different architectures are hard to evaluate, the barriers for adoption outside the members of the consortium are significant.

In many cases the project that developed an architecture also developed a policy and specification language. Some of these languages have been standardised through OASIS but their commercial adoption is subjected to even more uncertainties than novel IT architectures: the adoption of a policy language requires the adoption of the corresponding enforcement engine and therefore the existence of a company that commits to provide an open source or a commercial engine.

4.1 Success Stories

Many projects in Trust and Security have achieved significant impact and were able to deliver innovative products and to improve security for an "average user". Among those we could mention, for example, SECURESCM and AVANTSSAR.

The SECURESCM project to achieve its goal of securing supply chain management in the cloud, has worked on protocols for secure multy-party computation technology that allows several parties to compute jointly some necessary result without revealing the sensitive data of each party. The results from the project are at present exploited by SAP (the coordinator of the project) for secure benchmarking in the SAP Benchmarking Suite.

As mentioned earlier, AVANTSSAR has worked on protocol verification for security. The project studied the implementation of the Single-Sign-On (SSO) protocol used by Google in its Google Apps product, which is used for essential business services by millions of businesses. Formal specifications of the protocol expressed in the ASLan++ language (one of the project results) were analysed with the AVANTSSAR platform, and a bug in the implementation was revealed. This vulnerability allowed the man-in-the-middle attack, when a malicious service provider could access all user accounts in its federated service environment. The problem was reported to Google who fixed the problem and acknowledged AVANTSSAR for closing the security hole.

4.2 The Last Mile

Several project coordinators interviewed noted that after an R&D project is done, the road towards innovation is still very long. They were not referring to the additional effort needed to transform research results into full-fledged products but the efforts needed to run a real pilot.

Security solutions have to be woven into a "normal" application, as well the base system of the final target beneficiaries has to be adapted in order to accommodate the solution. In other words, nobody buys a flexible privacy policy as such but people might buy a social network with a flexible privacy policy if it improves ones user experience.

The technological or operational base might not be ready to incorporate a new security feature or use a new security model. The main idea might be really interesting but the technical gaps in the target system require additional efforts in order to be tried out. For example, accessing a web system with facial biometrics instead of passwords requires a high resolution webcam and this extra cost might not be justified by the functional services offered by the base system.

This additional effort cannot usually done within the timeframe and the resources of the research project for two reasons: this gap is not interesting from the viewpoint of research or technological development (it will not increase the project rating by the reviewers, or the research standing of the academics) and it requires significant efforts for the integration at operational level that needs to be done after the research results have been completed and validated.

Occasionally some projects "continue" the work of a previous research project with a strand dedicated to more detailed experiments in a new research project (for example the informal follow-ups PRIME, PRIMELIFE, ABC4TRUST sequence of projects). However this line of action is sub-optimal for the innovation. Being "new" projects they are subjected to all hurdles in the competition as if they were never reviewed before and besides being "research" projects they need to come out with new research results were the majority of effort needs to go.

Many coordinators suggested to introduce a specific financial instrument where (a subset of) the consortium could go ahead with a simplified proce- dure for project whose only focus is a medium or large scale user-trial with a focus on commercialisation.

This could still be a competitive call available to all concluded or near comple- tion projects but, considering the narrower focus (user trial) and the obligatory starting point (a result from a research project), it could be simplified along the calls for international cooperation or enlargement to partners from new member states.

5   Conclusions and Recommendations

In this paper we have presented the results of a study conducted on the European R&D projects in Trust and Security. The analysis of the constituency of the projects considered in the study revealed a dynamic, collaborative environment with few major players but without a clear market dominance. A variety of companies representing the software industry, the telecommunication sector and proper security services participate to the research projects.

To understand the technology transfer potential, we have classified the projects based on the end-users of their results. We have identified many research results that can stimulate product, service and process innovation in Europe. Some projects have clear innovative results that are usable by citizens and IT industries; many projects also delivered important potential innovations in tools and methods for ICT specialists. These results have the potential to be used well beyond the consortium, albeit the path to commercial product might be fraught with difficulties.

A weakness of the field, with few notable exceptions, is the lack of well reported empirical trials and pilots. Indeed, the results of well-designed pilots could provide crucial information to potential investors in the technology and thus act as a spur to innovation. As summarised by a project coordinator: "there is never enough time for user trials."

Another key weakness identified by our investigation is the lack of information on security incidents and benchmarks. Without information on past incidents it is not possible to learn from them as a community. In avionics safety accidents are thoroughly investigated and the recommendations become new industry requirements or prescribed operational procedures. Security is still very far from this level of knowledge sharing. This can only be achieved by an European regulatory initiative on the controlled disclosure of security incidents.

The analysis also identified gaps in the "last mile" that could be addressed by a mixture of organisational, funding, and regulatory measures. Many project coordinators stressed the importance of setting up structured relations with product groups or users from the projects start. However, to cover the distance from a research result to a product, more work is necessary after the research results have been achieved. A possible solution could be a specific co-funding mechanism by the EC for experimenting large scale follow-up trials of research results with a simplified funding procedure.

Acknowledgements. We would like to thank the Head, the current and past Project Officers of the F5 Unit and the project and technical coordinators of the FP7 Security and Trust Projects for providing us the necessary bootstrapping information. Without their guide and their support this report would not have been feasible.

At the University of Trento F. Dalpiaz, G. Oligeri, and F. Paci contributed to the analysis of project deliverables. From the EFFECTS+ and SECCORD consortia the suggestions from M. Bezzi, F. Clearly, N. Papanikolaou and N. Wainwright were extremely helpful.

The work leading to this report was supported by the EU under the FP7 ICT EFFECTS+ and SECCORD projects. This paper presents only the authors' point of view, and does not reflect the opinion of the EC.

References

1. Effects+ Project: D2.2 The Innovation Potential of FP7 Security & Trust Projects (2013)
2. Ernst & Young: Into the cloud, out of the fog. global information security survey (2011)
3. Lerner, E.: Biometric identification. Ind. Physicist **6**(1), 20–23 (2000)
4. Rasmussen, M., McClean, C.: Trends in governance, risk and compliance. forrester research (2007). http://mthink.com/sites/default/files/legacy/cfoproject/content/pdf/cfo3_3_86_wp_forrester_rasmussen.pdf
5. Frost & Sullivan: Demand for geographically dispersed scada in oil and gas sector poised to drive growth in world scada market (2010). http://www.frost.com/prod/servlet/press-release.pag?docid=218949720

Author Index